MARK JOHNSTON
PHENOMENON

MARK
JOHNSTON
PHENOMENON

The Authorised Biography

Nick Townsend

WELBECK

Published by Welbeck
An imprint of Welbeck Non-Fiction Limited,
part of Welbeck Publishing Group.
20 Mortimer Street,
London W1T 3JW

First published by Welbeck in 2021

A CIP catalogue record for this book is available from the British Library

ISBN
Hardback - 9781787398856

Typeset by EnvyDesign
Printed and bound by CPI Group (UK) Ltd, Croydon, CR0 4YY

10 9 8 7 6 5 4 3 2 1

www.welbeckpublishing.com

To the memory of Barney

CONTENTS

INTRODUCTION

In June 2020, Mark Johnston enjoyed the cachet of being the castaway on BBC Radio's *Desert Island Discs*, joining approaching 3,000 notable individuals who, since the programme was launched in 1942, have variously achieved status, prestige, glory and achievement in their field.

At the conclusion, the racehorse trainer who could be said to have embodied all those qualities, was asked by presenter Lauren Laverne which of his choice of the eight records he regarded most highly he would save if they were all in danger of being washed away. Without hesitation he named Fleetwood Mac's "Don't Stop."[1]

An addictive, catchy song, sure enough, suggesting good taste, but also apposite.

"Don't Stop – thinking about tomorrow" is the chorus line, sung by Christine McVie and Lindsey Buckingham. Penned by McVie, it was 'inspired' – if that is the correct word – by the break-up with her husband, the band's bass player John. And, of course, it would become Bill Clinton's Presidential theme song in 1992.

However, it also neatly encapsulates Johnston's philosophy for the majority of his 34-year career.

The song comes to mind on a dark, dank December afternoon as I drive through the ancient market town of Middleham, in Wensleydale, north Yorkshire, before turning into the entrance to Kingsley House, with its adjoining stables where over three decades earlier, Johnston and his wife Deirdre had arrived with seemingly audacious plans to establish a training base to rival any in Britain – in the midst of an area which was on the wane as a racehorse centre.

It is one of those days when the sun barely appears to rise. Nothing stirs – except maybe just a dog barking. To the uninitiated, it would be difficult to imagine that there is a thriving industry behind this façade of tranquillity, a veritable powerhouse of British horseracing.

With seemingly grandiose ideas, the Scot, an interloper, has constructed a behemoth of a training facility. From the dilapidated stables he and his wife encountered in 1988, he dominates, one could say has consumed, much of the area and his three yards – the hub Kingsley Park, Kingsley House and Warwick House – now have no fewer than 230 horses standing there.

Middleham is thriving once more. Indeed, it has done so for many years in the Johnston era. When Chancellor, and Richmond MP, Rishi Sunak, visited in October 2020, he described it as one of racing's "centres of excellence" and this is in significant part because of a visionary, a man with a single-minded mission.

When we meet, in the kitchen of Kingsley House, once a medieval rectory, to discuss the content of this book, it is inevitable that, firstly, we would return briefly to 23 August 2018 and a particular race at York. It was the day an outsider prevailed, and not just because Frankie Dettori's poise and persistence was sufficient to ensure that the Mark Johnston-trained 20-1 chance Poet's Society claimed the one-mile Clipper Logistics Handicap by a neck on Yorkshire Oaks day.

In another year, it would have been just another race, and soon just another page in the Form Book. But not this renewal of the event. This was also the moment that Johnston finally thrust his own head over the line to record a 4,194th winner – eclipsing the record set by Richard Hannon Snr, who retired with a tally of 4,193, making the Scot the most prolific trainer in British racing history.

There were no klaxons, flashing lights, or pyrotechnics illuminating the skies, just a contented, rather than triumphant glow, on the features of a man who could have been excused a verbal volley at those who had doubted him early in his career. He confined himself to a modest statement, expressing his relief that his "winning machine" as one headline deemed his operation, had finally produced that record-breaking winner, and containing the most relevant line: "From where we started it is unthinkable."

Among many plaudits was this from Cornelius Lysaght, the former BBC racing correspondent: "The way he has climbed from the most unpromising of starts, with a handful of moderate horses and plenty of debt, to the very summit where he now stands, is one of the great racing stories."

It was, indeed, and was also the instant that inspired this writer to tell Johnston's story – not just because of a record registered, but because of the phenomenal journey in his ascent into rarefied atmosphere, without the equivalent of oxygen support or Sherpas, just a degree in veterinary medicine and what can only be described as Caledonian chutzpah.

From the start, he questioned orthodoxy, the doctrines of those who came before him, and progressed from a self-taught novice to a Classic-winning trainer within seven years.

No-one could have ever confused him with a man content with a mundane existence. Tellingly, he once told me that, even in that first year as a trainer, 1987, he had watched Henry Cecil finish as leading trainer at Royal Ascot with seven winners, and promised himself: "One day that could be me."

It *would* be him, incidentally. By the start of 2021, the Scot had despatched 46 Royal Ascot winners, and been top trainer twice, in 2002 and 2003. Also, for good measure, he has been leading trainer at Glorious Goodwood on 12 occasions.

Throughout, his fearsome sense of national pride has been his spear and shield. The blood that pulses through him – and which is also frequently found in his compatriots who achieve distinction in public life, including in government and opposition, entertainment and sport – has empowered him.

If you're part of the Johnston operation, you become adopted sons and daughters of the Johnston Clan. At the racecourse, his staff are *all* turned out in tartan ties and waistcoats.

In fact, Johnston suggested, albeit with a touch of mischief, that this book should be titled *Scottish Power*, after the energy company that the trainer says he'd most like to have as his sponsor. He even offered to don a kilt for the cover photo.

But it was decided on *Phenomenon*, a word defined as a rare occurrence, a wonder. Because this character does not fit the typical trainer template.

He had never been an ace in the saddle – nothing could be further from the truth, we learn – nor a scion of a celebrated racing name, nor studied at the foot of a distinguished racing mentor.

To some, he is an irritant, a bristling malcontent, who continues to question everything about the industry in which he announced himself as a man with unconstrained ambition when he persuaded the Jockey Club to grant him a training licence all those years ago.

He refuses to play the political game, and relishes puncturing balloons of conventional wisdom. It certainly doesn't take much to provoke the former president of the National Trainers' Federation, who has been a columnist in many newspapers and periodicals, including the *Racing Post*, *The Times* and *Horse & Hound*, but now restricts himself to offering his take on racing, and the world beyond, in his own monthly magazine, the *Kingsley Klarion*.

Yet, his achievements are undeniable. There are few better placed to pass judgement on what the Scot has brought to the sport than the five-times champion trainer John Gosden. He told me early in 2021: "I admire totally his originality of thought. He looks at things from his own angle, and has a very fresh perspective on everything, from training of a racehorse through to the structure of the racing industry. I find him a fascinating, interesting and exciting person to be around. I've been on endless meetings with him and he's always impressive as an individual, intellectually.

"He's a great friend, Mark, and Deirdre, too. I went up to stay the night with them last September. I hadn't been there for 14 years, and I was just amazed at what he and Deirdre had created there – an absolutely splendid set-up for the training of horses.

"I have nothing but admiration for him; the way he goes to the sales; the way he operates. He's just a wonderful breath of fresh air, quite frankly. I think what he has achieved is something anyone else is going to struggle to match."

Johnston is quite simply the rarest of individuals in this industry: an entirely self-made man. Johnston is different.

---

*Johnston confides, incidentally, that his selection of the Fleetwood Mac song as the one he'd most want to avoid being washed away was an embarrassing error, and one he has not been allowed to forget. The disc he should have opted to save was "You're Still The One". Not Shania Twain's 1998 hit, but the excellent lockdown performance by Deirdre and Angus Johnston, a story to which I will return.

ACKNOWLEDGEMENTS

This is far more than a story of one man. As much as this book was first mooted in recognition of Mark Johnston becoming the most prolific British trainer, it is also the tale of one family – those connected by blood, but also an enormous extended family; those who are, and have been, linked and driven by a common purpose: the staff, owners and jockeys.

The material for this book is based on interviews and conversations with them over many years, and the author is grateful to all the following for their contributions:

First and foremost, Mark and Deirdre Johnston, who have both readily given their time to co-operate with the author, as has son Charlie, and Mark's sister Sharon. There has also been much valued assistance from owners Ron Huggins and the late Duke of Roxburghe, and members of the Johnston Racing team, including Mark's assistants Jock Bennett, Hayley Kelly and Andrew Bottomley, as well as Patrick Trainor. Thanks must also go to Mikaelle Lebreton for her great help in organising photographs, and John Scanlon, writer for the Kingsley Klarion. My thanks also go to former jockeys Jason Weaver and Bobby Elliott for their input, as well as to Joe Fanning – and to John Gosden.

In addition, this book cannot have been completed without the sterling work of my agent Melanie Michael-Greer, and at Welbeck Publishing Group, Ross Hamilton, as well as copy-editor David Ballheimer and proofreader Guy Croton.

Finally, my appreciation goes to Graham Dench and my brother Steve, who both painstaking reviewed the proofs – and finally to my wife Louise for her support and forbearance over many months.

Nick Townsend
Oxfordshire, August 2021

A CHANGING OF
THE GUARD

R ight up until late in 2020, the dying embers of the Flat
racing year were still being raked for winners by the Johnston
poker, with runners despatched to the all-weather Flat fixtures
at Lingfield, Kempton, Wolverhampton, Newcastle, Southwell
and Chelmsford.

Winter was once a dormant period for Flat yards in terms of
racing fixtures; a time when the National Hunt season swaggered
belligerently into the consciousness of many racing folk,
culminating in the Cheltenham Festival and Grand National.
From early November to late March, Flat racing was nudged aside.

But that all began to change in 1989 when all-weather Flat
racing (on Fibresand, Polytrack and, most recently, Tapeta) was
introduced. Initially, Johnston was a great enthusiast and supporter
of this development and, though he would not necessarily be
enamoured by its increasing prevalence – not if it came at the
expense of racing on the turf – the trainer readily harvests winners
on these surfaces, with the justification: "I didn't make the rules."

As will be observed, that is a phrase oft-repeated by the Scot in various contexts. He may not fully agree with a policy, but will not indulge in acts of self-harm just to make a point.

At the end of a year interrupted by the cancellation of 74 days of racing by the British Horseracing Authority (BHA)[1], following government advice, the nation's most numerically successful trainer has finished third in the championship table, which is based on prize money won rather than totals of winners. Johnston has amassed 169 winners and 471 places from 1,274 runners, with total prize money won of £2,134,037.

It means a 27th consecutive season of centuries for the Scot, nine of those double centuries – a total which almost certainly would have been ten had racecourses not been closed for more than two months.

If the trainers' championship had been based on victories recorded, it would have been an emphatic triumph for Johnston. Even as it is, above him in the table are only John Gosden (150 wins) and Irish trainer Aidan O'Brien (13 wins in Britain), the private trainer for John Magnier and his powerful Coolmore operation.

Johnston has never been champion trainer, but it is not something he dwells upon. "How many times would I have been champion if based on numbers? Twelve, maybe, 14, I don't remember," he says. "But I'm not crying over that."

Amongst Johnston's talented performers in 2020 was Elarqam, who took his final curtain call with a Group 3 success at Newbury in September.

The son of the mighty Frankel, and Johnston's dual 2004 English

---

[1] The British Horseracing Authority (BHA) was founded on 31 July 2007; it replaced the British Horseracing Board (BHB) as the governing authority for UK horse racing. The BHB itself had only been formed on 10 June 1993 and had taken on the responsibilities of The Jockey Club.

and Irish 1,000 Guineas victor Attraction, had set his owner Sheikh Hamdan Al Maktoum back 1.6m guineas. He had been retired to stand at the French stud Haras de Saint Arnoult.

There were also significant Group 1[2] victories in France: Gear Up in the Criterium de Saint-Cloud and Subjectivist in the Prix Royal-Oak at Longchamp. Both had been purchased for a relative pittance in bloodstock terms by Johnston but had progressed to emphatically defy their hammer price at auction.

The Covid restrictions meant no socialising at Christmas and, at Hogmanay, Johnston and Deirdre were at home alone for only the second time in their married life but, as he reported in his influential newsletter, the *Kingsley Klarion*, "rest assured, I raised a glass to you all and toasted you with the words: '*Here's tae us, wha's like us, damn few, and they're aw deid. Mair's the pity.*'"

This, according to *The Scotsman*: is a classic, traditional Scottish toast showing drunken sentimentality at its very best, and can be translated as "Here's to us; who is as good as us? Damn few, and they're all dead. More's the pity."

There's no escaping it; the past year has been a hellish one; a harrowing period for most, traumatic for some, deadly for many. Too many have lost their lives, many their business or employment, and then there has been the collateral health damage, physical and mental.

During that period in which all sport was cancelled, Johnston lost 12 days in bed and days more recovering from Covid. Although there was no racing at the time, the yard continued to operate

---

[2] Group 1 races are the zenith of achievement, and include the Classics: the 1,000 and 2,000 Guineas Stakes (at Newmarket), The Oaks and The Derby (at Epsom), and the St Leger Stakes (at Doncaster). Group 2 and 3 races are also highly prized – particularly when breeders are assessing the quality of prospective stallions and mares. Listed races are lesser events but also confirm quality. In a sales catalogue, the form of any horse that has won or been placed in a Group or Listed race is printed in bold, more commonly known as 'black type'.

cohesively under the direction of the Johnstons' eldest son Charlie, who is one of his father's four assistants (veteran Brian 'Jock' Bennett, Hayley Kelly and Andrew Bottomley, all-long-serving at the yard, are the others), together with Deirdre.

If ever there was an inevitability in racing it was the destiny of Charlie, who, to put it in equine terms, had been sired by a humbly-bred, constantly-improving, top-class stayer out of a redoubtable, talented, versatile mare.

I first encountered Charlie as an engaging, thoroughly normal, teenager, who could be heard listening to the Kaiser Chiefs in his bedroom. Yet, his first point of reference each morning before school was a review of the pages of the *Racing Post*. He scoured it for reports, statistics, his father's planned runners and, though too young legally to place a bet, frequently asked them to do so on his behalf.

As his father had conceded wryly, the *Post* was where he learned to read. Charlie's first words, according to Johnston were 'Carson' and 'Hills', after jockeys Willie and the twin brothers Michael and Richard.

The Johnstons' elder son also rode work, was thoroughly conversant with the complexities of form and, even as a precocious 15-year-old, was already representing his father on the Channel 4 racing preview show *The Morning Line*.

Assured and confident back then, if you had cast your mind ahead, say, 15, 20, years, you could envisage him ruling this mighty kingdom in his own right one day. Charlie and the Winner Factory, you might say, though it would be quite some hand-me-down when the time came. Even in his twenties, he had been named in a prestigious list of the most influential under-35 'rising stars' in racing.

Yet, the Johnstons were understandably concerned that such a presumption on Charlie's part could adversely affect his education. Why study hard at school or university if your future is already assured? – was their thinking.

Johnston decreed – not to put too fine a point on it – that Charlie should study for a veterinary degree, just as he had done, a course that he insisted "had been a tremendous selling point for me".

His argument was clearly persuasive. Johnston Jnr did, indeed, return to Kingsley House a qualified vet, after seven years at Glasgow University Veterinary School, his father's alma mater, and became an assistant trainer – to his father.

Now it would be just a question of time. But when would be the correct moment to usher in the next generation? In the Johnstons' kitchen at Kingsley House, where Charlie and his younger brother Angus spent so much of their formative years, we talk accession of the former to the family seat.

It's long been on Johnston Snr's mind, but he has been exceedingly circumspect. Whatever the qualities of Charlie, it has been the name of Mark Johnston that is on the metaphorical nameplate above the door; not so much licensed to sell alcohol as to sell dreams to existing and prospective owners.

It's not difficult for anyone with a love of the Turf to appreciate why racehorse training, particularly at such a rarefied level, can be so addictive to an able practitioner, and why to walk away would bring on cold turkey.

Earlier this century, Johnston told me he planned to retire at 55. It was a forecast that, frankly, never appeared likely to become reality. And, indeed, it hasn't.

On this day, a few days before the turn of 2020, he is 61 and is still the controlling figure. As much as the business was re-branded a few years ago as 'Johnston Racing' to allow for the eventual transition, 'Mark Johnston' is the name inextricably associated with winners and whose consistency of performance simply cannot be rebutted.

Yet, there must be a time when even an acknowledged master of his craft begins to relinquish control of his life's work. It is his penultimate year as a 'sole trader' or, to put it more formally, of holding a training licence under his own name.

By the start of 2022, it is planned that Charlie will join his father in a partnership – under an innovative concept introduced in May 2020 by the BHA – and will eventually run the operation under his name. For Johnston Snr as an individual, it is approaching the end of an era.

So, as the New Year dawns, the pair are set to amalgamate as licensed trainers. But precisely when, Johnston Snr has yet to decide. All that is certain is that 2021 will be a climactic one in Johnston's 34-year career and another reason to write this book now.

A crucial caveat to this otherwise ideal solution: the joint partnership would start afresh, with zero winners. At that point, there could be no addition to Johnston's tally of what is now approaching 5,000 winners in his own right.

What has been so important about the set-up in Middleham is that, despite the vast scale of the Johnston enterprise, it has always been, and will remain, essentially a family affair.

When you talk of 'the yard', you refer not just to the trainer but to Deirdre, his vivacious wife of 36 years, who has been instrumental in her husband's success and still rides work every day, and to Charlie and the Johnstons' younger son Angus.

While never sharing his brother's absolute obsession with the Turf, Angus has focused on a singing career and also runs a flat-renting business in Glasgow. Yet, he, too, is increasingly involved in the family business.

Charlie, who was not even born when his father and mother arrived here in 1988, has participated in and viewed, with some incredulity, the early scenes from a professionally-made family video, entitled *Then to Now*.

It comprises images and footage of the unlikely start made by Johnston, training at a stables adjacent to an RAF bombing range in Lincolnshire in 1987, and his progression to become a record-breaker.

Speaking in the video, Charlie admits: "You look at that run-down yard in Lincolnshire, and horses out on the beach and struggle to comprehend that you could take that from there and turn it into one of, if not the, best training establishments in the world. For that to have come from where they began takes a level of drive and determination that few are blessed with."

Charlie is not alone in his sense of wonderment at how Johnston made such a dramatic transformation in his fortunes, and became, well, a phenomenon.

DRIVEN BY A DREAD
OF FAILURE

L et's be clear. For all the assumption that savouring those elusive, tantalising moments of glory, while remaining in the top echelon of racehorse trainers, is what motivates him, Mark Johnston is fired just as much by a dread that all he has created could decline. It is a characteristic he maintains is a Scottish trait. "It's fear," he says. "Fear that the whole thing will collapse around my ears – that's why I can't take my eyes off the ball for a minute."

Initially, that revelation took me aback slightly, as the foundations here are seemingly cast in reinforced concrete. Yet, if you think about it, the advantages of large-scale production are only in play if investment – and by that, I mean the horses consigned to him by his owners and the accompanying fees – remains at a sufficiently high level to support a workforce geared to care for up to 270 charges.

He is acutely aware that hubris, or mere complacency, can so easily precede a fall from grace in this ultra-competitive industry. He has seen it too often amongst his peers; the decline of men revered in the sport who have struck fallow periods when the winners no longer flow, when once-fashionable names lose their lustre.

He does not want to become like some of the great trainers of the past whose careers entered dark periods. Being Britain's most successful trainer doesn't confer permanent unqualified support for Johnston or his operation.

Just because he enjoys the patronage of major owners now, including that of His Highness Sheikh Mohammed bin Rashid Al Maktoum (normally known as simply Sheikh Mohammed), and the Maktoum family as a whole, he is acutely aware how stable numbers can decline, with mega-wealthy individuals transferring their patronage to rivals. He has seen it happen to esteemed trainers, even the late Sir Henry Cecil.

Cecil accumulated ten trainers' championships between 1976 and 1993 and, yet, in 2005, won a mere dozen races, with his stable having declined to 50 horses. And this charismatic character, seemingly an unassailable force in British racing, who once instilled fear in the opposition whenever he introduced an unraced two-year-old and whose Classic victories at that time stood at 23 domestic and 11 in Ireland and France, was fortunate in that he retained the patronage of Prince Khalid Abdullah, who entrusted him with a horse named Frankel…

That champion, undefeated in a 14-race career and now, as a stallion, one of the leading sires in Europe, restored Cecil's reputation in the years before his death in 2013. But as Johnston says: "With Frankel, Henry died seemingly top of the tree. But it shouldn't be forgotten there were a few dark years before that."

This is a precarious business. No doubt about that. There are so many rivals who would relish adding the Johnston horses, and their owners, to their rosters if fissures began to appear in the superstructure of the operation.

To demonstrate what a competitive industry this is, the BHA lists just under five hundred trainers of Flat horses. True, they range from big-hitters to those who stable a select few, and many included are National Hunt trainers who may, on occasion, have a Flat runner, but it is a significant total, all vying for what *can* be a fickle owner's pound.

The capacity of a trainer to be fashionable is dependent on form and the kind of major-race winners that create headlines on television and in the racing and non-racing media. Form can so easily fluctuate. Johnston has told me in the past of at least one owner who'd switched his allegiance to another trainer purely because of an indifferent results sequence.

Though, in time, Johnston will hand over the business in its entirety to Charlie, he has remained insistent on these points: he would not want to hand over a failing business, which could give owners the opportunity to withdraw their horses from the yard. Yet, nor would he desire to overstay his welcome.

When I suggested to Johnston in 2018, and only partly in jest, that he would continue to be the pre-eminent force until he drops, he had forcibly refuted the notion. "I've looked at some other trainers where I've felt they've hung on far too long when it was clear the son was running the show. I don't want to be like that," he says. "It wouldn't be fair to Charlie and it wouldn't be good for the business."

Some handovers could scarcely have been conducted more smoothly, you submit. Richard Hannon Snr, having recorded a fourth trainers' championship, relinquished formal control of his Herridge Stables near Marlborough at the age of 68 to Richard Hannon Jnr, his son and former assistant. Hannon Jnr, then 38, duly became champion trainer in 2014, his first year in charge.

"Yes," agrees Johnston. "Although Richard [Jnr] was an awful lot older than Charlie when he took over – and named Richard, which probably helped a bit…"

He adds: "Certain other sons of notable fathers haven't found the succession process straightforward, and initially lost owners. They had to build the business back up again, so I wouldn't want to do that. I wouldn't want to see it run down."

Johnston Jnr has long been acutely aware of why it is so crucial the edifice shouldn't crumble, even slightly. "Because the business has got so big now and employs so many staff, our break-even number of horses is very, very high. I couldn't afford to start training with 150 horses, and the business still run as it does," Charlie explained to me in 2018. "It would start losing money very quickly. With 150 horses, I wouldn't have 200-plus winners a year, which is our target. So, people would view it as a failure. It's a downward spiral from there."

Such stories of decline, and his own innate circumspection, explain why, when I meet Johnston just before the turn of the year, his mind is focused fully on 2021, and most immediately on his more precocious two-year-olds ready to run once the Turf season starts in March, as well as the later-maturing types who will emerge come summer and autumn.

In horseracing, money generally shouts loudest – but not always. Among these hundred newcomers, many bought on spec by Johnston at the Autumn yearling sales, or sent to him by his patrons, could there be anything to compare with the miracle mare that was Attraction, bred by her owner the late Duke of Roxburghe, and who arrived at Middleham with crooked forelegs but proceeded to become the first horse to win the English and Irish 1,000 Guineas?

Or could any of them begin to emulate the achievements of the stable's redoubtable stayer Double Trigger, who cost IR7,200; or a

Mister Baileys, Johnston's 1994 2,000 Guineas victor, bought for 10,500gns and which gave a timely turbo-charge to his nascent training career?

The fact is that you never quite know; not until they begin their work on the gallops – as was the case with Shamardal, the horse Johnston regards as the best he has trained – and many not until they reach the racecourse.

The opening month of 2021 bodes well. Barely had the crowd-free New Year's Eve fireworks show in London fizzled out than the Johnston yard had responded with its own missiles of intent, recording its most successful January since he began training in 1987.

The operation shows every indication of producing a tenth year of a double century of winners. And, as Johnston is constantly at pains to emphasise, winners are as attractive to owners as lavender to bees. A double century come December 2021 will mean that he can rest relatively easy as he prepares for 2022. However, a dip too far below, and he would contemplate a winter of discontent as he prepares to forge an official partnership with Charlie.

"I WAS ALWAYS REBELLIOUS AND QUESTIONING AUTHORITY"

Lord Howard de Walden, regarded as the last of the great British owner-breeders and a name associated with the likes of 1985 Derby victor Slip Anchor and the great miler Kris, once gave me a considered verdict on racehorse trainers.

"Well," he had pondered my question during an interview, before responding: "They drive around in their expensive cars, but they're just glorified grooms, really, aren't they?"

I suspected this irreverence was a touch of mischief on the peer's part, but when I related this to Mark Johnston, expecting to be corrected, he smiled and retorted: "Part of my success story is that, from the outset, I've never made any excuses for my failures. The buck stops here. But at the same time, there are times when I think, 'Anybody could do this job, it's not rocket science. It's not particularly clever to be a good racehorse trainer.'"

Though the Scot has often prayed at the unorthodox church of training strategy and has long had his preferred methods, he does not attempt to create some great mystique out of the skill of preparing racehorses to win races.

His declaration is not one that would be necessarily appreciated by his fellow trainers, particularly those who buy into the belief that they are 'little gods', as the late racing writer Paul Haigh once described the breed.

The reality is, however, that *not* everyone could train racehorses, and certainly not successfully. It not only requires comprehensive knowledge of, and the ability to cajole the optimum from, the *Equus caballus*, the solid-hoofed herbivorous quadruped, but also an understanding of, and the ability to understand, the behaviour of the human biped.

It requires the ability to handle sometimes intractable equines as expertly as awkward, demanding owners, while also managing the expectations and occasionally the peccadillos of staff. It also demands some business acumen and ideally an appreciation of social intercourse.

As broached earlier, many are born into this world as the sons and daughters of trainers. Others have honed their skills as assistants to successful exponents. A number are ex-jockeys. Johnston was none of these. He simply recognised where his destiny lay as a young teenager.

To fully appreciate the influences that propelled him from such an unlikely genesis to where he now stands proudly atop the Sport of Kings, as it was once grandly known, it is necessary to return to his formative years when the seeds of his obsession were sown as a child by a father who owned and bred racehorses on a very small scale.

A father, who, it should be stressed, enjoyed a conspicuous lack of success.

* * *

Mark Johnston entered the world on 10 October 1959, at Bellshill Maternity Hospital, south-east of Glasgow, the son of *working-class* parents (he deliberately emphasises the adjective) Ron and Mary. The couple already had two daughters, Lyn and Sharon.

Sadly, Lyn died in 2014, and in his tribute to her in the *Kingsley Klarion*, Johnston related that "Lyn had been born on 30 March 1953 and I didn't come along until six and a half years later. During that time my mother gave birth to a still-born boy, who would have been Mark, and my sister Sharon. So Lyn was my biggest, big sister – all 5'2" of her – and I was the baby of the family."

His parents were both Glaswegians; his father hailing from Bridgeton in the city, his mother from Knightswood; though the family moved on to Springburn.

"Both Bridgeton and Knightswood are now inner-city areas, and are still not exactly upmarket, but then they were deprived areas, dominated by thirties tenement estates," emphasises Johnston. "It was pretty grim. Not quite as notorious as the Gorbals, but there wasn't much in it."

Ron had been evacuated to Aberdeen during the war and attended the high school there. "But my grandfather died when my father was 14 and, as I understand it, without that paternal influence, my father constantly verged on crossing the line and getting into trouble," Johnston says. "The result was that he was packed off to the Army, the Scots Guards, just after the end of World War II, with the reputation of being a bit of a rebel." A trait that clearly has been inherited by his son.

Ron Johnston had never displayed any athletic prowess at school, but once in the Army, he won medals for running – apparently, he was the Forces three-mile champion and he took up boxing, a sport that came naturally to him. According to his son: "He was from a very rough, poor background – in fact, I believe, quite a violent background. He was only 5ft 4ins tall, but he would fight anyone. He could take a drink and was a very aggressive guy, but never to us."

He adds: "If someone swore in front of us, he'd be liable to get hold of them, and remind them how to behave. I'd call his attitude very principled, and I guess that's where I got it from."

It would be easy to perceive Ron as a stereotypical hard-drinking Glaswegian who enforced his point of view with his knuckles, rather reminiscent of Robert Carlyle's character Begbie in the film *Trainspotting*. Carlyle played him as 'a cartoon caricature of a Glasgow hard man.'

But that would be untrue, and unfair. Ron Johnston was actually a pacifist by nature. He was also anti-establishment and, according to Mark, disliked being in the Army. He was opposed to serving in Tripoli and Palestine.

One facet of the Army did appeal to him, though. When his unit was asked whether anyone knew anything about horses, he volunteered. He didn't know anything. He also claimed to be able to ride. He couldn't. Ron Johnston's only connection with horses was that his cousin Jack, to whom he'd been close, had worked with carthorses at a stable in Glasgow.

And, so, Private Ronald Johnston went off to work in the Army stables as a groom. Johnston recalls the regiment had a racehorse called Nonesuch, which his father rode in at least one Army race. "That was some achievement because he was basically self-taught," Mark says.

After Army service, Ron Johnston worked in London with his brother Jimmy. "They worked in hotels and then joined the airlines; my Dad as a steward for BOAC [British Overseas Airways Corporation]. That's where he met my mother, Mary who was a stewardess for BEA [British European Airways – BOAC and BEA were the forerunners of British Airways]. My Uncle Jim and Auntie

Jean, his wife, were also stewards and stewardesses and they all shared a flat in London together."

Ron and Mary married in 1951 and, after Lyn was born, the couple moved to Birmingham. "Sharon was born there in 1953, but by the time I came along in 1959 my parents were living in East Kilbride, a new town," says Johnston.

And so, the Johnstons gravitated back from England and moved into a new council house in East Kilbride, south of Glasgow. It was just a village until the end of World War II, but became the first and most successful of Scotland's post-war new towns.

It was here, living in The Murray area of the town, that a young Johnston was first introduced to racing when his father, at that time a hotel night porter, would sneak him into a bookmaker on Saturdays to place bets. Being considerably under-age, he'd either wait outside or he would be smuggled in by his father and stand under the counter. "We'd then go to my grandmother's house in Calderwood where my dad and his step-father would watch the racing."

The two families, his parents' and his uncle's, tended to move as a group, and when they decided to up sticks once more, it was a significant moment in Johnston's life. The transition took the then six-year-old from the prosaic austerity of a new town to an exciting new world for a young boy to explore, albeit only 25 miles north of Glasgow.

"When my Uncle Jimmy moved to the holiday village of Aberfoyle in the Lomond and Trossachs National Park, one of Europe's most beautiful locations, and bought a hotel there, my parents, sisters and I followed them up there," says Johnston. "My father bought five acres of land at Gartmore Bridge, near Aberfoyle, and got planning permission to build a house."

He adds: "We lived in a mobile home, on that land. The idea was that we should live in that while the house was built. But it took years to build, and after a few years we moved out and rented a house in Aberfoyle village."

While the family were still in East Kilbride, the younger of his two sisters, Sharon, was bought a pony, and both she, her elder sister Lyn and her kid brother had riding lessons.

The pony came with them to Aberfoyle, and young Johnston seized every opportunity to ride it. "I had to steal her pony if I wanted to ride it," he says. "I used to climb in through the boarded-up window of the shed where she kept her tack. I'd pull the board away and squeeze in. I couldn't get the saddle out, could only get the bridle, but that was sufficient."

Meanwhile, his enterprising father Ron Johnston became a Scottish representative for S&H Pink Stamps. These were trading stamps, which you received at petrol stations and some stores, and exchanged for goods available in a catalogue. His Uncle Jim became a representative for Green Shield stamps.

Ron Johnston was also a Scottish representative for Alba Television, at one time a significant contributor to the development of the British radio and television industry. "He left the job when I was four, but my mother took it on, and she was there for close to 20 years, until it went out of business."

Johnston adds: "When she took the Alba job, my father set up his own business, initially specialising in loft insulations and television aerials from a storeroom he rented in East Kilbride. He also increasingly developed the electronic side, and based his business, Ron Johnston Agencies, in Duke Street, Glasgow. He was the sole Scottish representative for [electronics manufacturer] Pye Labgear.

"That business took off. He ran it for around ten years and then sold it, possibly under-sold it, but it was that which provided him with sufficient capital to fund his hobby of owning racehorses. That really spawned my interest…"

His father's obsession with the thoroughbred certainly stirred young Johnston's imagination. By his teens, he had his bedroom wall decorated with posters, not of pop groups, but the supreme racehorses of that era: Mill Reef, Nijinsky, Brigadier Gerard. "In my slightly later teens, I had a record of *The Story of Mill Reef* which I used to listen to, a vinyl LP! I had that, and the book, and pictures on my bedroom wall, pictures of Nijinsky. I even had two wooden chairs in my bedroom that were painted with names of great horses. I painted them myself."

He did not completely reject the rituals of typical teenage life. As he explained, nearly 50 years later, on *Desert Island Discs* in selecting Slade's 1971 hit "Get Down and Get with It": "In my very early teens, or before I'd reached my teens, I'd already started to listen to music, although I wasn't buying records. I decided I should have a group that I was a fan of and I wanted to follow, and I chose Slade. That has remained until this day and this song, which is a cover, is the ringtone on my phone."

So, in his company, you're highly likely to be treated to a loud blast of a song with lyrics somewhat incongruous for a man generally perceived as possessing a certain gravitas: "Want to see ev'rybody get up off their seat, Clap your hands stamp your feet, get down get with it, I said a-get down get with it and do the jerk."

To return to Aberfoyle, this charming village on the banks of the River Forth – once important for its slate quarries – is known as the 'Gateway to the Trossachs'. Its history and literary legacy have long entranced visitors from around the world, principally because of Sir Walter Scott, who was a familiar presence as he rode along the forest tracks and would stay in the Old Manse House.

It was this wooded location he used as a backdrop to his novel

Rob Roy and his poem "Lady of the Lake", the lake being Lake Katrine. He wrote the poem while on holiday there in 1809 with his wife Charlotte and daughter Sofia.

> *"The summer dawn's reflected hue,*
> *To purple changed Loch Katrine blue,*
> *Mildly and soft the western breeze,*
> *Just kissed the Lake, just stirr'd the breeze…"*

Now located in the Queen Elizabeth Forest Park, it's an idyllic haven for any child to develop in, particularly one like the young Johnston, whose curiosity in animal life of all kinds was becoming apparent.

"From childhood, I was always an animal person," he says. "Anything I could get hold of, I wanted to keep. Not just chickens and dogs but wild animals: snakes and lizards, birds and fish. I went out and caught minnows, newts and snakes and slow-worms. Fortunately, I soon learned the folly of keeping wild animals in captivity. What I did was not fair on the animals, but I learned a lot from it. It was probably what eventually led me to go to vet school."

He adds with a laugh: "I had animals my parents had no idea I had! I did daft things. When I was 11, I bought a calf from the market for £1.50. I kept it in the garden shed and tried to rear it. But it died after about a week. It wasn't the brightest thing to do, but I learned a lot from the experience."

However, he harboured no sentimental love for animals. "Later I'd go fishing and shooting rabbits, or laying snares for them. I'd feed them to my dogs. Killing wild animals – that didn't bother me at all."

Though he knew a few children locally, his closest friend through his early school years was his cousin David, who lived in the same village. Johnston says: "I suppose, looking back, I was a bit of a loner, a bit different from the rest of the crowd. Maybe it was because I'd arrived in Aberfoyle from the Big Smoke, or close to it, East Kilbride. I was always rebellious and questioning authority."

Johnston stresses it was school rather than parental authority that was the subject of his disaffection. He would often skip school, but with his parents' consent. "I would go to work with my father at his office in Glasgow, or I'd go in the van when he was delivering TV aerials. We also went to a lot of auctions. Most of the things in our house were bought at auctions. We'd go to antique auctions, vehicle auctions, ex-Army auctions, cattle auctions, horse auctions, all kinds. He liked auctions, and so did I."

However, he is forced to admit: "My attendance record at school was horrendous. I found some report cards recently, which had my attendances on it, and it was just unbelievable the number of days off I had."

He adds: "Deirdre's parents and I both went to the same secondary school, McLaren High School, in Callander, about ten miles from Aberfoyle, but 20 years apart. I absolutely hated it, and don't have a good word to say about the place whereas Deirdre's parents loved it. Afterwards they were in all the old pupils' groups.

"There was a teacher I really didn't like. I think she may have been at school with Kathleen [Deirdre's mother]. And, before I married Deirdre, this teacher said to Kathleen: 'Oh, yes, Mark Johnston – always thought he was smarter than he really was…'"

Johnston's sister Sharon, four years his senior, has recalled Mark being doted upon by their parents. "He was quite spoilt," she says, in a tone of affection for her brother. "As the boy, he got treated differently from us girls. When we were old enough to drive, we got an old banger. He was given an MG Midget."

Johnston has a slightly different version of events, protesting that, actually, "Lyn *and* I got the car." He says: "When I was 17, and Lyn 23, my dad lost his licence for drink driving, and he let Lyn and me go and trade in his Vauxhall Victor for an MG Midget. We also had an old Volkswagen one-ton pick-up, and we swapped them around until Lyn crashed the MG. We got it repaired, but she never drove it again after that, and I just commandeered it – until I blew up the engine, and got another one."

What would not be disputed was that the Johnston children were the offspring of parents who were vociferous supporters of the Scottish National Party. So staunch was that support that their mother, Mary, was not only a member of the SNP, as was Ron, but she also stood as a parliamentary candidate for the party in Motherwell and Coatbridge. She also ran the trade union wing of the SNP.

It was perhaps inevitable that Johnston would inherit a profound love for his nation. Sharon says: "He couldn't avoid having feelings like that. It was in our blood. Our parents had a huge influence on our upbringing. Other children would be taken out at the weekends to enjoy themselves; we'd have to do leaflet drops for the Scots Nats."

She adds: "Our parents were very committed to the cause. Meetings were held at our house. I'd go so far to say that their views were quite extreme – at one time we thought our phone was being tapped. You don't grow up in a house like that without having strong nationalistic tendencies. Mark's got huge pride in where he came from. I'm sure that's why he gets an extra kick out of his winners at the big meetings down south."

Those days lay a long way ahead for Johnston. And had he followed his father's example, certainly when it came to buying and breeding horses, they would never have arrived. "I would say he taught me how *not* to do it," is his considered verdict.

BECOMING A CHAMPION – AS A WHIPPET TRAINER

Ron Johnston's first horse was trained by Paddy Chesmore, an Irish former jump jockey. He had been appointed by Sir Hugh Fraser, at one time chairman of the House of Fraser department stores, to train on a farm he owned at Drymen, eight miles from the Johnston home.

"We went to see this new racing stable that had opened and my father bought a horse. It was named Torso. I can still remember its pedigree: Sir Tor, out of Celestial Body. It was placed God knows how many times, but never won a race. But that was me hooked."

When Chesmore died from a brain haemorrhage, his widow Sue took over the licence. Johnston's father then bought another horse, called Sure Jumper, so had two horses in training with Sue Chesmore. At this time, Mark began to go racing with his father. He also worked at Chesmore's stables at weekends.

"When we went to the races to watch our horses, I used to sit in the back seat of the car and listen to my father and Sue chatting in the front and say to myself: 'I *want* her job'. I wanted to be paid for it, rather than watch someone else do it."

You can almost imagine the teenage Johnston believing that if he thought about it hard enough, he would be granted wish fulfilment. It would certainly prove to be a critical moment in his short life.

Also significant was that there were horses at the Johnston home as his father became an amateur breeder in a minor way. "It was his hobby and he probably had three mares on the go at the peak and various foals and yearlings," recalls Johnston. "But he wasn't very good at it – he never bred a winner – but it got me used to being around horses. I'd muck them out and occasionally ride them."

Apart from the five acres around the house being built, his father rented a further forty acres of land from the Forestry Commission between Gartmore and Aberfoyle. "I remember, for my tenth birthday, my present was a two-year-old filly, with the idea that I would eventually ride her," remembers Johnston. "I didn't. She ended up as a brood mare."

In truth, though, that breeding project became more of a frustration than an inspiration to young Johnston. "I was becoming irritated by the way my father dealt with these horses. We were on a hiding to nothing."

Johnston elucidates. "He was doing it on a shoestring. The house was littered with copies of the *Stud Book* [a breed registry for horses in Great Britain and Ireland] and *Ruff's Guide to the Turf* [a record of every race run, and horse bought]. He used to read every page of it and would go through all these statistics."

He adds: "He was one of these people who was looking at the third generation of a pedigree, because he couldn't afford the Frankels and Dubawis of that time. Instead, he was dreaming of in-breeding them to Hyperion[3], but put bad mares to cheap stallions.

---

[3] Hyperion is considered one of the most important thoroughbreds of the twentieth century, both as a runner and as a sire.

He was looking at using £100 stallions to try and breed himself a Derby winner – which I now realise was nonsense. It doesn't work like that."

You could argue that it was a learning experience for his father, who had actually displayed great enterprise. "But it was also the way he kept them, in muddy fields, with bad fences, the way he fed them," Johnston explains. "He fed them lots. But he didn't really know how to handle them properly. They grew up wild."

Johnston adds: "I see lots of people like him now, trying to breed a racehorse. And they know nothing about it. That's why I say that I learnt from him how not to do it. He bought cheap, moderate horses at the sales, knowing nothing about what he was buying."

Ron Johnston's vain attempt to breed a winning racehorse did have one beneficial consequence, however. "One of my father's home-bred yearlings, named Yes Indeed, was broken by Sue Chesmore. But she didn't have a Flat training licence. So, it was sent to Tommy Craig [a local trainer], based on the coast at Dunbar. That's how I first came across him." It was to prove a valuable connection.

Yet, for all young Johnston's ever-developing interest in racehorses, it was the greyhound track rather than racecourse where he could more commonly be discovered.

"From my early teens, I used to go greyhound racing more than I went horseracing. At one time, I went two nights a week, after school. My dad would take me into Glasgow, and we'd go dog racing: at White City during the week, Shawfield at the weekend.

"I really believed I could train a greyhound, but my parents wouldn't let me own a dog of any kind. I didn't necessarily want a dog to race; it was just to catch rabbits and so on. In the end, they relented and let me buy a whippet."

It was more than a pet. Johnston, by now aged 14, decided he'd like to enter his dog in a show. Except he knew nothing about such events. It was pure providence – on two counts, as it would transpire – that he came across a woman named Flora Lindsay, who lived nearby in Kippen, a village in West Stirlingshire.

Flora knew all there was to know about whippets. She and her husband Denis had competed in dog shows, jointly founded the Scottish Pedigree Whippet Racing Club and been, respectively, secretary and treasurer of the Club since 1965.

"She agreed to help, explained how to show it, and trim its nails. For six months, I'd take it to shows and we came away with rosettes," says Johnston.

"Later, she persuaded me to bring my dog along to races, and I got to know her well. I would travel with her and Denis round the country, racing our dogs."

He adds: "There wasn't much pedigree whippet racing in Britain at the time. We had to race against the non-pedigree dogs, and the non-pedigrees beat us out of sight. But we would still try it. We'd go to Forfar, Armadale and West Lothian. I went there with the Lindsays, or my father would take me there, to train our dogs and race them. We went as far as Macclesfield, I remember.

"It was all very amateurish. You're talking about a club with only a handful of dogs, maybe ten, dogs in it. My bitch didn't have a racing dog in eight generations of her pedigree. But mine became Scottish bitch champion."

Later, he would breed from her. "I put her in pup to a show dog, and I bred two pups. They were quite successful racing dogs. I then put her in pup to one of Flora's dogs and that produced one of Flora's best litters."

His sister Sharon recalls that first whippet well. "She was called Flip, as in the flip side of the coin. He'd actually wanted another of the litter but ended up with her. But she did well for him, and

Mark went on to breed from her a couple of times. He wanted to keep the puppies but, remember, he was still at home, and our parents put their foot down and told him: 'We're not having a house full of dogs.'

"So Mark, clever little blighter, agreed that, no, *he* wouldn't keep the offspring. He gave the rest of the pups from the litter to all of us as presents. That's how he kept them. We had about seven at one time."

Throughout this period, young Johnston wasn't just looking to win races. He was cultivating his own ideas about the amount of exercise and diet a racing animal required.

"There were all these guys at the Club who had been training dogs for 20 years, whatever, and I believed I could train dogs better than them," says Johnston.

His training regime was straightforward enough. "I just thought: 'I'll feed my whippets more and work them harder.' So, that's what I did, it worked, and my dogs were fitter than everybody else's. I walked them three miles every morning before I went to school. But at the weekends, if they weren't racing or going training, I'd take them out and they'd go chasing hares, anything that got up and ran, and walk for miles. They were as fit as the proverbial butcher's dog. I also fed them as much as they could eat."

He even worked after school, washing dishes in a hotel – not so much for the 25p an hour, but to retrieve the leftover pieces of steaks from the plates to feed his dogs.

There was a crucial by-product of his association with the Lindsays. "Flora asked me what school I attended, what subjects I was studying, and what I wanted to be. I told her: 'I want to be a vet.' It had been at that time that I started planning to get into vet school. She told me: '*I'm* a vet.'"

She was actually rather more than that. Even more fortuitously, it transpired Flora had spent almost her entire career as lecturer, then senior lecturer, of anatomy at Glasgow University's Veterinary School in Buccleuch Street and latterly at the Garscube campus in Bearsden.

"I'm not sure if, when the time came, she helped me get in there," says Johnston. "But she was certainly supportive through all the time I was there." To say that Johnston was blessed by this association is not to overstate what it would ultimately mean to him.

You feel compelled to ask: why whippets? Johnston responds: "I suppose it's like some people race greyhounds, or pigeons, because they can't afford horses, and they're cheaper. I raced whippets because it was what was accessible to me."

Intriguingly, he adds: "I've always loved animals that have a function, a purpose. I once had a Staffordshire Bull Terrier [I recall him – he was named Gnasher, after Dennis the Menace's dog and was a ferocious-looking but thoroughly amiable creature].

"Now, I wouldn't even remotely condone dogfighting [he emphasises this point], I've never seen one, not even a video, and I've no desire to – if there are such things on the internet, I wouldn't want to watch it. But I love dogs like Staffordshire Bull Terriers and Pit Bull Terriers. I spent a summer in the States, and all the Mexicans had Pit Bulls. I regard them as physical, magnificent dogs because they're so strong and powerful, and fantastic characters."

He adds: "Obviously organised bull terrier fighting is almost completely eradicated here, but they do get into scraps, they *are* inclined to fight. You'd get them in the practice [when later he was employed as a vet] to stitch up wounds, and they'd stand there wagging their tail while you're sewing a scar on its face."

Johnston continues: "I've never owned a working collie, but I've tremendous admiration for them, watching them work, and I like seeing greyhounds. With my whippets, I had this crazy idea about how I was going to do it better than anyone else. It was mostly based on 'I'm going to feed 'em more and work 'em harder'. And I wasn't far wrong."

Johnston's father, though primarily devoted to his equine interests, began to accompany his son to dog races. "It didn't always go to plan," says Sharon. "They left some of the dogs in a car once while a race was on and came back to find the interior of the vehicle entirely ripped up, and I mean ripped up. Another time, Mark left a couple of bitches for half an hour and came back to find they'd nearly killed each other."

To this day, Mark has a strong affection for racing dogs, and years later would fulfil that teenage desire to train greyhounds.

But crucially, the ideas he formulated about training whippets would also provide the groundwork for his future career. He could train racing dogs. For young Johnston, it was confirmation to him that he could train racehorses. That aspiration was rarely far from his thoughts.

During this period, however, another character had entered his life; one who, had not equine pursuits preoccupied her, could you suspect, have trodden a very different stage.

Deirdre Ferguson was then 14 and would become an indomitable presence in her husband's life and career.

"MARK TOLD ME HE'D BE A MILLIONAIRE BY 24. HE LIED…"

To briefly fast-forward to recent times, and early in Lockdown Mk I in 2020, Deirdre Johnston combined with her younger son Angus to record their own cover version of Shania Twain's 1998 hit "You're Still the One". A splendid rendition, it featured as the fourth record on Mark Johnston's list compiled for *Desert Island Discs*.

Angus played guitar and performed lead vocals and Deirdre supplied backing vocals. Indeed, the duo became something of social media celebrities during the shutdown with their 'Kingsley House Acoustic Sessions', and made TV appearances on Racing TV and ITV Racing. It drew one particular Tweet of admiration: "Amazing… I keep thinking Charlie and Mark are going to appear from the kitchen banging pots and pans! Can we please have the full Von Trapp family ensemble?" Probably fortunately, that never materialised.

Johnston explained the relevance of the song to presenter Lauren Laverne:

"Deirdre and I have had quite a tumultuous relationship. It started when she was 14 and I was 17. She went off to college and a lot of people said it wouldn't last but this song sums it up: 'you're still the one'."

Deirdre is a natural entertainer, both in the social sense and in the showbiz sense, and clearly that talent has been inherited by her younger son.

In another world – one in which Deirdre had remained Deirdre Ferguson and, as a teenager, had never fallen for a certain young man whom she describes as having a reputation for being "quite wild" at the time – you would quite probably have discovered her treading the boards. And today? A television or film star, perhaps?

When she recalls her time spent in amateur dramatics, it doesn't require too much of a leap of imagination to see her portraying Sally Bowles performing "Tomorrow Belongs to Me" at the seedy, decadent Kit Kat Club in 1929 Berlin.

"I played the lead in *Cabaret*. I was also in Gilbert and Sullivan productions, and *The Boyfriend*. I did everything, singing, dancing. I never thought about it [a career on the stage], but Mark used to say that I should have studied drama at college."

You suggest to her that she could have made a success as a professional showbiz performer. "I've always enjoyed singing and dancing, used to win lots of singing competitions when I was at school and when I was first doing my degree, and I loved doing the amateur dramatics. It would have been musical theatre I would have gone in, but everyone says it's so tough. I never took it far enough to even have an inkling." Deirdre pauses and, perhaps reflecting on what this alternative life has brought her, says: "I certainly don't regret it."

That said, visitors can be assured of a "*wilkommen, bienvenue,* welcome", with all the effervescence of a Liza Minelli when they visit Kingsley House.

The boyfriend, the real one who would become her husband, first entered her consciousness at the age of ten. He was three years her senior. "But it was not until I was about 14 that the attraction started. I used to notice him driving up and down the road in his sports car!"

She adds: "From the moment I met him, it was apparent that all he ever wanted to do was become a racehorse trainer. I always thought that was absolutely great because I had it in my mind that all I ever wanted to do was work with horses."

She recalls her father Duncan initially being not entirely persuaded by such a prospect for his daughter. "There's no money in it," he told her. "You just concentrate on your education." Deirdre did. Her future husband did anything but.

They began going out together when Deirdre was approaching 15, by which time Johnston was about to start further education. "Deirdre's grandparents lived in Aberfoyle," explains Johnston. "When they died, the house was kept on as a holiday home. Deirdre, her sister and their parents would stay there for a month in the summer – and that's how we met."

Deirdre was raised on the outskirts of Glasgow, though her parents came from only a few miles from Aberfoyle. Her mother was a farmer's daughter from Thornhill, originally a staging post on the Glasgow to Dumfries road. Her father, an anaesthetist, was from Stronachlachar, a small hamlet on the banks of Lake Katrine.

"My family were city people who lived in the country," explains Johnston. Deirdre's family, who are Fergusons, would be what we call 'Teuchters' [pronounced Tooch-ters] or semi-Highlanders."

I later discover that this *could* be considered a somewhat derisory term; what a Lowland Scot might term a Highlander in an argument – an expression used by Billy Connolly and other prominent Glaswegians at the expense of those who hail from the Highlands.

"There's a tendency for English people to think of Scots as all being alike, but there's a great difference, depending on your origins," says Johnston. "For example, Deirdre's father Duncan, who was from the borders of the Highlands, a countryman who happened to live in the city, would always wear a kilt as formal dress. My father wouldn't have dreamt of wearing one."

Deirdre's affinity with horses began at the age of five when she convinced her non-horsey parents that they should pay for her to have riding lessons. "Later, I managed to persuade them that I should have a pony," she says. "My sister and I shared it, and we used to take it out to Aberfoyle in the summer. Eventually, I would keep it in Mark's field."

It turns out that Mark's 'field' was actually the acreage where his father kept his horses. "Deirdre jokes that she had a pony and I had a field," says Johnston, laughing. "For her, that was the attraction…"

Deirdre's features crease into a rueful smile as she recalls the teenage Johnston: "Very early on, his reputation in the village was he was a bit wild and boisterous. His Dad didn't always make him go to school, and he'd get up to mischief with his cousin David. They would find a car in the woods and drive it off. Young lad things, nothing dramatic."

Indeed, there was apparently an occasion when he was asked to leave the Fergusons' garden by Deirdre's mother "for swearing". Deirdre adds: "I remember my uncle didn't think he was at all the kind of boy I should be socialising with. But my mum always loved him, just thought that he was great. My parents got on really well with him and were very fond of him."

Curiously, Johnston's own memory cannot bring to mind such an image of his teenage self, but the evidence suggests that he certainly appears to have had an impetuous, self-willed side.

His sister Sharon remembers an incident when Mark and the boy next door discovered a can of liquid and, determined to discover what it was, put a match to it. It turned out to be paraffin. They managed to set fire to the toilet of a station of an old disused railway line near where they lived.

As has already been emphasised, education had been far from a priority in young Johnston's existence. However, he was sufficiently aware that if he was to pursue his ambition to become a racehorse trainer, such minor details as passing examinations would have to intrude into his life of whippet-training and racehorse-obsessing.

He had left school at 16, having been what he readily concedes, "a bad student with a terrible attendance record who received low grades in all his exams". Johnston duly sought out a further education college where he could obtain higher grades in the subjects required to be accepted at Glasgow University's School of Veterinary Medicine. He believed that qualification could be his admission card to the training fraternity. If he achieved that, it would unlock a door that was closed to many.

The best further education establishment to study at at the time was said to be Langside College in the south of the city. "I told them I had got four Cs in my Highers [Highers are the equivalent of A, AS and A2 levels in England], and needed two As and three Bs because I wanted to be accepted at vet school," says Johnston. "The guy looked at me as though I was completely crazy and told me: 'Choose another career...'

"I was so depressed at that, but then I enquired at Glasgow Cardonald College of Further Education [now Glasgow Clyde

College – Cardonald Campus], which was full of immigrants who didn't have the best English and were trying to get an 'O' level or two.

"I told them the same story: how I wanted to do Physics, Chemistry, Maths and Biology because I wanted to get into vet school. They weren't really interested in what my ultimate aims were. They just said: 'Sign here, start on Thursday'. I was almost *more* depressed at that. I started thinking: 'What are these guys going to teach me?'"

Indeed, in the introductory stage, in the Physics class, Johnston and a fellow student, who also required to improve his school exam results in order to study medicine, were asked what they wanted to achieve.

"We both said we needed As – which prompted the lecturer, who was a bit of a character, to quip: 'So, what are you doing at a dump like this?!' Well, we both did get As. I owe him a lot. He was an excellent teacher."

Johnston concedes he "scraped into" vet school, having initially been rejected. But, after having set out on what one could almost describe as a pilgrimage, such was his nigh-on religious zeal to become a trainer, he presumably got his head down to do some serious studying?

Johnston shakes his head ruefully as he recalls: "When I say I was a 'bad student' I mean it. Yes, I know I have a reputation now as a workaholic, but I'm certainly not one by nature. When you end up working for yourself, you have no option. The problem is that I've always had a short attention span. I get bored very quickly. That's why I was never going to make a good student."

In truth, in attending vet school, he was always looking way beyond obtaining a degree. "He was terrible," recalls Deirdre. "He just wouldn't do any work at all. I'd be working on my

'O' levels and Highers and I'd go to the university reading room with him, sit over him and get him to learn while I was preparing for my exams."

He has always possessed a reputation for being something of a 'last-minute Johnston'. "And he's never really changed in that respect," Deirdre continues. "When, years later, he used to write articles for the *Racing Post*, he'd do them at midnight the night before he had to submit them. Until he actually has to do something, he won't. His exam revision was just like that."

When you consider what a marathon subject veterinary medicine is – normally a five-year term – you do wonder that Johnston stayed the course. Or was permitted to do so. Commitment clearly wasn't his byword. Skipping lectures became a habit. Instead, he admits, "I was always swanning off doing ridiculous things. To an extent, that's the nature of vet school. There were around 70 of us who started together on the course, went to all the same classes, and finished together, so we knew each other pretty well. We had more parties than other faculties, and we'd have these AVS weekends – the Association of Veterinary Students – where two bus-loads of us would go down to London and run riot for a few days."

He adds: "I simply got fed up with lectures, or sitting there in a histology lab, looking down a microscope. I thought that was as boring as hell. One day, Gordon Lonsdale, a friend of mine – we shared a flat together – were sitting in an anatomy lecture. We looked out of the window to see the Campsie Hills had snow on them and thought: 'If there's snow on the Campsies, think what it must be like up north. Let's go for a drive, looking for snow.' So, we did."

And not just the once. "We'd sneak out and just set off for some crazy places, like Thurso [the northernmost town on the British mainland and a 550-mile return journey]. We'd just drive around, looking for snow – and drive to the north of Scotland, the Lake District and Hadrian's Wall.

"One time, we were supposed to go to a meat inspection lecture. But after some debate, we decided to go to Paris instead, hitch-hiking. We arrived, spent a day there, sent postcards to the folks in the class, and arrived back about six days later."

"Any reason?" – you ask. He shrugs, and replies rather lamely: "It was just to show we could do it, I suppose…"

It was Gordon Lonsdale who apparently had a hand in his friend's entry in the Glasgow University Veterinary School yearbook (1978–83). The student Johnston is described in the following terms:

"An intensely private person about whom, until now, little or nothing was known…Mark's scruffy barrow-boy appearance initially failed him as a playboy while attempting to set up the James Bond Club, a renovated outhouse in Aberfoyle" ("this was my cousin David's restaurant that we all used to trek out to," Johnston explains).

"Mind you, the club, dedicated to good dining and not-so-good women, obviously taught him something. He developed a rapport with the young, high-spirited girls of Park School, in particular with the daughter (Deirdre) of an eminent Bearsden Gas consultant" (as mentioned, her father was an anaesthetist).

Johnston paid the price for his lax attitude towards studying. In his first year, he failed his Chemistry examination. When he fluffed the re-sit, too, the rule was that you couldn't stay on the course. He appealed and was allowed to continue but then spent a year re-sitting just Chemistry. Then he had re-sits in his second year, in Anatomy and Physiology, and in his third year in Pathology and Parasitology.

"In my fourth year, there were no degree examinations, but

there were a lot of class exams. You had to pass them in order to be allowed to sit your finals at the end of the final year. Most of them were oral exams, and you had to keep re-sitting them until you passed. I had heaps of these things.

"In the final year, I was absolutely convinced that I would have to do re-sits again. Yet, my finals were the only time I passed at the first attempt. It was a huge shock to everyone – and most of all me."

Johnston had been wracked with dread as he arrived at the main university building on the evening the results were posted. "It was one of the worst moments of my life," recalls a man who, because of that Chemistry resit, had already spent six years rather than the usual five to complete the course.

"I remember the results were presented in a certain way. One list read: 'The following people have satisfied the examiners…' That meant you had passed. You'd got your degree. Below that, another list read: 'The following people have passed Medicine, or Surgery, or Pharmacology, which meant you had failed something, so you hadn't got your degree.

"I started at the bottom. I wasn't on the pharmacology list, I wasn't on the surgery list, I wasn't on the medicine list. I said to myself: 'Shit, I've failed them all!' Then someone said: 'Look, your name's up here.' I couldn't believe it – I'd passed at the first attempt."

In fact, it was discovered in the university records that no-one in the history of the course who had done re-sits every year had passed their finals at the first attempt. He was setting records even then.

His strong suspicion remains that Flora Lindsay, the Glasgow vet school lecturer, who had advised him on whippets, had played a crucial part in his entrance to, and rough passage through, vet school. "She never told me, but I've no doubt she helped me get in there," he says. "And when I was a bad student, having all these resits every year, I've no doubt she helped keep me in there when I could have been chucked out."

Johnston had met up again with Flora at her husband's funeral. She insisted that he was *not* a bad student. They just didn't recognise talent when they saw it!

"'Look at what you achieved,' she told me. 'It proves you weren't a bad student.' That was nice of her, but the truth is I *was* a bad student. I scraped through by the skin of my teeth."

Flora died in 2013, aged 92. In her obituary in the *Glasgow Herald*, it told of her 38 years at the university, and how "she sought to enlighten and nurture the minds of the almost 2,000 veterinary students she taught" including "those troubled young students who were regarded by others as rebels, fools and ne'er do wells." To whom could she have been referring?

* * *

Meanwhile, in studied contrast, the far more education-serious Deirdre was completing her schooling, uncertain as to which direction to take. She had plenty of choices.

"I had a place at the University of St Andrews to do English and History, and another at I.M. Marsh College of Physical Education in Liverpool. I could have gone into teacher training in Glasgow. But my parents were very keen on Dunfermline College of Physical Education. There were very few places; it was hard to get in and was very prestigious. So, that's what I did."

She adds: "I'd got all my exams in my fifth year, so I spent the sixth year having a great time, and doing lots of sport, lots of singing." As for her relationship with Johnston, it had continued to flourish, albeit in a fitful way.

"I was at school in Glasgow, not far from where he was at

university, so I saw him nearly every day." Except when he was off on one of his junkets...

However, theirs was a romance that evolved over time, punctuated by break-ups. "It was a relationship that was on for six months, off for six months, on for eighteen months, off for two years," recalls Johnston. "And finally, we got back together when I was in my final year at vet school and Deirdre was in her third year of a four-year course at teacher training college."

It was when Deirdre went to college in Edinburgh that she and Johnston had their most serious parting of the ways. This was a period punctuated by constant duelling with the demands of academia and the angst of relationship difficulties.

It was at this time that Johnston put the Dire Straits song "Romeo and Juliet" on a cassette tape and sent it to Deirdre. As he told Lauren Laverne when it featured among his choices on *Desert Island Discs*: "There's a line 'when you gonna realise it was just that the time was wrong?' Eventually, the time was right and we got back together."

Throughout, Johnston's eyes were firmly fixed on his guiding star, which would lead him to his kismet. "He talked about his ambitions a lot," says Deirdre. "He always knew exactly what he wanted to do and I believed everything he told me."

Hmm. Possibly an error? "He told me he'd be a millionaire by the time he was 24, and he wasn't," she says, bursting into her typically infectious laugh, and pausing before adding with theatrical timing: "He lied..."

However, she swiftly continues: "No, I never had any doubts. He must have been very convincing. He gave off a great air of confidence. He didn't strike me as a dreamer. He was very practical."

Johnston was true to his word about such financial rewards; it just took him rather longer than he had scheduled and, as will become apparent, not without profound discomfort in the early years.

CHAPTER 6

HELPING TO SAVE THE GRAND NATIONAL

For all that Johnston's studies may have lacked focus, his desire to become a racehorse trainer never abated. Never for a moment. Every spare minute away from his educational course was spent preparing for what he never doubted would be his future life.

During the holidays of their first year, students had to gain work experience at veterinary practices. Johnston spent time with a small-animal veterinarian in Edinburgh. In the second and third years, the work experience had to be somewhere that specialised in lambing, dairy and pigs.

"So, I looked through the *Directory of the Turf* to find somewhere where I could do those things and there'd also be racehorses," he says. "I found a place at Stetchworth in Newmarket, run by a woman named Hermione Bartholomew. She called herself a dairy farmer, although it turned out she had only 13 Jersey cows. There was an old gelding in the field she'd 'rescued' from Cambridge market rather than it going to the knacker's yard. She said she didn't know its background. I looked at it and noticed that its legs had been pin-fired [at one time, commonly used to treat tendon injuries]. I thought: 'It looks like a thoroughbred, and if it's been pin-fired, it must be broken.' So, I put a saddle on the horse and rode it."

"Hermione told me, 'Oh, you ride fine. Why don't you go and ride out for [the Newmarket trainer] John Winter?' She knew John well and arranged for me to ride for him during the fortnight I was there. I wasn't very good, but I coped, coped well enough to think that when I got home, I'd phone Tommy Craig and ask him if I could go and ride out for him."

Few would have argued with his modest self-assessment of his riding abilities at the time. His sister Sharon recalls one worried phone call from her father. "'Mark's having problems with his horses,' he told me. 'He gets on them and they're running away with him all the time.'"

Fortunately, not least for his own welfare, Johnston didn't have to pursue riding as a career. "He discovered that training horses was all about using the mind," Sharon adds. "And he had a brilliant one." As future events would demonstrate.

Johnston continued to ride out over the next four years, principally when he was home from vet school, even though it was about 70 miles each way from Aberfoyle to Tommy Craig's Tilton House Stables at West Barns, Dunbar, which meant that he had to leave at four every morning.

Craig's uncle was George Boyd, the only Scottish-based trainer to train a Classic winner – the 66-1 shot Rockavon, triumphant in the 1961 2,000 Guineas. Craig had been head lad to Boyd until the latter retired in 1969, and he then inherited the stable.

"Tommy was always a small, struggling – probably gambling – trainer, but I probably learnt as much about training racehorses there as anywhere else," admits Johnston. "Tommy trained on the beach. It gave me the confidence that I could do that too. I didn't feel that, when the time came, I would necessarily need any grass gallops." That belief would prove remarkably prescient.

By the time Johnston was 23, and in his fifth and final year of vet school, he had already come to the conclusion that he might have to adopt unconventional methods if he was to gain a foothold in the industry. From somewhere, a thought formulated in a mind that was constantly open to new ideas.

That scheme yielded evidence of qualities that would later come to the fore: Johnston's enterprise, radical thinking and capacity for self-promotion.

It was spring 1983, and extraordinary as it may appear today, the future of the Grand National was in jeopardy. That year, the marathon spectacular was sponsored by *The Sun* newspaper, but reports at the time suggested that £4 million was needed to save Aintree racecourse from closure, and a campaign to save the iconic steeplechase had been launched.

For one young veterinary student, determined to machete his way through the impenetrable forest that he perceived to be the world of horseracing to discover a clearing of opportunity, it presented the ideal chance to promote himself.

At that time, Johnston had a two-year-old colt, sired by Scallywag, who had finished third to Crow in the 1976 St Leger. He had bred him from a ten-year-old mare, Kimbo, who had been bought at Ascot Sales by his father. "I had broken this colt, but he was doing nothing," he says. "Going nowhere. There was no prospect of me putting it into training. I couldn't afford it."

However, the colt, which he had named Mister, was a good-looking animal by a sire who stamped his progeny with his imposing physique. "All through that period, I was trying to get a job in horseracing, or some kind of break into the industry," Johnston explains. So, he offered his three-year-old dark grey colt to be auctioned on behalf of the appeal before the big race.

"It was a bit of a brainwave," he says. "I had this idea that I would do my bit by giving this horse to be auctioned, with the proceeds going to the Grand National campaign. I offered it, and the campaign people accepted it."

Before the auction, the colt went to Ken Oliver's stable in Hawick. Oliver predicted it could fetch between £5,000 and £10,000. The young student was interviewed by the BBC, and the story also featured prominently in local and national newspapers. An earnest Johnston told the *Glasgow Herald*: "We will feel really proud when we see the colt paraded at Aintree in front of all those people. It will be a big wrench for me to lose him. But I have no prospect of being able to afford the training fees, so I decided to do the best thing for the horse and help the National campaign at the same time."

Half an hour before the big race, Johnston, who was accompanied to Aintree by his father, proudly led his colt into the winner's enclosure to be sold. To his delight, expectations were exceeded *and* the horse stayed in Scotland.

The successful bidder was Arthur McCluskey, a director of a Glasgow kitchen furniture contract firm. He paid 10,500gns. McCluskey had also owned The Grey Bomber, another son of Scallywag. The colt was to be put into training with Michael Cunningham in Ireland.

It was an emotional day all round. This was the year when the National was won by Corbiere, trained by 'the First Lady of Aintree', a tearful Jenny Pitman. The following year, Seagram stepped in to sponsor the National.

Johnston has never lost his affection for the Aintree spectacular.

He still regards it as his favourite race. Yet, that certainly wasn't the end of the affair for him. Scallywag was owned by the De Rothschild family, and Mrs James de Rothschild rewarded the student for his generosity by offering him a free nomination to the sire. Before he could act on that gesture, Johnston found himself embroiled in controversy; a precursor to the many that would follow.

A correspondent to the *Glasgow Herald*, one Ian Turner from Kippen, Stirlingshire, protested in a reader's letter that Johnston's support of the Grand National condemned him as being "no animal lover" and that "his desire to see the continuation of the Grand National, and therefore the cruelty that is part of it, demonstrates to me that he has no time for the feelings of horses".

The family rallied around Johnston. His cousin, Jill, was moved to pen a supportive letter to the newspaper in which she condemned Mr Turner's views. This would, no doubt, have been welcomed by Johnston, even if everything we have learnt since suggests that he is not a man who has ever required too much advocacy on his behalf.

What no one could contest was that his contribution to the Grand National campaign was an astute piece of initiative. "I got a bit of fame out of this, in a small way," he reflects. "And I was given a free nomination to send my mare Kimbo back to the stallion Scallywag. The colt was born and, when I qualified as a vet, I took the mare away with me, and her foal, down to where I was then living at Yarm, where I was in practice."

That may have been the end of that episode, but then Johnston noticed in *The Sporting Life* that someone had paid a record sum of 28,000gns for a Scallywag yearling at Doncaster's National Hunt sales.

"The purchaser's name was Edward Stenton," says Johnston. "I tracked down his number, phoned him and said, 'You paid 28,000 guineas for a Scallywag colt. I've got a Scallywag colt. Do you want to see mine?' It turned out that he was a life insurance salesman, who had horses in training. He came to see my colt and, though he never bought it, I stayed in touch with him."

With vet school behind him, there followed a three-year period spent in general veterinary practice. Johnston started out at Newtonstewart, between Omagh and Strabane, County Tyrone. He recalls: "I started in Northern Ireland with Bob Smith, a guy who has shares in horses with us now. He is still a close friend. I really enjoyed my time with him, both the work and the people. I still have fantastic memories, like calving cows."

I shoot him a quizzical look. He nods and continues: "I still say that sitting in a farmer's house, after he's been trying to calf the cow, and you've come along and calved the cow or done a Caesarean, and you've got a live cow and a live calf and you're sitting in the farmer's house having a cup of tea at two in the morning – that's better than a winner. Perfect. Much better than a winner. Greatest thing I've ever done. A fantastic thrill."

After seven months, he moved on to the market town of Yarm in North Yorkshire, and then, a year later, relocated to Braintree in Essex. During his holidays, Johnston seized every opportunity to work in racing yards. He even travelled abroad: to Charlie Milbank in France and the late John Russell in California, and Alan Bailey, then based at Tarporley, Cheshire, as he sought a means to establish himself in horseracing. It nagged away at him like a tooth requiring urgent filling.

Ultimately, he decided on the most obvious route to enter the industry – find his own stables to start training. "So, I looked at a yard to be let at Tupgill, near Middleham, and another at Wetherby. I made stupid offers, knowing, really, that I wouldn't get them. And

at the same time, I was also applying for jobs, in any shape or form."
Apparently, there was no ceiling to his search parameters – or
his audacity.

"I wrote to trainers, and owners," he says. "I applied to be racing
manager to the late [Prince] Fahd Salman [who later was the owner
of the Epsom and Irish Derby winner Generous, the champion
racehorse of 1991]. I didn't get it, obviously."

He adds: "I phoned Martin Pipe [the prolific jumps trainer,
who would end his career with 15 championships] and asked if he
needed an assistant. Nothing came of it. I also applied for a job with
Sheikh Mohammed, in 1985." And the response? "I wrote twice
and then I went and handed him a letter at Newmarket October
Sales. I didn't get a reply."

One contract was sealed that year, though, and it remains a
lifelong one: Johnston and Deirdre were married on 8 June. The
happy couple were 25 and 22, respectively.

Johnston had apparently taken some persuading to go down the
conventional route. "He would have been quite happy for us just
to live together," Deirdre says. "But I told him, 'I'm not doing that.
If you want me, you take me lock, stock and barrel!'

"Then he didn't want to get married in a church, because neither
of us were particularly churchgoers, but I said, 'Well, I'm not doing
it any other way. I want the white wedding, the whole works.' So,
he left it to me to organise."

The wedding took place near Aberfoyle at a church in Brig
o'Turk, situated on the western shore of Loch Achray, a popular
venue for traditional weddings. Deirdre was determined to ensure
that their day would not be forgotten.

"I wanted it to be a fun occasion, and for everybody to have a
really good time. I got buses to take everybody from the hotel to
the church, we had the service, and then the buses took the guests

to the end of the loch," she recalls. "I'd got special permission from the water board for us to go on a steamer from one end of the loch to the other. The buses were allowed to drive around the private road while we were on board. So, we had a band and champagne on the steamer, and then were driven back to the hotel. At the end, Mark said he was really glad we'd done it, because he'd had a brilliant day."

Deirdre had done far more than tie the proverbial knot; she knew that, in doing so, she had bound herself to a man empowered by a powerful conviction in his own potential. She was buying into a belief system just as much as she was taking his hand in marriage.

"At the time, I knew nothing about racing," Deirdre admits, "I just knew about horses. But I just believed in him, believed in him completely, and in what we were trying to do."

It cannot be understated just how much that faith has been a crucial component of her husband's development. As Mark's sister Sharon empathises: "Deirdre's been a huge part of what he has achieved. Mark would have been a success anyway, but maybe not to the same degree."

Brian 'Jock' Bennett, one of Johnston's assistants today, a man who has worked with them both for a quarter of a century, takes a similar view. "When it was just him and Deirdre [running the operation], he wouldn't do anything without asking her – probably still doesn't, although now there's Charlie on the scene as well. They've been a very good team considering it's probably very difficult to work with your wife in the same business. Because they're so close, it's worked."

But such commitment does require complete faith in your partner. And though, almost invariably there would be financial headaches down the track, there was not a scintilla of scepticism about her husband's objectives as Johnston desperately sought the key to what increasingly appeared to be a closed shop.

He discovered it not long after his marriage to Deirdre when he chanced upon an advert in the *Horse & Hound*. It read: "Racing Yard: 20 boxes. Three-bedroomed house. Lincolnshire. Offers over £95,000."

Johnston called the agents and asked for details to be sent. "That night Edward Stenton, the fellow I had spoken to about my Scallywag yearling, phoned me about something completely different," he recalls. "I knew he came from Lincolnshire, so I said, 'Oh, I've just sent for details of a racing yard in your area.'

"He asked, "Who's selling it? It's not Mawer, Mason and Bell [estate agents], is it?' I told him it was. He said that he knew them and that he'd find out more about it. The following morning, he called and said, 'Don't panic, but I've made an offer for you, on your behalf. I've found out that they [Mawer, Mason and Bell] are owed £33,000, so I've offered them that. You'd better come and see it.'"

That precise moment was the genesis of what would become a racing dynasty when Mark and Deirdre, a vet in practice and a teacher, both in their 20s, set out on an expedition of discovery in the precarious world of horseracing.

CHAPTER 7

GOOD VIBRATIONS FOR
THE BEACH BOYS

When, in the autumn of 1986, racing's newest recruit to the training ranks, Mark Johnston, together with wife Deirdre, two staff and 12 "moderate and injured" horses, arrived at Bank End Stables in North Somercotes, Lincolnshire – their first base camp on what was expected to be a long and arduous ascent to the summit of their ambitions – it felt like they'd been transported to the Russian steppes or the landscape of some distant planet.

Johnston still recalls wryly that the stables, 15 miles down the coast from Grimsby, were located in "the coldest place on Earth." A slight exaggeration? "Well, it's certainly the coldest place in Britain," he says. "The wind blows straight in from Russia." It would be fair to say that the area was not for anyone with agoraphobic tendencies. "It was all reclaimed land," Johnston recalls. "Completely flat for miles around." Today there is a nature reserve, populated by seals.

However, it was another feature that most would have found

rather more of a deterrent. "We were a mile from Donna Nook beach, which was used – and still is – by the RAF as a bombing range," he says. So, when Johnston first started galloping his horses along the shoreline, he was not exactly doing so in an oasis of tranquility.

Now, it must be emphasised that this site was some way removed from that scene in the film *Apocalypse Now* (the one where Robert Duvall's character declares "I love the smell of napalm in the morning" as his air strike devastates a Vietnamese village).

Yet, if you'd imagine that training activity would be highly restricted during target practice, you'd be wrong. "We trained the horses while they were using the bombing range," says Johnston insouciantly, as though it was the most obvious reality of training life.

He explains: "The stables were sitting on the sea wall and we used the shoreline for gallops. It was a large flat beach and there were telegraph poles with a big cross on the top. If a red flag was flying, the bombing range was live. They were mostly A10 Gunships, American aeroplanes, which were firing shells at big square canvas targets. The firing was repetitive, like a big machine gun. I say bombs but they weren't really. They were empty shells and didn't explode when they hit the ground."

Johnston adds: "You couldn't go beyond the telegraph poles. The targets were 300–400 yards beyond them. So, we worked horses along the edge of the poles because the poles were two furlongs apart. I used to climb up one to get a better view of the horses working.

"The riders would trot down, trot back, talk to me, they'd tell me what the beach was like, and I'd say 'go down to the third pole and come back again. Hack down and canter back'. Sometimes I used to ride out myself because we didn't have any staff."

What if a rider was thrown, and his horse ran loose and ran on to the range? "It would be seen by men in a nearby tower," Johnston assures me. "The sirens would go off. The aeroplanes would go away, and the guys from the RAF would come out in a jeep and help you catch it."

The trainer insists this commotion didn't frighten the horses. "No, but it spooked Bobby Elliott [one of the yard's first work-riders], first time he came! He ran for cover, getting off one horse, and getting on another as the bombs went off."

Elliott himself laughs as he recalls: "You're walking down to the beach and, all of a sudden, 'boom, boom, boom', there's rockets flying around. I said to Mark 'At least they're bomb-proof, your horses.'"

You remind Johnston that Red Rum, the three-times Grand National-winning legend in the 1970s had famously been trained on the beach at Southport by Ginger McCain. He thrived on it. Johnston nods. "But I don't think you can train a big string on the beach. Both there, and at Tommy Craig's, you galloped the horses when conditions were suitable – which wasn't very often."

He adds: "You couldn't have said 'Oh, Frankie, come next Wednesday because we're going to gallop Enable on the beach.' No, it didn't work like that. You tailored your work around what the condition of the beach was like. It was fine for a small handful of horses."

Johnston is quite candid about the stable's appeal. "We went there, in the autumn of 1986, because it was available. And, eventually, cheap."

Frankly, the bombing range aside, their first view of the yard hadn't been the most propitious sighting for a prospective buyer. "We drove up there one Sunday, and the whole area was enveloped in fog," he says "But we could see enough to tell us that the yard was a mess, and completely overgrown with weeds. It looked a complete disaster area. But Edward Stenton was rushing me into it. We'd only been there an hour and he was saying, 'Do you want it, or don't you?' Well, I'd been looking for a yard for ages, so there was only one answer. 'Yes, we want it.'"

It transpired that the yard had been owned by a woman named Kate Bull, who had trained there but had gone bankrupt. The estate agents were selling the property for the building society, which had repossessed it. According to Johnston, "it was cheap, shoddy and only three parts finished, and dilapidated. However, a coat of paint would make a big difference to its value."

That first viewing was around April 1986, and the purchasing saga continued throughout that summer as they attempted to negotiate a price they could afford, with Edward Stenton acting as a go-between.

By then, it had got to the stage where the Johnstons thought a deal was never going to materialise. So, they organised a holiday. "Deirdre wanted to visit a college friend in Canada. We had £1,000 in the bank. So, we said, 'Oh, stuff the yard. We'll go and spend the thousand quid on a holiday to Canada.'"

"I went to the travel agent to book it. I came home and Deirdre was standing at the back door. She said, 'I don't know whether to laugh or cry. We've got that yard in Lincolnshire – for £50,000.'"

Johnston adds: "Edward arranged a mortgage for us. It was a 90 per cent mortgage, so we needed a 10 per cent deposit – £5,000.

We phoned Deirdre's father and Deirdre told him we'd just spent £1,000 at the travel agent. He told her: "You'd better have your holiday. It'll be the last one you'll have for a long time. I'll give you the deposit.' So, we borrowed £45,000 and the yard was ours. Everything was fine."

Well, not quite. There was the small matter of some working

capital. "I went to the Midland Bank in Braintree where I had £200 on deposit, and I took along with me two little business plans, cash-flows really, written on graph paper," recalls Johnston. "I'd bought a book on business which explained how to do it."

Johnston showed the manager photographs and particulars and told him that he needed an overdraft so that he had working capital. "I then explained to the manager: 'Everybody says I should be starting a vet practice. Here's the cash-flow for that. But the truth is that I want to start a racing stable. Here's the cash-flow for that.'

"Fortunately, we got on because his daughter had a pony and our [Braintree] practice looked after it. The manager explained that it was out of his area, but he'd forward the details to the Midland Bank in nearby Louth and get back to me in a week."

The manager's counterpart in Louth was not impressed, however. "His verdict was: 'It's not very nice, it's damp, and it's in a mess,' and he declined to authorise a release of funds. Johnston was dumbfounded. He admitted the blood drained from him at that moment. Surely, he and Deirdre weren't to be frustrated after all these protracted negotiations?

"But then the local manager had a thought. He told me, 'I cannot believe you've bought a 20-box stable, with a three-bedroom house and a flat, all for £50,000, so *I'll* lend it to you.' And that's what he did. He also gave us a £15,000 overdraft facility, which over two years increased to £30,000. I just kept phoning him up and saying, 'I need a bit more, I need a bit more.' He'd say, 'OK.' And that's how we existed."

Hand to mouth, and overdraft to empty wallet.

"The mortgage company we never spoke to," says Johnston. "I worked on the basis that as long as I made the repayments of £60 a week, they wouldn't ask me any questions about whether the business was doing well or badly. The only person I had to convince was the man giving me the overdraft."

That early business was organised on a no-expense-wasted basis from the outset. "I bought an old horsebox in Perth, which had been constructed circa 1961," says Johnston. "We called it Thomas the Tank Engine. In October we crammed all our furniture in it and moved to Lincolnshire, although Deirdre stayed with friends in Essex until Christmas that year."

That was because, by then, Deirdre was teaching in Chelmsford. It had never been her vocation, but after she left college her naturally gregarious character and ability to communicate meant it ideally suited her.

"At the time we got married, Mark was in practice in Essex, and I needed a job," she says. "I just looked around for anything that was available. I'm not the sort of person who likes sitting around, doing nothing. I hadn't really wanted to teach, actually, but a job came up in a school in Chelmsford, I applied for it, I got it, and that's how I started teaching." She had to work a term's notice, and would teach during the week then drive up to Lincolnshire at the weekend.

They weren't exactly in penury, but finances had been so restricted after the move to Lincolnshire that it was decided that Deirdre should continue teaching even after she left the Chelmsford school. "There didn't seem to be any permanent jobs around there, so I wrote to all the schools in the area saying I'd be available on supply," she recalls. "I spent two terms doing that before I was offered a full-time job in Cleethorpes, teaching English and Drama."

Deirdre also assisted her husband when work permitted, along with – for the first year – Deirdre's sister Donna and her husband Peter, who lived with them. Peter would drive the horsebox; Donna would help with the mucking-out at weekends. "Donna was a pharmacist," says Deirdre, "So she would go away to where she was working at Bawtry on a Monday morning and return on a Friday night. We had two staff, one in a little flat next door and one in a mobile home."

Deirdre also prepared fully for their life ahead. "We'd got the yard in Lincolnshire, but we had no idea how to do the office stuff, so Mark organised for me to go to Newmarket and spend two or three days with the secretary of trainer Lord Huntingdon [formerly one of the Queen's trainers], to learn about entries and declarations, the running of a racing office."

Once at Bank End, her weekday schedule left no time for winding down. "I used to ride out first lot, run home, have a shower, drive to school, teach all day. Then come back and do evening stables," says Deirdre. "We all had to muck in. I wanted to be at home full-time, working with the horses, but I couldn't afford it. I had to teach for the two years we were in Lincolnshire."

Deirdre was a natural when it came to riding out. "I had a few lessons on my pony when I was young. When I started out, I rode the worst horses, like everybody, and you just gradually get better, until over time I rode the better horses. But it took me a while."

CHAPTER 8

GAINING ADMISSION TO AN EXCLUSIVE CLUB

It needs to be emphasised at this point that there was one large impediment to the Johnstons' plans which had to be overcome. All the preparations for the venture would have counted for nothing if Johnston had been unable to obtain his licence to train from the Jockey Club.

That institution, thought to have been founded in 1750, was then racing's ruling body and rightly didn't exactly dispense such an entitlement with abandon.

Possession of a noble racing name – say, Cecil, Stoute or Balding – or a close relationship with one, or having worked for a major name in the industry, would have helped. But Johnston was an unknown, beyond Tommy Craig's stables near Dunbar.

As soon as it was confirmed that the Bank End yard was his, he phoned the Jockey Club. The number soon became familiar to him, but on that first occasion he had to search for it in *The Directory of the Turf* – an annual volume he regarded as "my indispensable bible".

"I asked for application forms for a trainer's licence. Frankly, I just wanted to see the forms, see what was involved. I had no idea at all. The girl put me through to Licensing, and I spoke to Kevin Dwyer, Secretary to the Licensing Committee. He said to me, 'What experience do you have?' Well, I wasn't expecting that, so I said to him, 'I'm a vet in practice.' He retorted, 'Just because you're a vet doesn't mean you can train a horse.'"

Now, some may contend that an understandably sceptical Mr Dwyer, who did not know Mark Johnston from Mark Twain, and certainly could not have imagined what he would go on to achieve, may have had a point.

It will surprise no one that Johnston viewed things rather differently. "It was like a red rag to a bull," he says. "I was absolutely fuming. My first instinct was to say, 'Stuff you, I'll go and train in America,' and put the phone down. Working in the USA had always been in the back of my mind anyway. As a student, I thought it would be very easy there, in comparison to here."

He adds: "I'd just been told I'd got this yard, I was in total disarray, and this guy does that to me. Yet he actually did me a huge favour because he made me realise what I was going to come up against. I suddenly realised it wouldn't be straightforward."

Johnston knew that, as a man who had no experience other than riding out for the trainer Tommy Craig in Scotland and spending his holidays with trainers here and abroad, he needed to establish a strong supporting case for a licence, and that he would require some substantial backing prior to putting his application before the Licensing Committee. "What an uphill struggle that was," he recalls.

He laboured tirelessly to organise it. "For a start, I knew I needed a minimum of 12 horses. I needed to gather as many potential owners as I could. So, I visited, wrote to, or phoned everybody I knew who had racehorses and asked them to send me a horse, or at least to write me a letter which I could show to the Jockey Club, saying that they'd send me one. I got 20 promises from people who would send me horses, and they were invaluable when I went to the Jockey Club."

In fact, only two owners materialised initially, although other owners became involved once he was up and running. Significantly, his first owner was Paul Venner. For Johnston, it was the case of the stars aligning when Venner, co-founder of Baileys Horse Feeds, became his first patron.

"Paul, personally, along with his partner George Knowles, and his company, sent us horses. We would repay him with a Classic winner seven years later. The other was Brian Palmer, founder of the electronics firm Hinari," says Johnston whose uncle Jimmy had introduced Palmer to horseracing, having worked for him. "He would become my business partner when we moved here to Middleham. Half our horses were owned by those two, and there were other bits and bobs."

Yet, as crucial as that backing was from those owners, it was the support of Major Michael Pope, then president of the National Trainers' Federation, which almost certainly produced dividends for Johnston. "I went to see him and told him all about my background. Probably it was my connection with Tommy Craig, who was my mentor and who had taught me the little bit I knew, that made him positive towards me."

He adds: "I think Michael Pope felt the industry owed Tommy a debt because he had been warned off for a year for using anabolic steroids in the mid-seventies – at a time when they were in common use. The Major thought that Tommy had been made a scapegoat for all the others, and the industry owed him a favour. I was the lucky recipient. The backing from Tommy Craig wouldn't have pulled much weight in itself, but the support of Michael Pope did."

There was one further hurdle to overcome. "The Jockey Club

wouldn't accept that our gallops were the beach," says Johnston. "Fortunately, we found a local farmer, Cliff Dawson, who had 2,000 acres. He was master of the local hunt and point-to-point. He was prepared to confirm that we used his land as gallops."

Finally, the moment that would decide the future course of events for Johnston arrived, an appointment with the licensing panel. It was in early 1987 when one rather anxious would-be trainer arrived at Portman Square, home to the Jockey Club, an anonymous building close to the heart of London. It was a location traditionally visited with great apprehension by trainers and jockeys because serious disciplinary cases were referred to and heard there.

"I sat before them and they asked me strange questions like: 'Have you ever saddled a winner?' I thought: 'They know I haven't got a licence and have never had a runner, let alone a winner. Do they mean 'do I know how to put a saddle on a horse?' Did they really think it was going to take me more than half an hour to learn how to do that?

"So, I asked rather lamely, 'Is that important?' Anyway, I managed to negotiate my way through the interview. They sent me out so they could consider my case. When they called me back in, the chairman of the panel said to me: 'We think you should have a jumps licence. Start just in the winter.'"

From somewhere, Johnston summoned as much brass nerve as he could muster and retorted: "No thanks. I'm going to give everything to this. I can't do it part-time. I need a licence for 12 months of the year. Give me a combined licence or no licence at all."

The panel were almost certainly not familiar with what could easily have been interpreted as impertinence. Had they been, Johnston's aspirations could have been dealt a serious reverse there and then – though the suspicion is that it would have been only a temporary impediment to his aspirations.

"They sent me back out again, called me back in, and basically said 'OK'. Where I got the balls to come out with that I don't know. But thank God I did."

So, Johnston now had a yard, owners, horses and a combined Flat and National Hunt licence. But one rather important consideration remained: could he train them successfully after undergoing what amounted to a process of self-education?

It may not be rocket science, as Johnston has always stressed, but it is a far from easily acquired art; that of nurturing half a ton of sometimes capricious, injury- and sickness-prone, highly tuned equine athlete to a pitch of fitness.

His grounding for the task had been a veterinary degree and riding out for a quartet of trainers, scrutinising how they operated. He had watched and listened and devised his own ideas which he was eager to put into practice. But could that satisfactorily prepare him for this moment? There are, after all, far more familiar routes before gaining admission to the industry.

So how, back in those days, did a Scot without a racing background penetrate a world that has always been full of mystique; one containing as many enigmas as the tomb of an Egyptian pharaoh? It is remarkable that an essentially self-taught man transformed himself so rapidly from a novice to a Classic-winning trainer.

In simple terms, it was down to a conviction in his own potential – one that could be occasionally scratched and slightly dented, but would never suffer irreparable damage. As far as Johnston was concerned, he may not have begun as a Grade-A genius with the Form Book or a Lester Piggott in the saddle, but he *understood* horses, their anatomy, their physiology.

Johnston knew how they were put together, how they might fall apart, and, most crucially, had developed his own theories about how to get them to run to their optimum potential.

There is much in common about the progress from inauspicious beginnings of Johnston and that of Martin Pipe, who, at one time, also held the record for total winners before it was broken by Richard Hannon Snr.

Both were outsiders. Pipe was the son of a West Country bookie, of whom the *Racing Post*'s Peter Thomas wrote that "starting off with no more than a derelict farm and a shelf of dog-eared old equine text books, the untutored horseman took out a licence in 1974 and began reading his way to some form of understanding. With his mind uncluttered by years spent learning at the feet of people who played by the old rules, he learned the hard way, by means of hard financial necessity."

The writer also opined that "eschewing the horseman's eye and the instinctive approach, Martin adopted blood tests, the meticulous keeping of data and the use of new-fangled interval training on an all-weather gallop to produce the kind of lean, wiry and relentless front-running beasts far removed from the burly, old-fashioned chasers of yore."

In certain respects, he could have been referring to Johnston who, despite his obeisance to the likes of Vincent O'Brien and Richard Hannon Snr., has come to realise that the West Country champion was, in truth, his model.

Yes, the backgrounds of Pipe and Johnston and their initial aspirations differed. Unlike Johnston, who, from his teenage years harboured a single-minded ambition to be a trainer, Pipe wanted to be a jockey. He worked for his father, David, in his betting shops, and had a few point-to-pointers down on the farm, Pond House, in the hamlet of Nicholashayne, on the border between Devon and Somerset.

He rode one point-to-point winner, but then broke his thigh. That fracture was to prove the catalyst for a new career. True, also,

Pipe was raised in an equine environment, the family farm, while Johnston wasn't, beyond the minor owner-breeding interest of his father. But those contrasts apart, there are fascinating parallels.

Pipe went back to basics, questioned and learned. Maybe it wasn't quite on a par with Leonardo da Vinci dissecting corpses to learn about the working of the human body, but Pipe even went into the operating theatre and helped to dissect horses. As we know, Johnston went the whole hog in terms of educating himself about the inner workings of the horse.

Over the years, when discussing how he developed his training skills, Johnston has invariably returned to the dogs he bred, showed and raced as a teenager. "I always had ideas about how I was going to do it differently," he says. "How my horses were going to be out for two hours and work hard and eat more. I based that on my whippets. I had young, naïve ideas that everyone else was daft."

He adds: "The biggest joke in the world to me was seeing old men or kids out walking their dogs. My thinking was: 'if those dogs couldn't walk faster than old men or children, if that's as much exercise as they did, what chance did they have of winning a race?' I sort of thought the same about racehorses, that trainers probably didn't work them hard enough."

That summation, however, was not the only time he would review an opinion with the benefit of experience. "Over the years, my thinking has changed on that," he says. "Having worked with racehorses now for as many years as I have, it's staggered me how little work a fit horse can get away with. It's unbelievable how little work you have to give them. I now realise that there is a balancing act between fitness and freshness. You have to walk that tightrope. Just more and more work isn't the answer."

He has always been self-deprecating enough to conclude of his own progress: "I don't think I've revolutionised training. I probably started off with some quite extreme theories about how I was going to change the way people trained racehorses, and gradually, through trial and error, I learned I didn't need to change things that dramatically. What made me different from many trainers is that I was open to new ideas."

In essence, he refused to genuflect before conventional wisdom, even when there were many surrounding him prepared to impart the advice: "That's the way it's always been done."

Johnston once told me: "I remember our first head lad when we came here to Middleham, Declan [Condell], talking to me about shins and bandages and claiming that so-and-so was saying something, with which I profoundly disagreed, and that he must be right because 'he's been training for 50 years'," Johnston recalls. "My attitude was that he had probably been training badly for 50 years."

He added: "There's a terrible lot of arrogance within the medical profession, including on the veterinary side of things. But the fact was that I knew a lot about animal husbandry, and still do. I think that's vitally important. I've always tried to get that across to Charlie. My horses weren't going to be sick, ill, undernourished or under-cared for. I may have been naïve in many ways, but I did know how to look after my horses."

Indeed, that's why the reaction from the Jockey Club's licensing department when he first called to seek advice about applying for a licence still galls him, even today.

"If you know how to look after your horses, to my mind, they had no right *not* to give you a licence. You *are* qualified to do the job. I was not going to bring racing or the Jockey Club into disrepute. Instead of that, they ask you stupid questions like 'Have you ever saddled a winner?'"

That wouldn't be long in arriving.

A FIRST WINNER – AND IT'S BOBBY ON THE BEAT

The first runner from the yard of M. S. Johnston – as his name appeared in racecards early on – just four weeks after having acquired his licence, was over the jumps at Towcester. It was a momentous occasion for the family. Even Ron Johnston came down from Scotland.

When that chestnut nine-year-old, General Billy, approached the start under jockey Richard Rowe, amid a snow flurry on a bitter late winter's day, to set off in the last race of the card at an emptying course at just after 4.30pm on 17 February 1987, it would have been absurd to envision those first strides would culminate in a career of such eminence – on the Flat.

The race was a two-mile-five-furlong handicap hurdle worth £1,671.30 to the winner. Not that the prize was of any relevance to the novice trainer.

Challenging for the lead briefly, the 16-1 shot faded in the closing stages to finish ninth of 21, but it served notice that Johnston had arrived, albeit at the periphery, of his chosen profession.

The *Glasgow Herald* deemed that run "an insignificant event in an undistinguished career, but a significant milestone in the life of a young Scottish vet who made racing headlines four years ago when he helped save the Grand National."

"We thought he would win," Deirdre recalls, "and we were devastated when he didn't. We thought the jockey hadn't given it a very good ride. He'd obviously thought 'small trainer, don't know him' and we questioned how hard he had tried. We were very put out."

This may well have been disappointment talking, but more importantly, the suggestion that anybody connected with the yard was *not trying* was to become anathema where Johnston runners were concerned over the years. The legend 'Always Trying' would, in time, become the stable maxim and part of the Johnston branding.

A week later, the yard despatched its second runner, Rosie Oh, to contest a novice hurdle at Huntingdon. She was partnered by a conditional jockey, David Hood, and was the stable's first placed horse, finishing fourth.

By then the Flat season was fast approaching. Although, later in his career, there would be victories over National Hunt obstacles, Johnston had always believed that the Flat would be his forte. It was where serious money was invested in bloodstock and decent prize money was won, or relatively so, anyway.

With the Flat in mind, Johnston had purchased two horses for Brian Palmer, one of his two principal owners, at the breeze up sales[4]. "At the time, Brian wanted to promote Hinari, the fastest-growing electronics company in Europe, and he wanted to do it through racing," explains Johnston.

---

[4] Breeze up sales are where a young horse is worked over two furlongs in front of prospective buyers.

The colt was named Hinari Video and the filly became Hinari Hi Fi. "As you can imagine, I was pretty naïve in those days about entries and declarations. Brian said he wanted to entertain his customers at Haydock on 22 and 23 May, which were Friday and Saturday meetings. He'd told me back in April that he'd like both horses to run there in the maiden five-furlong two-year-old races on each day. I said 'OK' and duly entered them. That was it. Never mind what the opposition was. We thought from their work that Hinari Video was our 'star' horse of the two."

At the time, Johnston didn't even have a regular work-rider. "So, I rang Tommy Craig and he recommended Mark Beecroft, who was based in our area. Tommy said, 'He's good, but he's struggling. He'll come and ride out for you.'"

The horses worked on the beach at home, and then Johnston galloped both horses on the racecourse at Beverley. "I told Mark Beecroft that he'd be riding work on Hinari Video because the colt was the better of the two, and then I asked him whether he could organise a jockey for the other one."

Beecroft duly asked a jockey named RP (Robert Peter), known as 'Bobby' Elliott, if he fancied staying behind to ride work on a couple of horses for a rookie trainer called Mark Johnston. At the time, the young trainer had never heard of Elliott, but it was an association that would transform both their careers.

"Most people, in the situation that we were in, a young trainer, with 12 moderate and injured horses, and a beach in Lincolnshire, if they'd got a stable jockey, they would basically have got a bad one. And that's the last thing you want," says Johnston. "We just got lucky. Bobby was in a different league."

"When he came to ride work, Bobby Elliott made some comment to me about how he'd ridden the sprinter Song, who was Hinari Hi Fi's sire. I looked Elliott up in my *Directory of the Turf.* There it was, under his entry: best horses ridden: 'Brigadier Gerard and Song'."

That first-named would be Brigadier Gerard, regarded by many as the best racehorse of the twentieth century. He was partnered by Joe Mercer in all his races, of which he won 17 of 18, between 1970 and 1972.

"I later discovered Bobby was Joe Mercer's sidekick for quite a long time, through various yards that Joe was in. When Joe was away, riding in India, Bobby was writing to him and telling him that Major Dick Hern had this superstar, Brigadier Gerard, in his yard."

All went smoothly until just before the first of Brian Palmer's horses was due to run at Haydock. Mark Beecroft was to ride them both. "Unbelievably, about four days before the meeting, he told me he wasn't available," Johnston recalls. "So, I booked Rae Guest to ride the filly on the first day and Willie Carson to ride Hinari Video, whom I regarded as my winner." In the event, Hinari Hi Fi finished 12th, though not far adrift of the winner.

In the paddock before Hinari Video's race the following day, Carson was in typically impudent mood. "Willie, as I later learnt, could be very dismissive," Johnston has told me. "Now, you have to remember that the owner, Brian, and his wife, Val, knew nothing about racing. Val, just making conversation really, said chattily to Willie [five feet tall and riding at 7st 10lbs] 'So, what do you actually weigh, Willie?'"

"Willie looked her up and down before replying 'A lot less than you, love.'" Followed, no doubt, by that familiar high-pitched cackle. "That was our introduction to Willie Carson, a great rider who always came across as super-confident, but could be a difficult personality to work with," was Johnston's opinion of his compatriot.

"He could be very stubborn. And you always got a smart reply."

"That was our introduction to Willie Carson, a great rider who always came across as super-confident, but a horrendous personality until he retired," is Johnston's opinion of his compatriot.

"He was very stubborn and difficult to work with. And you always got a smart reply. That's probably because he is a smart guy, very streetwise, and well able to market himself. It was only once he retired and started working in the media, appearing on *A Question of Sport* and as the BBC's racing pundit and so on, that he developed a more positive side to his personality."

Later, Johnston was to employ, and enjoy conspicuous success with, another jockey whom he regarded as equally competent and intelligent.

That was Jason Weaver, who has also prospered by turning to a TV career after retiring from the saddle. Carson and Weaver could hardly have been more opposite in terms of their out-of-saddle demeanours.

"I used to try and tell Jason this," says Johnston. "Willie used to ride a horse and come in, having got beaten, and he'd say something along the lines of 'Oh, if I'd done this or done that, I'd have won. I just didn't know such and such about the horse, but next time, I'll know better.'

"You see, the owner is then instinctively made to feel that he or she wants Willie Carson next time. It's a very clever way of making sure he gets the next ride. Blame yourself. Not too much, just a little bit. And maybe bring the trainer into it too. In contrast, Jason would never blame himself. I think that's a fault. Even if Jason knew he was wrong, he'd never blame himself."

In the race at Haydock, Hinari Video finished towards the rear, like his stable-mate had, in tenth. Carson's faith was unshaken, however. As Johnston recalls: "Willie came back and said, 'Teach it to come out of the stalls, take it up north, and it'll win next time.' [The tracks in the 'north' were then perceived as a likelier location for winners.]

"I asked him something else. 'Has he run green[5]?', something like that. He repeated, rather impatiently, 'Teach it to come out of the stalls, take it up north, and it'll win next time.' That was typical of him.

"Then Willie added, 'I pushed the button today, so give him a couple of weeks off before you run him again.'"

The horse had more time than that to recover as he came home with slightly sore shins. Also, in those days, entries had to be made three weeks in advance. Hinari Video was entered to run at Carlisle on 1 July. Meanwhile, the filly, Hinari Hi Fi, was declared to run at Carlisle on 1 June. "We thought 'stuff Mark Beecroft' and booked Rae Guest to ride Hi Fi," says Johnston, "But the day before the race he told us that he wasn't well and couldn't ride the following day. It was late on in the day and we couldn't get a jockey.

"We were really scraping around, phoning everybody. Then I thought to myself, 'What about that guy who rode her in the gallop at Beverley?' I phoned Bobby Elliott at home and asked if he'd be available. He of course said yes, though it was his only ride of the day. He rode Hi Fi and she finished fourth. We were very pleased with that."

Afterwards, Johnston told Elliott that he needed a jockey to come down to Lincolnshire and ride out. "'If you could do that,' I said, 'you could ride our horses. I've got another one running soon.' Bobby agreed. He came down within a few days and rapidly became our principal jockey."

Elliott, born in Hackney during the Blitz, had started his career,

---

[5] A horse is said to have 'run green' when it has shown signs of inexperience.

aged 14 and weighing just 4st 7lbs, with trainer Tom Masson, who had stables at Lewes in Sussex. He rode his first winner, Dante's Inferno, at Lewes Racecourse at 17, had been champion apprentice in 1960 and 1961 and would ride around 1,200 winners worldwide. He also recalls being the only apprentice retained by the Queen to ride her horses requiring a lightweight jockey, and partnered three winners for her.

Elliott had gone to ride in the United States and Hong Kong, where he was top jockey from 1971 to 1974, and returned to England in 1981. With opportunities hard to come by in the south, he moved north to ride for Thomas 'Squeak' Fairhurst, based in Middleham.

At Carlisle a month later, Elliott rode Hinari Video in his second outing. The horse won convincingly. The Form Book comment was: "Made all. Clear 2f out. Stayed on." That could have been cast as a template for the running of so many Johnston winners, to the present day.

Possibly the most exhilarated of those connected to that first of more than 4,000 winners was Deirdre – and she wasn't even at the course. "We couldn't quite believe it," she recalls. "I was teaching my last class of the day. The race was at 2.30 and I finished at 4.15. I couldn't wait to get out and phone. I ran out to the phone box to discover that it had won. I put the phone down, ran back to the staff room and screamed, 'We've won! We've won!'

"My colleagues were obviously thinking, 'What an odd woman.' When I got back, I switched on Teletext, and it was still on when Mark got back four hours later. It was just fantastic to see his name up there."

Mark adds: "My abiding memory was coming home, seeing the result on Teletext, and watching nothing else all night!" He laughs at how ridiculous that sounds in today's world of immediate communications but adds: "There were no racing channels in those days and if you wanted a video, you had to send off for it, and it arrived in about three weeks."

What a stalwart Hinari Video would be – the horse would proceed to run in another 127 races for Johnston, winning 11, before retiring as a ten-year-old. "He ended up in a riding school," says Johnston. "I can still picture him – more than some of the horses that I've got in the yard now."

Elliott, who would ride 57 winners for the yard, remained attached to the Johnston operation until the end of 1996, when he left to work for Michael Dickinson in the United States. He later returned to Middleham to work for Johnston before setting up as a trainer in his own right. "He was a fantastic work-rider," reflects Johnston. "As good as I've ever seen. He made an invaluable contribution to the yard."

The winners didn't flow immediately, however. In that first year, 1987, Hinari Video was the stable's sole success. That tally of Johnston winners increased to five the following year. A modest start, but the portents were auspicious – particularly as he would soon be bound for rather more productive pastures.

Watching Mark Johnston reminiscing about those intoxicating days of 1987 and 1988, when placing every winner gave him an almost spiritual uplift, is like witnessing a bon vivant stumbling across a long-forgotten cellar of vintage wine.

The trainer rattles through those early victories. Apart from Hinari Video there were Hinari Disk Deck and Hinari Televideo (both for Brian Palmer, and both partnered by Bobby Elliott, at Beverley and Ayr, respectively), and Just Precious for Paul Venner (successful in handicaps at Beverley and Doncaster, ridden by Greville Starkey and Ray Cochrane). And there was Craft Express, again in the hands of Elliott, at Catterick.

Craft Express would proceed to secure the Portland Handicap at Doncaster the following year. That was his first big handicap[6] win, at 25-1. Ah, nostalgia, guaranteed to inject an emotional supplement into a past life. It makes the good times feel even better, the tedious and troubled times bearable.

"Oh, we had great fun, and Bank End in 1987 and 1988 really was a great way to learn," Johnston says. He adds: "It clearly wasn't a sustainable business, but that never worried us. Life was so different then. All we knew was that this was what we wanted to be doing and we had enough cash-flow to be able to eat."

Deirdre agrees. "It was a fun period," she says. "We made a lot of friends, some of whom we still have now, and some helped us out. It must have been tough, but looking back, it seems easier. Now it's such a way of life. Every day you're racing and riding out. Then, we didn't have that many horses. There were only three in the string. We always look back on it fondly."

Johnston can relate stories aplenty about those two years at Bank End. "I remember one winter's day I was up at 5 a.m. to feed the horses, and it was snowing. There was a girl living in the flat which was part of the yard, and my then brother-in-law and I built a wall of snow against her door and above her windows before she got up. For a minute she thought it had snowed so much it had buried her flat!"

He adds: "At night, we'd play games like Trivial Pursuit while drinking bottles of lager until it was time to feed the horses at nine or ten. One horse was called Bestbuybaileys. He'd stand in the corner of his box and wait for his food, then charge at the door when you entered. The penalty for losing the game was to feed Bestbuybaileys!"

---

[6] Handicap races enable horses of varied ability to race competitively against each other via the allocation of weight. The higher their handicap rating – between 0-140 for Flat horses, and between 0-170 for National Hunt horses – the more weight a horse is required to carry.

If it sounds like elements of a script for *Carry on Up the Humber*, and in stark contrast to the ultra-disciplined routine of Middleham today, that wouldn't be too far amiss. "Back then we had time to do stupid things like that," Johnston says. "It was a very different atmosphere to today. There was nowhere near the same pressure."

Which, if you consider it, is a curious observation. Certainly, Johnston's reputation demands consistent success now. But wasn't there an urgency then for the yard to demonstrate that it could produce winners; to announce itself to major owners?

As a virtual unknown, questions would soon begin to be asked about his prowess, wouldn't they? "Sure," he responds. "I know that people who have small yards now look at us and think, 'Well, what the hell has he got to worry about? So many winners already this year. Why's he walking about with a face like a fist?'

"Yet, I look back and realise it was much easier when you have one winner a year. We could go months without a winner. It didn't matter. I don't remember it worrying me that much. Things were rolling along much as we'd planned. It was very different from all this." With a sweep of his hand, he gestures at his kingdom in North Yorkshire.

However, he pondered the question further, before adding, "No, I can't say I was satisfied with that first year. But for me, at 27, it was a huge achievement just to have a trainer's licence. That was an ambition I'd been thinking about for half my life. I'd achieved the number one goal. For a while, nothing else mattered."

However, the lure of training more horses and garnering more winners was increasingly seductive, and that would require a capacity to develop and expand. That would be impossible at Bank End, using the beach to work horses. The location was also well off the motorways and arterial roads.

CHAPTER 9

The move onwards and upwards was not immediate – in most part because of the finances involved in acquiring premises on a rather grander and more conventional scale than Bank End Stables.

By the time Johnston had begun searching for a new yard, he had established a business partnership with Brian Palmer. "We went to Goffs [bloodstock sales in Co. Kildare] at the end of 1987 and paid fifty grand for a yearling that would be called Hinari Televideo. That was the same as we had paid for our Lincolnshire yard, so I was very excited about this."

He adds: "We bought the filly on the first day and we spent the next two days in Ireland, discussing whether we were going to go into business together, or not. Before we'd left Ireland, we'd struck a deal. I phoned Bobby Elliott, to tell him about Brian Palmer, and I told him we were going to look for a new yard."

This had been a wise move, according to Elliott. "The beach gallop wasn't suitable for training decent horses. I told Mark: 'You're getting better horses now. You can't train them down here.'"

He adds: "They looked around for a suitable place and eventually I said: 'I don't know why you don't come up to Middleham'. There's a lovely yard, well an old yard, up here."

The location he had in mind was Kingsley House Stables.

MAKING HIS MARK IN MIDDLEHAM

Today, Middleham is much more than home to the Johnston operation. It has become almost the family's domain. It may be rather overstating things to suggest that Mark Johnston is rather like a feudal baron, but certainly the trainer has accumulated many of the acres he surveys into his ownership over the years.

There are 12 other stables within this rugged idyll, situated between the rivers Cove and Ure. Eight of them are located in Middleham; the others are at nearby Coverham. However, it is the blue and green livery of the Johnston yard that dominates.

Today, over 230 staff make their living at his three yards: Kingsley House, Warwick House, and at Kingsley Park, the most recent of Johnston's acquisitions and now the hub of the operation.

Their responsibilities range across the full gamut: groom-riders, two full-time vets (as well as Johnston and Charlie), administration staff, cooks, nightwatchmen, estate workers, night feed people. In addition, the families who directly or indirectly take an interest in Mark Johnston's fortunes probably quadruple that number.

Even a rough tally of the staff, the jockeys, the owners – including members of Kingsley Park partnerships – and all their families confirms that there are thousands whose lives are influenced by the success, or otherwise, of this leviathan.

Yet, in November 1988, no-one would have dared to prophesy the scale of the transformation of this bucolic North Yorkshire setting. Indeed, many of the locals registered outright scorn when the Johnstons, a few staff and 13 racehorses arrived here at their new base, Kingsley House Stables, a dilapidated 39-box yard offering nothing more than, as an estate agent might enthuse to prospective buyers, "exciting potential to modernise and improve."

Then, more than three decades ago, they must have felt like Old West pioneers following their wagon as it rolled into a desolate township. They surveyed weeds which had grown to chest height. All that was missing was tumbleweed.

"The local reaction was that they thought we wouldn't last five minutes," says Johnston. "They thought I was completely mad; that I didn't know what I was doing." His satisfaction today stems in part from having emphatically disproved those doubters.

In truth, there were other reasons for that scepticism, other than they thought this character was just another deluded dreamer. The Johnstons' predecessor, George Dawes, who had won £750,000 on the football pools in 1983, installed George Moore as his trainer, but then went bankrupt. A similar fate had befallen trainer Ken Payne before that. Steve Nesbitt trained here from the 1970s until his death in 1982. A pattern, of sorts, was emerging. "They thought we were next," says Johnston.

However, those brow-raisers hadn't bargained with the conviction of this self-starter, and indeed, the confidence that his backer, Brian Palmer, had in Johnston's potential.

With Palmer's financial support, Mark and Deirdre emerged

from the relative obscurity of Lincolnshire determined to make a statement in an area which had a horseracing heritage, and at least had turf gallops. This location had scope. As it transpired, enormous scope.

The trainer explains: "We had this idea to build something unique; a yard with every facility, including a swimming pool. I had all these great ideas about veterinary and other gadgets and equipment I wanted to include."

Though Johnston now enjoyed the backing to fund such aspirations, he undoubtedly provoked a sense of intrigue by arriving with a business partner who had founded a company called Hinari.

You can imagine the rumours circulating, and the suppositions. A Japanese company, wasn't it? Something big in Tokyo or Yokohama. Or maybe they were Chinese? They make electrical goods, don't they?

Well, not quite. "Brian just made it up, to sound Japanese, because electrical products from the Far East were the big thing at the time," Johnston explains.

"The locals used to nod knowingly, and say, 'Have you heard about Kingsley House? The Chinese have bought it.' They thought I had Oriental backers.

"Now Brian actually did do a lot of business in the Far East, and I think he probably brought some Chinese people here at one point early on."

So, why Middleham? Certainly, the area boasted a tradition of Classic winners stretching back to the late eighteenth century, when John Mangle produced no fewer than five St Leger victors, and it has long been believed locally that the High Moor gallops, on the site of what was once a racecourse, offered the advantages of 'altitude training'.

I can recall many years later, when the stable's Road To Love had scorched home by seven lengths at Ascot, it had the BBC's pundit Willie Carson eulogising about "Mr Johnston's horses" and alluding mysteriously to the way he works them "up on the moors" as though those contours might contain some mystic power, distilled by a wizard.

In the real world, in the late eighties the scent of conspicuous success hardly permeated the area, and given the bankruptcies of his two predecessors, it didn't appear the wisest investment for the prodigiously ambitious Johnston and his equally committed wife.

Why not Newmarket, long-acknowledged as the 'Headquarters' of Flat racing, or Lambourn, or any base in the wealthier, in equine terms, south of the country?

In fact, the intrepid duo had considered many other options but ultimately their decision was financial. When the Johnstons decided they must move on from Lincolnshire, they had a budget of more than half a million pounds.

Johnston recalls: "We'd bought our yard in Lincolnshire for £50,000, and we'd run up debts of £30,000. We sold it for £130,000, which meant we walked away with a net £50,000. Brian Palmer matched our net profit of £50,000 on Bank End when we sold, and he ended up lending the business a further £125,000. So, we started off with £225,000 and borrowed another £400,000 from Barclays Bank. To us, then, it was a huge amount."

He adds: "Brian Palmer used to come down quite a lot to Lincolnshire [from his base in the North East], but he wanted us to be closer. He talked about us going to Scotland, and him buying a yard and me becoming a private trainer, but I wouldn't do that.

"We went with Brian Palmer to look at three places. The first was Kingsley House, there was Bill Pearce's yard at Hambleton, which is now Kevin Ryan's, and Bill Elsey's yard in Malton, and also a farm around the York area because we had decided that area was the most central place in the country to train.

"We met at a hotel near York racecourse, and all the way in the car – Deirdre and me in ours, Brian and Val Palmer in theirs – we were saying to each other: 'They're not going to like that place in Middleham, but we like it because it's got a tap, it's got boxes, it's got gallops. Although it's a mess and a wreck, you can train horses from there. And it'll be cheap.'"

Johnston, fired with the optimism of a gold prospector, saw way beyond what he observed. That was October, but it took until the following May to buy it. "The man selling it, Dawes, had gone bankrupt and Kingsley House was empty. We offered him £160,000. He turned it down. We gave him a deadline to accept it. We thought he couldn't afford to turn it down. He's got no buyer for it, he's got no money. But he still turned it down. So, we spent seven months looking at other places, including Newmarket.

"The Jockey Club was leasing sites in the Hamilton Road at the time – for trainers to build their own yards – but we thought for the money we had, well, all we'd get was a bungalow and 40 boxes," Johnston explains. "We just couldn't do it there; it was too expensive.

"In the end, he [George Dawes] came back to us, and we settled on £162,500, to include the light fittings and the carpets – there was one in the lounge which we still have to this day!"

Johnston has always asserted: "Now, I've got no desire to be anywhere else," and has added: "People promoting Middleham will tell you that we came here because of the best gallops in the world. The truth of it was that we came here because it was the cheapest."

And yet, there is no disputing that these verdant acres possess an inescapable allure. You'd need to be a confirmed townie, damned with a soul of stone, not to be captivated by the scene before you. Newmarket may boast a greater equine population, but the horses there do not pound hooves within such a glorious vista as Wensleydale, the largest valley in the Yorkshire Dales.

The town itself, granted a market charter in 1389, is the smallest in Yorkshire, you are told. Which is probably why everyone appears to refer to it as 'the village'. Here, the ghosts of equine legends gallop, nurtured to the finest pitch by the skills of men such as Captain Neville Crump, who once trained at the now Johnston-owned Warwick House Stables, the entrance to which stands across the road from Kingsley House.

'The Captain' trained his three Grand National winners here: Sheila's Cottage in 1948, Teal in 1952, and the 1960 victor Merryman II. Crump, who also trained five Scottish and two Welsh National winners, died in 1997, aged 86, and is buried in Middleham cemetery.

Middleham itself was once the capital of Wensleydale and an important market town. It was the home of King Richard III, who lived at Middleham Castle and, much visited by royalty and nobility, it became known as 'the Windsor of the North'. Situated just below St. Alkelda's Church, Kingsley House is named after Charles Kingsley, author of children's fantasy *The Water-Babies*. Kingsley lived there and was a canon at the church.

Racehorses have been trained in the area for some 250 years. Isaac Cape, who was a jockey in the first half of the eighteenth century, became the first specialist racehorse trainer here in 1765. The Cistercian monks of nearby Jervaulx Abbey were breeding horses even before then.

Race meetings on the High Moor, 750m above the town, were staged as early as 1739, but they ended in 1873 after disputes between trainers and local gait owners, the landowners with grazing rights on the moorland.

Since then, the High Moor has been used only for training and the surrounding area has become a haven for its practitioners who have settled here. Frankly, it is not for anyone but the hardy. In winter, a raw, blustery wind chastises you as harshly as a Victorian mother scolding a recalcitrant child.

And this is not just the author's opinion. The stable's former stable jockey-turned broadcaster, Jason Weaver, opined after a victory for a Johnston-trained filly at Lingfield on a blustery day in March: "She's been up in that incredible set-up they have in Middleham. As Bobby Elliott always used to remind me, up on the high and low moor, it was always nine months of winter and three months of bad weather, so she won't mind at all the conditions this afternoon."

It is here that a man who is a compulsive expansionist has made huge tracts of this land his own. While many racehorse trainers are content with, say, stables for 50, maybe 100 horses, Johnston recognised relatively early on that size matters, numbers mean everything.

It took a while for him to heed that reality, and he will concede that a large complement of horses was not penned on his original blueprint for success.

"When I started out, I was naïve, and didn't realise that if you want to train Classic winners, you need 150-plus horses," he says. "In football, it is often said that the strength of a team on the pitch is dictated by the strength of those sitting on the bench. The same applies to us to some extent."

That has been his maxim throughout his career, although there are exceptions to that rule as he agrees: "We actually hit our first Classic winner [Mister Baileys in the 1994 2,000 Guineas] when we had around 70 horses."

However, he is disdainful of those trainers who settle for less as though it is some kind of badge of honour; an optimum for the industry. There is a belief in some quarters that some yards have too large an equine population, and the trainers fail to have an intimate knowledge of every horse.

Indeed, I once confirmed to him that, as a journalist, I had interviewed many of his counterparts who talk about being 'comfortable' with, say, 50-, 60-, 70-horse stables. He retorted: "That's what they say…but that's only because they can't get any more. My view is that if you're not moving forward, you're moving back."

As an example, and briefly throwing the story forward, he referred to James Given, also a vet, who was Johnston's vet-assistant from 1995 to 1998, at which point he left to launch his own training career in Gainsborough, Lincolnshire, and enjoyed Group race success with the likes of Dandino, Indian Days, and Wunders Dream.

"I remember James being quoted as saying after a couple of years (training on his own account) 'Seventy horses is as many as I want. When you have over 100, it gets too much like a factory'." Johnston admitted he took umbrage at that observation. Though he added, with some satisfaction: "It's strange that James now has over 100 horses…" Given retired from training at the end of 2020. He was appointed the new BHA director of equine health and took up that role in 2021.

Sceptics will argue that a trainer like Johnston cannot possibly possess an intimate knowledge of all his horses. That was the author's suspicion too, but he was swiftly disabused of that notion. For those which aren't at his fingertips, his mobile phone doubles as a mini-computer and contains details of every horse's current progress. He consults it constantly.

The fact is that the very term "comfortable" is anathema to Johnston. Indeed, he has lived in mortal fear of having to post a

'House full' sign and turn away horses – or, worse, much worse, not be sent them.

Complacency is not in his lexicon. You sense that some trainers believe that their names alone will always be a magnet for owners, regardless of results. Not this character. He knows that owners can have a roving eye if a stable has a decline in form, and they observe positive results elsewhere.

He cites an example closer to home. His own. Going back a few years, the yard underwent a particularly indifferent run, and he told me: "You know you'll lose horses when that happens. We did lose horses, two or three that I would directly blame on the fact that we were out of form. We had one new owner took their horse away before it had even run!"

For Johnston, a stable in form is not *purely* about winners. He is very sensitive to trends of how his horses are performing. The *Racing Post* has a section that gives handlers' records over the previous fortnight, in terms of wins, places and runners. It offers a telling insight, he believes. "The measure is to look at the percentage of horses getting win *and* place from runs," Johnston says. "If we're hitting 50 per cent then we're really flying. That's incredible. It usually only happens at certain parts of the year. If we're running at one-third everything's fine. But if it drops below 25 per cent we're in dire straits."

But winners are what the public and, crucially, owners, see. That explains why he has constantly demanded that the business has to grow, must progress. "I've spent my whole career building and expanding," Johnston has told me. "Once I stop doing that, I'll give up."

The ultimate project manager, he has a rapacious desire to transform fallow land into gallops and derelict sheds into rows of boxes. The Scot is so driven with naked ambition, there are rivals who would probably contend he should be arrested for indecent exposure. But he is unapologetic about it.

Thirty-three years on from an unostentatious start, he may be about to transform the management profile of the operation to Mark & Charlie Johnston. But the philosophy behind the business has never changed, will never change, while he has a breath left in him.

CHAPTER 11

ALWAYS TRYING AND THE CREATION OF RACING'S BEST-KNOWN LOGO

Tan Le, a Vietnamese–Australian telecommunications entrepreneur once reflected: "It is okay to be an outsider, a recent arrival, new on the scene – and not just okay, but something to be thankful for...Because being an insider can so easily mean collapsing the horizons, can so easily mean accepting the presumptions of your province."

Johnston took a similar belief into his new operation. From those early days, it would be fair to say that he made an impression with his training philosophies and, in doing so, provoked the bemusement of many.

"When we arrived here, we worked our horses considerably harder than the average Middleham trainer," Johnston once told me. "Though it wasn't exactly unheard of, they'd all got into this habit of believing that you couldn't take a horse out on a Sunday, or take all the horses from Middleham village all the way up to the High Moor, but we started doing those things. They thought we were crazy. Then I started taking two-year-olds, and they said, 'You *definitely* can't take two-year-olds all the way to the High Moor.'"

He adds: "The fact was they couldn't be bothered. They maybe didn't have the staff. In fact, it's good for the two-year-olds. There's a lot of that kind of thinking in racing. I'm sure a lot of unsuccessful yards convince themselves that certain practices aren't the thing to do because it's not the convenient thing to do or the economic thing to do. But if you look at Michael Stoute, John Gosden, over the years, they don't cut corners. Sir Mark Prescott doesn't either. I'm a firm believer that training racehorses is about not cutting corners. That was my strong belief from the start."

Indeed, Johnston found the industry so hidebound with custom and practice in those early days, he deliberately sought young stable staff in the expectation that they wouldn't arrive with preconceptions about how to train horses.

This is what he told me in 2006, when we discussed the issue and, bear in mind, he had by then trained two Classic winners:

"The older fellows all thought they knew more than me. Probably still do, a bunch of them here now, but they don't get much say in it now." He reflected on what he'd just stated. "No, that's not true. Everybody gets more say in it than they did in those days. But the truth remains that I found that the best staff were the youngest staff. They were open to new ideas.

He added: "Out in that yard, there's approaching 125 staff and there's probably about 25 of them who think they know more about horses than I do; that I run this business from an office and my success is based on knowing how to run a business. If you asked 20 trainers who are less successful than us, probably 19 would say the same, that I know more about running a business than they do.

"That's crap. Yes, when it's all going well, I can sit there reading my emails and run everything from my office. If it goes wrong, I have to get out there and get among the horses. At the outset, I had to know about horses."

It's unthinkable that any member of staff would harbour such a view today, of course. But his words reflect the attitude Johnston knew existed amongst some earlier in his career. Had he been a distinguished trainer's son, you suspect that wouldn't have been the case.

But this was Mark Johnston, two years into his training career, but dismissed by some as *just* a vet with grandiose ideas.

Returning to that first year at Kingsley House, 13 horses had made the move from Lincolnshire to Middleham. In Johnston's first year here, that tally rose to 27 charges. It was promising, but the Scot knew that the priority was new patrons, and many of them, and plans were made early on for the construction of new boxes.

As Irish trainer Willie Mullins once opined, "I'd rather have a good owner than a good horse. One of the former can lead to several of the latter. Word of mouth is an important vehicle of communication."

Johnston had no delusions about that reality. He was acutely aware that he had entered a fiercely competitive marketplace in which he would have to sell himself. And if that meant doing so as brazenly as a Kim Kardashian or Paris Hilton, so be it.

When Johnston arrived in Middleham, for all the town's historical horseracing associations, there was little then to commend it to prospective new owners. There was simply no particular reason why anyone should send a racehorse to Middleham to be trained. Johnston needed to offer them one. Even while still in Lincolnshire, he had formulated a publicity plan.

"I needed winners, but I wanted quality as well," Johnston explains. "I wanted to win televised races because I was desperate to be interviewed on telly. Not because of my ego, but to publicise the yard. I knew what I was going to say; I had it planned maybe for six months before I appeared." Johnston was totally calculating. He'd even worked out the best place to stand after a televised victory to make sure he'd be interviewed.

The opportunity arose after Just Precious, a three-year-old, won a handicap at Doncaster. It was in his second year of training, in September 1988, just before the move to Middleham.

He adds: "Channel 4 Racing's Derek Thompson interviewed me, and I'd prepared myself fully. I knew I had to talk about owner Paul Venner, and his company Baileys Horse Feeds, and the fact that we fed the horses with that. I had to mention Hinari too because they were our biggest supporter; and I had to talk about our impending relocation to Middleham and our plans there.

"I had this list of things, and I had to answer his one question and get everything into the answer somehow. It was the best advertising I could get. All my interviews in those days were like that."

However, he stresses: "I didn't particularly enjoy them because I wasn't particularly outgoing in nature. It was one of the necessary evils if I wanted to get on."

During that first year at Kingsley House, Johnston compiled a brochure of the yard. His features are wreathed with a mischievous smile at the memory of it.

"We called it our 'Spanish Holiday Resort brochure' because it was a bit of a con," he admits. "The photographs weren't of this yard, or if they were, they were of selected, more prepossessing bits of the yard. The building site was kept well in the background. That wasn't our swimming pool, or our horse-walker, and those boxes weren't actually finished yet."

He then trawled through owners' names in his faithful *Directory of the Turf* and despatched the brochure to everyone who had more than one trainer. "We worked on the basis that there was no particular loyalty there."

"We had zero success initially, if I remember rightly, although some positive interest did come out of it within the year." It came from Robert Kennedy of the Greenland Park Stud, in Berkhamsted, Hertfordshire. Kennedy had initially told Johnston he was happy with his existing trainers, Peter Calver and Ian Balding, but a year later sent him a horse, Marina Park. "She would give us our first Group winner [in the Group 3 Princess Margaret Stakes at Ascot] in 1992."

The relationship between Johnston and Kennedy would bring further rewards. A decade later, they combined for another Group 3 success with Fight Your Corner – a rather apposite name, given Johnston's preparedness to climb into the ring to defend his stance over many issues. That colt won the Chester Vase, having won three of five starts as a two-year-old, before finishing fifth in the 2002 Derby.

To participate in the Classic involved a supplementary fee because the horse was a late entry. In Fight Your Corner's case this was the extraordinary sum of £90,000 just to run in the race though, admittedly, at the time he was being bought out of the yard by Sheikh Mohammed's Godolphin organisation. It is a subject which to this day incurs the Johnston wrath, and to which I will return.

Today, winners, particularly major successes, are far and away the yard's greatest marketing tool. But Johnston has always insisted that creating a positive image is crucial. "Take the guy down the road who's never had more than 20 horses and blames it on the horses being not much good. It's nothing to do with the horses being poor," he says. "I've always said that it's easier to win races with moderate horses than good ones. It's that he's not proving himself a good trainer by getting the best out of them – and, just as important, being seen to get the best out of them. He's not selling himself."

The trainer adds: "At a very early stage, in Lincolnshire, before Brian Palmer got involved, I knew none of the business-speak, the jargon. Brian came along and was immediately saying, 'We've got to look at our unique selling points', the USPs. 'We've got to get them across to potential customers. What's unique about our business that we can sell to the customers?'

"When we came to Middleham, people loved to laugh at everything we did. Yet all we did were the most obvious things in the world. We were concerned with making our horses and our staff look smarter than the others. It was the maxim 'If you can't *be* better, *look* better.' Our rivals' stable staff thought that was funny. They liked to sneer at that."

Branding, as will be seen, is highly important to Johnston. He raises the example of Godolphin and how the so-called 'Boys in Blue' became a familiar sight on the racecourse. "Nobody laughs at them," he says pointedly. "And do you remember Jack Berry [the former Cockerham, Lancashire, trainer] used to have all his horses in sheepskin nosebands, and all plaited, and for him to wear a red shirt? It created familiarity with his operation. It was branding. It was salesmanship. We were doing that from a very early stage."

As stated early on, the fact that the Johnston staff at the racecourse wear a tartan tie and waistcoat and are turned out in smart apparel makes a statement: the Johnston horses are here for serious business.

Was there any resistance to this, I had wondered, particularly by non-Scots? On a visit in 2021, I asked the previously-mentioned Jock Bennett, who has spent a quarter of a century at the yard, and is one of Johnston's assistants.

Now, admittedly, being Edinburgh-born, and blessed with the

epithet 'Jock', he could be considered a trifle biased, but he said: "They're quite happy to wear it. People laughed at Mark when he first introduced it. Now you hardly see a yard that hasn't got its own jacket, or uniform. You're out of place if you don't have one."

In fact, he believes that the fact that the yard's grooms are so smartly turned out may contribute to their charges being adjudged similarly in the parade ring. "Mark did all that before Godolphin; he had this idea of the emblem and the uniform and the jackets, and then started bringing in the tartan waistcoat. I've never actually had to wear one because I have a different role, but though I thought 'with the English staff, we could have a problem here' we never have. It gets them so many best-turned-outs [an award for the horse adjudged to have been best groomed for a race], so they get a few quid."

He explains: "It goes a long way because the judges are usually amateurs, and people just see the horse well plaited up, looking well, and then there's a groom with a waistcoat on who's different from the guy behind. I'm sure that influences a lot of best-turned-out judges." There's a lot of adopted Scots here then? – you ask. He laughs. "Yes, we have our own embassy."

The stable motto, and a statement of intent, 'Always Trying', would become an important part of the branding, too. Mark recalls: "We were working with Rory MacDonald [a long-serving chief executive of the British Racing School] on a staff training programme for us, and that's what triggered it. It also involved some marketing, training us to run the business as well.

"Rory and Brian Palmer came up with the idea of a logo. I thought this was naff, a stupid idea. I really didn't like it. I remember thinking that this was like British Airways painting the [union flag on the] tails of their airplanes. I just thought this was ridiculous.

"Anyway, I was at Hamilton one day, and this guy, as they do all the time – though you perhaps don't hear it so much these days – leant over the rails and said of one of my horses 'Is it trying?' It still angers me. It angered me so much, not just that someone should say this about our horse, but that's what they think horseracing's about."

The implication was clear. A commonly-held belief of the betting public is that, too often, their selections are by no means always trying, and Johnston adds: "The BHA allow this public perception that it's all down to whether it's trying, or not. That they allow this perception that the whole game's bent. They do nothing but almost encourage that perception."

He refers to an explanation being sought after a horse has performed poorly, "when the truth is that on the day the others ran better. Why do you have to have an explanation for something getting beat? It's ridiculous. The only logical explanation is that it didn't run fast enough. You shouldn't spend your life looking for the reasons."

On that particular day at Hamilton, Johnston had grown weary of being asked if his horses were 'trying', or if they were 'off' to use racecourse parlance?

"Of course, he's trying. They're *always trying*," he retorted perfunctorily, as though that was an obvious statement of fact.

For Johnston, this was his 'Eureka!' moment. "By the time I'd driven home from Hamilton I'd thought 'this is just brilliant'. That was one of my best ideas in 30 years. I knew full well that other trainers and people would perceive that was me saying theirs are not always trying. But I've got my answer ready: 'This is not about us. This is about everyone in the business.' I say to the staff: 'You're *always trying* to do the best for the owners, the best for the business, and the best for yourself.'"

He adds: "I knew it would get publicity – because of how people would take it. So, I went from not wanting to have this logo, to thinking it was naff, to 'this is a coup'."

Indeed, so many articles on Johnston refer to that slogan, I tell him. "What a good logo it was. Still is. The best," he agrees. "If people laugh at it, they laugh out of jealousy. Look at all those who have copied us now, with slogans like 'The horse comes first' [a BHA initiative, promoting horse welfare] and so on. But we've got the best one, and we got it first."

Now, there may be those who would contend that Johnston himself is always trying, some might suggest: *very* trying. Anyway, it stuck.

That innovation would come. For the moment, the move to Middleham, and a considerably larger yard, won new owners and the graph of winners soon showed a healthy upturn.

But it was not too long before business truths began to dispel the aura of optimism.

MAKING A PROFIT?
A NOVEL PROPOSITION

The Johnstons had been in situ at their new base for about 18 months, when a new bank manager at the nearby Leyburn branch visited and brought with him an icy blast of realism.

"When we came to Middleham, in partnership with Brian Palmer, he largely pushed it all through financially and we thought that winners-wise everything was hunky-dory. It was going great," Mark Johnston once told me. And in many ways, it was. After that sole winner in their first season and five in their second in Lincolnshire, the tally rose to 15 for 1989, their first season at Middleham.

In that year, the yard also secured its first victory at Ascot, with Hinari Televideo, partnered by Bobby Elliott, and for the first time a Johnston horse gained 'black type' when the same jockey secured a Listed event, the Cock of the North Stakes at Haydock with Lifewatch Vision. The following year, 1990, the total of Johnston winners rose to 28.

"But then came my biggest eye-opener. I would never forget it,"

Johnston said. "The winners were flowing. Everything was going the right way. But interest rates were going through the roof and we were paying £70,000 in interest. We hadn't budgeted for that, and we were losing money. The bank manager came and sat in the kitchen and gave me a lecture, telling me that I should be putting our fees up."

He added: "I felt really insulted. I thought: 'Who's he to try to tell me how to do the job? It's no business of yours.' We were all about filling the place with horses and getting winners, because if we didn't do that it wouldn't matter what we charged – we wouldn't have any customers."

The real shock came when Johnston realised that the bank not only wanted him to make the repayments on the loan and stay within the overdraft limit, but demanded that he present accounts to show that he was making a profit.

Profit? This was a novel proposition; a term that was then alien to him. "I thought, 'Why? What business is it of theirs whether I'm making a profit or not?' In those days, we weren't making a profit – and I didn't care. I only cared about surviving and training winners. I thought 'I'm eating, I'm living, I'm getting around, I'm training winners, and I'm meeting the repayments.'

"I couldn't understand that they could threaten to call in the loan or cancel the overdraft if I didn't make a profit. I thought, 'How can you be expected to make a profit as well?' I was pretty naïve about running a business. I now realise that is *exactly* what they expected."

He may have entered the business with a solid knowledge of equine physiology and with grand plans to expand and introduce the most cutting-edge facilities, but nothing had prepared Johnston for this.

He added: "From the very early stages we'd done very regular, disciplined management accounts, with profit and loss, but although I used to get a balance sheet, I never looked at it, or really understood it. It never really occurred to me in those days that we were probably insolvent.

"'Got to make the repayments.' That was my only thought. I'd also got a £100,000 overdraft facility, so as long as I didn't go over that, it would be fine. Everybody'll be happy. I couldn't have imagined that anyone would come and sit in our kitchen and tell me how to run the business.

"I'd blithely ignored most of the financial advice I was given initially. I went through a terribly risky time, without even realising it. We had some pretty sleepless nights. We needed money more than at any other time in our business life but we couldn't get it in."

The explanation for that was simple. "Some people didn't pay us," Johnston admitted. "We were no good at collecting the money even though we needed it desperately. We tried chasing people up but we weren't very good at it."

There is a commonly held belief that training is one of the safest businesses in which to operate. The BHA publishes a 'Forfeit List' of owners who are non-payers of their training fees. They are disqualified until they make good their arrears. But that doesn't guarantee that they will ever pay off that debt.

"It was a serious problem for us at one time. And, of course, you're scared to put too much pressure on them because you fear they may take the horses away. And we needed winners to raise our profile."

Deirdre, possibly more than her husband, found this a desperately troubling period, "It was an horrendous time," she once told me. "I'd never done accounting before, yet here I was doing cash-flows and reconciling bank statements on a daily basis so that we knew where we stood. At one stage, we couldn't pay our own bills. We had to sit on them until some more money came in. It was a frightening situation, owing money, feeling under pressure to pay and not having any money."

She added: "We'd gone into business with Brian Palmer, and that gave us loads of confidence. But it was only when things got tough that we suddenly realised how much money we'd borrowed. I just didn't like being in debt. Didn't like it at all."

This could not have come at a worst time. It was essential that they renovated the yard and the house, which in itself had required a dampcourse and central heating, and they also needed to expand. The problem was doing so when income could never be guaranteed.

They came close to going bust. Things were that fraught. "When we had arrived, there were 27 boxes, and 12 wooden ones. We got rid of the 12 wooden boxes and we built more to give us 42. We had already rented boxes from other yards – Chris Thornton's and Chris Fairhurst's – but we needed more of our own," said Johnston. "We wanted to build 15 more loose boxes here at Kingsley House, which would take us to a total of 57 initially, and eventually up to 67."

"We'd had a verbal agreement from our Barclays Bank manager in Leyburn that we'd get the money and had already started building. We were up at wall-plate level. It wasn't the builder we needed to pay at that stage – he'd already been paid – but VAT."

"Just at that moment, our bank manager told us that his regional office had apparently rejected the request. We couldn't have the money, which was around £20,000."

It doesn't sound a large amount today, but then, Johnston admitted: "We were in real trouble. At the level we were operating at then, we had five days to find an alternative to pay the Revenue. Having paid the builders, we were bang up to our overdraft limit. Brian Palmer's attitude at the time was, 'We're going out of business. We can't borrow the money.' He said it was against his principles to borrow from family and friends."

Fortunately, Deirdre's father Duncan stepped in, for a second time; quietly depositing the money into his daughter's personal Midland Bank account in Leyburn. Deirdre wrote out a cheque to the HMRC.

This backing of Deirdre's parents again proved vital. She recalled: "It was massively important. They lent us the deposit for our first yard and they were always there supporting us. My dad had an insurance policy that matured, and I said 'we can't take your money.' And he said: 'I know you'll pay me back'. We only ever used half of it, actually, to pay the HMRC, and that it was it. We never needed to ask for anything again."

Johnston has conceded that the whole affair was like an army camp reveille – loud, unwanted and unpleasant – but the wake-up call necessary to arouse him to the realities of commercial life. "Fortunately, we got through that period. We were bedding down those boxes, and staff were moving horses from one of the yards where we'd rented boxes, literally as the doors here were being screwed on. It enabled us to turn the whole business around. It was a defining moment, moving from 42 to 57 horses – and from losing money to breaking even. We paid Deirdre's father back within three months. It's been steady progress ever since."

It was a time when Deirdre's confidence in her husband's financial acumen took something of a bruising. "In those days, there were lots of tears and panic," Johnston remembered, grimacing. "I don't know whether Deirdre's always had faith in me. I think there were times when she felt it was a bit of a roller-coaster that she was caught on, and she never got any say in the matter."

He added: "In the early days, she agreed with me that there was nothing to lose. She became very frightened when she felt there was a lot to lose. No, at that time, I'd say she wasn't confident at all.

"I've always been driven to make money. But only as a means to provide for us. Becoming wealthy from racing never really entered my head. At the beginning, all I thought about was avoiding the downside. When we set up Bank End Stables, we had considered the negatives, not the positives. We didn't say that we could make it to the top. We just took the view that the worst that could happen was that we would end up back as a teacher and a vet."

From the moment the loan to Deirdre's father had been repaid, profit became the Johnstons' quest. Which, you suggest, somewhat tangentially, and possibly unfairly, could be perceived as a clash of ideologies. How did it sit comfortably with the world in which he was raised?

Now, nobody would have contended for a moment that Johnston was about to metamorphose into Michael Douglas's Gordon Gekko in *Wall Street*, who at the end of the eighties famously espoused the philosophy "Greed is good". Yet, for a man born into a socialist household and whose leanings earlier in his life were decidedly left-wing, surely 'profit' was a tricky concept to accept?

We have discussed this subject often over the years, and Johnston has always maintained there was no conflict for him.

"There was a strange contrast within my upbringing," he explains. "My father was in principle a communist, but was, in practice, nothing like one. Today, I don't believe I'm that different from everyone else. Politically, you've got this natural progression from when you're a teenager and you're the most left-wing, most rebellious of your life. As you go through life you become more conservative, with a small 'c'. You move to the right, probably, and become less rebellious."

He adds: 'My father used to quote Marx, you know: 'From each according to his ability, to each according to his needs.' He used to quote these things to us. But he didn't necessarily practise it. I certainly don't practise it either. And then, when he was doing well, he had racehorses. His excuse used to be 'we don't make the rules…you give your vote and if they [governments] reject it and write different rules, beat them at whatever rules they write.'"

You tend to say that, too. I remind him.

"I probably got it from him."

Johnston recalls that his father and uncle frequently took very different standpoints when it came to their political thinking. "Uncle Jim, who died the year before last, was a bit of an influence on me, maybe a bit of a help to me at times. But he used to really annoy me because he'd be dismissive of all my father's opinions and would say things like: 'It's dead simple. You put food down for two dogs in one dish, and one'll eat it all. It's nature.' I would tell him, 'It shouldn't be like that. We're better than dogs. We should share.'

Today, the trainer concedes that, "I have certainly become less radical and left wing in my political views. I look back at the Margaret Thatcher years. I was a student in Glasgow around the time Thatcher came to power and, like many in Scotland, I hated her.

"Today, I still don't agree with the idea that she was Britain's greatest PM, but I do realise that it was an achievement in dealing with the unions – unions who had become so powerful."

With age and experience, has come a healthy scepticism of all politicians. He has often told me that he regards *Animal Farm* as the greatest book ever written. "It's true: some animals are more equal than others. They're willing to fight for equality, until they can have more for themselves. Don't you see it in just about every walk of life?"

When it comes to employment of his own workforce, Johnston maintains that he has always attempted to be fair, but adds: "I'm not running a staff benefit. This is a Mark Johnston benefit. It's my business, and at the end of the day the principal gain is for me. First and foremost, this is my job and I employ a lot of people to help me with it."

He adds: "No, we'll not all get paid the same. Everybody's at a different level, but that doesn't mean they're not doing the best for themselves, or we're not doing the best we can for them. Or that we're not paying them a fair wage for the job."

He aims for wages to be between 38 and 42 per cent of turnover. If that percentage were to climb to 46, it would be too high to sustain, but if it was to fall below 36 per cent, staff would not be paid enough.

"I don't think we need to apologise for making a profit, or be at all ashamed for doing so. It's essential. The day we stop making a profit, we'll shut. Yes, this [he sweeps his hand around] makes money. It has not failed to make money now for many years. If it wasn't doing that, I'd be doing something else."

He argues that, apart from their knowledge and experience, the risk element for trainers is as significant as it is for any entrepreneur. Their businesses can flourish, they can struggle; some may crash and burn, just like any other small to medium concern.

"Though we've made money, there's been huge amounts of risk along the way," he says before adding: "This has *got* to bring a return. Sometimes I look at it and I wonder how trainers further down the scale survive. There must be an awful lot of them still applying my Bank End principles: eating and existing, making the repayments, and that's about it."

MAKTOUM QUALITY COMES TO MIDDLEHAM

Throughout his painful learning process during the early years at Middleham, one other thought had nagged away at Mark Johnston: how to be noticed by the Maktoum family? How to add them to his roster of patrons?

It was not merely that the yard would benefit from superior bloodstock. Just as significantly, in view of his financial woes, these were owners who didn't require reminders to pay their bills promptly.

Seven years after a rather gauche Mark Johnston, still in veterinary practice in Braintree, had made what turned out to be a fruitless approach to Sheikh Mohammed, asking to be considered for a job within his operation, he made another pitch to the ruler of the Emirate of Dubai, this time seeking the patronage of him and his family.

Johnston wrote again to the Sheikh in early 1992, the year of the inception of Godolphin, the gargantuan horseracing operation and brainchild of Sheikh Mohammed. The name comes from the Godolphin Arabian, one of three stallions that founded the modern thoroughbred.

The trainer explained that he could have his horses trained cheaper, but to the same standard, in Middleham. It was typically brazen Johnston. He believed that nothing would be gained by reticence.

At the time, members of the Maktoum family had their horses assigned to a range of trainers, many in Newmarket, with the likes of Henry Cecil and Harry Thomson Jones (known as 'Tom Jones'), but also elsewhere: with John Dunlop at Arundel; Major Dick Hern at West Ilsley; Barry Hills at Marlborough; Peter Walwyn at Lambourn; and Bill Watts at Richmond in Yorkshire. Johnston could only look on covetously.

"I got a nice letter back from Anthony Stroud [Sheikh Mohammed's racing manager at the time] just saying that they weren't planning, at that stage, to have any more horses in the north."

Watts, whose triumphs included the 1972 1,000 Guineas with Waterloo and the 1985 Arlington Million with the mighty Teleprompter, owned by Lord Derby, trained at Hurgill Lodge Stables in Richmond and was considered one of the Yorkshire power bases.

Johnston's determination to entice the Sheikh was undimmed when, coincidentally, he agreed to complete a Q&A in a lifestyle feature for *The Sporting Life*. "There were the usual daft questions, like 'Are you superstitious?'" Johnston recalls. "But one question was 'What's your favourite colour?' I said, 'I'd like it to be maroon and white [then the colours of Sheikh Mohammed's silks], but it isn't yet.'"

The trainer grins as he adds: "I couldn't resist it. A short time later I happened to see Simon Crisford, who was representing

Sheikh Mohammed [as Godolphin racing manager], at Sandown. He said: 'We saw the item in the *Sporting Life* – we all had a good laugh at that.'"

Johnston's transparent attempt to ingratiate himself with the country's most powerful family of owners may have ended there – in amusement for the subjects of his approach. Or so a less self-assured character might have assumed.

Unabashed, Johnston remained determined to make an impression and thought he had done so inadvertently in 1990 when Starstreak, one of the yard's early smart horses, won the White Rose Stakes at Ascot, defeating a short-priced favourite of Sheikh Mohammed's. That was when we thought, 'We've made it.'" He smiles at the memory. "I didn't think I cracked it with one horse, but there have been milestones, and I remember thinking then, 'Sheikh Mohammed *must* have noticed me now.'" He shrugs. "Probably he didn't notice me at all!"

Yet, finally, one of his arrows of intent struck the target. "I was sitting in the kitchen one day at the end of 1992," Johnston continues. "Our secretary put her head round the door and said, 'It's Anthony Stroud on the phone.'

"In a strange way, I was expecting the call. I felt I knew what he was going to say. Anthony just said, 'We wondered if you had room for one horse?'"

Kingsley House certainly did have room for this particular horse; this particular owner. The horse was a filly named Pearl Kite. She ran in the colours of Saeed Manana, a close friend of Sheikh Mohammed and, in 1993, she won on her debut, a maiden at York, by three lengths, ridden by Michael Roberts.

That would be her only victory, though she was placed in the Group 2 Ribblesdale Stakes at Royal Ascot and the Listed March Stakes at Goodwood. Later, she became a successful broodmare.

But for Johnston, that first race for an Arab owner was a significant breakthrough. It felt like he was joining a masonic society, although he was aware that he still had to win the full approval of the brotherhood.

"I didn't know if we were going to get any more horses from them [the Maktoum family]," he recalls. "Then, one day, we were sitting here, having our dinner, and we heard the fax machine whirring next door. The fax was headed 'Darley Stud' [based at Dalham Hall, on the outskirts of Newmarket – and home of Sheikh Mohammed's global breeding operation] and simply read, "Your yearling allocation is…and the details of four horses came shunting out of the machine. The whole yard was celebrating." Since then, Johnston has continued to attract significant Arab patronage.

This powerful extended group of family and friends is headed by His Highness Sheikh Mohammed bin Rashid al Maktoum, Ruler of Dubai, the largest owner and breeder of racehorses in the sport's history. His brothers, Maktoum al Maktoum and Hamdan al Maktoum, who died in 2006 and 2021 respectively, have also been prominent owners. Rabbah Bloodstock is a 20-strong group of Sheikh Mohammed's Dubaian friends, including Jaber Abdullah, Saeed Suhail, Mohammed Obaid al Maktoum and Saeed Manana.

Over the years, the Maktoum family has been accused of discouraging British owners by stripping the prize-money tree of too much of its prize fruit simply because they had the purchasing power and breeding operations to do so.

Julian Muscat wrote in *The Times* in 2009: "Some maintain that Sheikh Mohammed's dominating presence in Britain masks underlying problems; that bloodstock prices are prohibitively high, and that poor prize money levels are not being addressed. Owners are also being forced out by the intensely competitive nature of the sport." As one banking scion said after a poor season: "I am a taxpayer trying to compete against a tax collector."

The only beneficiary, it has been claimed, is an exclusive, highly fortunate elite of trainers who run a cosy cartel, vacuuming up Arab patronage.

There is now a more enlightened approach to the Maktoums. Johnston has told me that he regards any antipathy towards the Maktoum family as 'stupidity', although, of course, he does declare an interest as a trainer for the family and their friends, and someone who has been a frequent visitor to Dubai to contest the country's best races. It would be foolish not to do so. "We send horses there because it's fantastic prize money," he admits.

The situation in Britain, he added, was that: "For every £1 in prize money the Maktoums win, they put in £4 into running their horses. That's not a benefit to them, it's a benefit to us. So long as owners are net losers in this country, you want to welcome everyone you can get, wherever they come from. They're not taking it away, not taking a penny out of this country. They're only putting it in.

"A win for a Godolphin horse is a win for a British-based trainer. That money is re-invested in Britain, and much more is added to it. They're British owners, with horses cared for, on the whole, by British staff. Of course, there is an element of Dubai training, but there's a lot more British than anyone coming in from outside."

Johnston believes the Maktoums' crucial legacy is that they have maintained British racing's position among the world's elite during an era when otherwise it would have fallen dramatically. "Not only have they invested in racing stables, studs, staff, every aspect of British racing, but they have also brought the best American blood, and European as well. They win the top races with it, and they stand it here at stud. So, the next generation become British. Obviously, they may have a dream that some may become UAE–British, but really they've allowed us, despite poor prize money and funding, to stay up there, competing with Japan and the US."

There does though, remain concern in some quarters that the Maktoums, and it could be said the Coolmore[7] operation, skim off the cream of major races with their runners?

"The wonderful thing about horseracing is that's never the case," Johnston counters. "Of course, if money, or the best breeding, could guarantee success, then very few people would be in it. The wonderful thing is that every horse has a chance. We started with very cheap horses and climbed a long way up."

Securing the patronage of the Maktoum family and their friends was a crucial breakthrough. One that should never be understated, and was extraordinary, coming as it did less than six years after Johnston's arrival at what was then a 39-box yard in urgent need of renovation and expansion.

This development had not only provided an injection of quality; it yielded a much-needed cash-flow. "Suddenly, we had customers who we sent a bill saying 'please pay within 30 days' and they paid sooner!" says Johnston. "We could pay the staff without worrying about it. It was an education for us – and helped solve our cash-flow problems. Bad debts became a thing of the past."

Just as crucially, winners were on a significant upward curve. In 1992, the stable recorded 53 winners, 77 the following year and, in 1994, they registered their first century.

"We were really chuffed with ourselves. We were really flying at that time. I could never have imagined the business would grow so fast," says Johnston.

---

[7] Coolmore Stud, in Co. Tipperary, Ireland, is headquarters of the world's largest breeding operation of thoroughbred racehorses. Aidan O'Brien is trainer of the racing arm, Ballydoyle.

Despite those first years at Middleham being fraught with financial worries, Johnston was quietly achieving what he had planned from the beginning.

In essence, this was to accumulate an ever-larger complement of horses, and to become synonymous with winners; preferably consistent winners who would capture the imagination of the media and public.

He certainly achieved that with Lifewatch Vision, who won on seven occasions, and Quick Ransom, who cost only 6,000gns as a yearling but included the 1992 Ebor Handicap at York among his nine victories.

But if they were willing and able foot soldiers, it was the afore-mentioned Marina Park, bred and owned by Robert Kennedy, of Greenland Park Stud, who became the first standard-bearer for the stable and led the Johnston name into a battle for recognition from which the trainer would ultimately emerge triumphant.

The first horse Kennedy had sent to Johnston was Key Point, a horse with knee problems which it was believed could be solved by sessions in the Kingsley House swimming pool. Key Point never made it to the racetrack, but for many years he was ridden by Deirdre, who rode him in equestrian events and used him as a hack.

Marina Park was a different story, vindicating Kennedy's faith in her. She won four of her 20 starts, including the Group 3 Princess Margaret Stakes at Ascot in 1992, before being beaten by less than two lengths by Zafonic in the Group 1 Prix Morny at Deauville – Zafonic would win the 1993 2,000 Guineas. She was also defeated by just a neck in the Hong Kong International Bowl at Sha Tin.

Even in defeat, Marina Park kept esteemed company, and that, too, contributed to raising the stature of Kingsley House Stables, just as the arrival of the Maktoums as patrons had. The yard was now becoming recognised for nurturing quality as well as yielding winners.

In the nineties, Johnston would establish himself as an adept trainer of handicappers. Star Rage won nine Flat handicaps in 1994 alone, equalling the twentieth century seasonal record. Meanwhile, a remarkable three-year-old filly named Branston Abby had arrived at the yard.

The sprinter would end her career four years later with 25 victories from 97 runs between 1991 and 1996 (though her first two wins were for other trainers). She became an experienced world traveller. Evry (France), Munich (Germany) and Sha Tin (Hong Kong) were among her stop-offs.

With the lure of often far greater prize money purses, despatching his horses abroad always appealed to Johnston. "I first started sending horses over to Ireland when we were in Lincolnshire," he says. "I've no idea what triggered it, but I got a real taste for it. I even had a pacemaker in that first one. I ran our two-year-olds, Hinari Televideo and Hinari Disk Deck. Hinari Televideo finished third."

Star Rage boasted a prodigious record which spanned an astonishing ten seasons, during which time she had four trainers. This admirably versatile horse won 28 of 137 starts on the Flat, on turf and all-weather, and over hurdles.

The pinnacle of that latter career came in late 1997, when Dean Gallagher produced the gelding with a finely-judged run to secure the Fighting Fifth Hurdle at Newcastle for Johnston. It was a rare reversion to the National Hunt code in which he had begun a decade before.

It should be added that, at one time, the intrepid Johnston even sent horses to St Moritz, the Swiss village, 6,000 feet above sea level. It may well be a chic playground for the well-heeled and celebrity A-listers, but it was also a venue for the well-shod and forward among his string. The tri-annual race meeting, staged on a three-foot-deep frozen lake, provided inviting prize money and an opportunity to seek fitness before the turf Flat started at home. Johnston likens it to "a posh point-to-point, with furs instead of Barbours."

SUPER-SUB JASON SEIZES GUINEAS PRIZE FROM PAL FRANKIE

E arly in the Flat season of 1993, Mark Johnston stopped for a brief chat with fellow trainer Sally Hall as they passed on the Middleham gallops where the two-year-olds were placing their first skittish hoof-prints.

The Scot knew that Hall, niece of Sam, who trained more than 1,000 winners in a career starting in 1949, and a successful and knowledgeable handler in her own right, kept a few broodmares at her nearby Brecongill Stables.

He can still recall her words. "She said to me, 'What's that horse [sired] by...that one there, with a big white face?'

"I told her, 'Robellino.' She said, 'I like him. I think I'll send a mare to Robellino.'"

That sire, a son of the 1972 Derby winner Roberto, had won the 1980 Royal Lodge Stakes at Newmarket, but failed to fulfil that promise at three, with a sole victory from his eight races. He had finished 14th in the 1981 Derby won by Shergar.

In late June that season, Johnston happened to bump into Sally's partner and assistant, Paul Platts, at a meeting at Newcastle where the same bay juvenile was due for his introduction to a racecourse. "Paul said to me, 'Is that Sally's Robellino colt?' I nodded. 'Yes, that's the one.' He just said, 'I'll back it.'"

Sally Hall proved to be an astute judge. As Johnston will readily concede, her assessment of his charge was possibly keener than his own at the time. Clearly word had spread that this two-year-old had certainly looked the part on the gallops. "Sally had picked that horse out just from seeing it cantering past her," says Johnston.

The colt made a tardy start from the stalls before eventually striding seven lengths clear in a six-furlong juvenile event. Even at his most sanguine, Johnston could not have foreseen that this youngster who would transform the yard's prosperity, and his entire career, was taking his first exploratory steps.

His owner, Johnston's first patron Paul Venner, had originally bought the Robellino colt as a foal, paying 10,000gns, but ten months later sent him to Tattersalls as a yearling – and he was there to be sold.

The vendor was Petches Farm, Venner's own breeding enterprise, and he wanted 15,000gns for the yearling colt. Johnston recalls: "Paul said to me: 'Protect him to 15,000gns and then let him go. Buy it in for Baileys until 15,000gns. At 15,000gns he's gone.'"

He adds: "The bidding was between [trainers] Michael Bell and Giles Bravery. It stalled at 10,000gns, and I bid 10,500gns." The hammer came down.

"Michael Bell and probably Giles Bravery, too, looked round and saw it was me, and they just thought 'the owner is running me up' – which we were, basically."

'Running up' means an owner bidding for his own horse. It is a practice decried by some in the industry. In a *Racing Post* article in 2017, Thoroughbred Breeders' Association board member Bryan

Mayoh, said: "Even when the reserve is reached, the vendor can place bids on his own horse, aiming to 'run up' the genuine would-be buyer even though the reserve should surely reflect his real view of the horse's value. This is not only allowed by the auction house, it is practically encouraged."

Johnston can see no problem with this practice. "If you take your car to auction, and you think it's worth £20,000, and there's someone else there who thinks it's worth £20,000 – but there's only that one person, you're not going to get to £20,000 unless you bid against him. So, to my mind bidding against him is completely legitimate – so long as you're willing to take it on. We were saying 'we think he's worth 15,000gns and if he doesn't make that, we'll buy him back.'"

Once on the racecourse, that scintillating victory by his charge, who had been named Mister Baileys, partnered by Dean McKeown, was the beginning of a sequence that would enhance the lives of many involved.

Not least Johnston, who, after nearly five years at Middleham was still searching for that elusive Group 1 success. On the face of it, this cheaply-acquired individual had scarcely looked likely to overcome the Newmarket big players and fulfil that objective.

Yet, increasingly an aura of anticipation surrounded the colt with the ostentatious looks: a white blaze and three white feet. "Dean McKeown [then the yard's principal rider] kept telling me that Mister Baileys was the best we'd got," says Johnston. Deirdre, who had soon proved herself a sound evaluator of bloodstock, was also convinced that he possessed great potential.

"I never rode him at home," says Deirdre. "But it was great watching him. We were pretty bullish, by the time he ran at Newcastle, that he would win his maiden."

Recollecting the events of that entire period exposes Johnston at his most fervent; at his most candid, when his judgement subsequently comes under question; and at his most vindictive, towards anyone who dares to diminish his charge's achievements. He has never been cowed from hitching his wagon to a star, as the American poet Ralph Waldo Emerson expressed it.

"Mister Baileys went from winning that race at Newcastle to a Newbury conditions race where he got beat, boxed in during a five-horse race and only finishing third (though by half a length), but we thought so much of him that he went straight from getting beat to running in the [Group 3] Vintage Stakes at Goodwood," recalls Johnston. "He won that, went to the [Group 2] Gimcrack, where he was sixth of eight, but then won the [Group 2] Royal Lodge [now staged at Newmarket, but then run at Ascot]. Three of his five two-year-old starts were Group races."

The 2,000 Guineas had become a tantalisingly plausible project. Yet, the winter that separates a racehorse's two- and three-year-old careers – 217 days in the case of Mister Baileys – can feel like an eternity, particularly when you have care of a Classic contender. For Johnston, it was worse: he had never been in this position before.

But throughout, his belief in the colt was unwavering. Other arbiters were not so convinced by Mister Baileys' Classic credentials. *Timeform's* much-vaunted *Racehorses* annual for 1993 damned his charge with faint praise. "Mister Baileys represents the best chance for northern success in the Classics for several years, even if he cannot yet be regarded as up to Classic-winning standard," it stated, albeit with the concession that he was "Very much the type to train on".

In the spring of 1994 Johnston had some traditionalists muttering their disquiet when he despatched Mister Baileys directly to the 2,000 Guineas, with only the benefit of a racecourse gallop.

So, why did Johnston eschew a preparatory race for his Guineas contender – a strategy he would also employ 11 years later with Attraction? It was borne out of a question of practicality rather than being some piece of elaborate equine science. "The year Mister Baileys won the Guineas it was an atrocious winter," Johnston recalls. "The reason we got into racecourse gallops was because Middleham gallops weren't fit to use.

"We tried him on the turf at home. He just wasn't handling the soft ground at all. Then we gave him one bit of work on the all-weather which in those days was woodchip and not all that good. And then we thought: 'Stuff this for a lark. We'd better take him to a racecourse.' So, we did."

There were two other factors, according to Johnston, for not giving Mister Baileys, and, indeed, other Guineas horses, a preparatory race: "Horses like that, well, all we're doing is training them down to a racing weight, ready for the race.

"But also, in their early careers, I like horses to go through a progression of racing. I don't like them to win a Group 2 and then come back and win a Group 3. I usually don't like them to win a Group 2 and come back and run in another. Sometimes they'll jump a stage. But I don't like them going backwards." With Mister Baileys, there was nowhere else to go than Group 1 – and that meant the 2,000 Guineas."

There was one further crucial consideration – who would be in Mister Baileys' saddle come Guineas day? After the move to Middleham, Bobby Elliott had continued to partner the majority of the yard's horses before Dean McKeown had increasingly assumed that role. McKeown had partnered Mister Baileys in his first four races, but had departed to ride in Hong Kong.

So, fate decreed that Jason Weaver, who had begun his career with Luca Cumani as a 16-year-old and had been champion apprentice in 1993 with 60 winners, would enter the picture. "Jason had just lost his claim[8], and he appeared at the door one day, asking if he could ride out," recalls Johnston.

Weaver takes up the story: "You're champion apprentice and have lost your claim, and you're a young jockey, looking around. I had an agent named Terry Norman. I remember we met at the now-defunct snooker centre in Newmarket and we'd chit-chat over a game. He said 'right, I've got a list of trainers.' He'd obviously had his eye on what Mark was doing, thought that he was doing fantastic at the time, although I doubt he imagined then that he'd be where he is now! He told me: 'You go up there, ride work, and keep your head down.' So, that's what I did. I went up there, I rode out, and was as keen as mustard."

The association proved immediately fruitful. "Mark threw me on a few horses after a little while and I had a lot of luck," he says. "I think the way they train…it's not that I clicked in with them, I think everybody clicks with them, don't they? They're so professional and straightforward."

He adds: "If you look at all of Mark's horses, you very rarely see any of them being pushed along in the early part of the race or pulling in the early stage of a race. They seem to find that nice, fluent rhythm. They're quite happy. And that has to be something he has in his training ability."

Weaver rode his first winner for the Kingsley House trainer at Musselburgh in September 1993 and, five days later, while a trio of the stable's classy charges headed for Ascot, Weaver was despatched to Redcar to partner a two-year-old debutant. That colt's name was Double Trigger.

---

[8] An apprentice jockey, aged between 16–26, can "claim" a weight allowance for their mounts. This allowance (7lb, 5lb and 3lb) decreases in stages as the number of wins increases.

Over time, Johnston's partnership with Weaver could be likened to white-water rafting; frequently exhilarating but always liable to strike boulders. But in the autumn of 1993, the style and positive attitude of the Nottingham-born jockey was sufficient to impress Johnston enough to offer him a retainer, starting the following season, although Johnston concedes that not all his owners were prepared to have him ride their horses. Fortunately, Paul Venner was not amongst them.

Weaver rode Mister Baileys in his two racecourse gallops, and they remain vivid memories. "He went to Thirsk first, and it was an OK gallop. But he had so much balance and natural ability. It was so smooth, I'd compare it with riding in a top-of-the-range Bentley or Rolls Royce. He had a fantastic amount of speed and agility."

Weaver adds: "At Ripon, he was absolutely out of this world. I gave him a kick at the two-pole and, I'm thinking to myself: 'Jesus Christ, he's absolutely flying.' He was nothing short of spectacular. It didn't matter what price he was, and where he was trained. After that piece of work, I think everybody thought: 'we're going down to Newmarket with a massive chance.'"

Frankie Dettori had partnered Mister Baileys when the colt won the Royal Lodge and Johnston had initially intended that the pairing should remain intact at Newmarket for the first Classic and Weaver says: "I recall being told 'you're stable jockey, but you can't have him if Dettori is available.'"

Except Dettori wasn't available. The young Italian, who had begun his extraordinary career as apprentice and then stable jockey to Luca Cumani, by then had not only impressed himself on the public's consciousness with his flamboyance and garrulous repartee but also his exceptional riding prowess. He had opted instead to ride the Lord Howard de Walden-owned, William Jarvis-trained, Grand Lodge.

In the spring of 1994, Johnston might have been expected to summon an experienced, ideally Classic-winning, jockey as a substitute, but the trainer had other ideas, and offered the 22-year-old Weaver the chance to ride in his first Classic.

"It was very much a last-minute decision," says Johnston. "But by the time the Guineas arrived, Jason was doing very well for us." The young rider had already partnered 31 winners for Johnston that season. "Also, you mustn't forget that Frankie was not then the big star that he is now. He was pretty big, but not a champion." That said, the Italian would, though, proceed to claim his first title that season, with 233 winners.

The young replacement for Dettori was not a last resort, says Johnston. "But after two or three riders turned down the ride, Paul Venner said: 'Let's have Jason.'"

It must be stressed that when Johnston had arrived at Newmarket on 2,000 Guineas day, 30 April 1994, it had been only seven years on from him training a few horses on a Lincolnshire beach; his charge had not benefited from a preparatory race – a definite omission according to traditional thinking – and the ride had been rejected by Frankie Dettori, who had been replaced by a jockey not that long out of his apprenticeship.

The cumulative effect was that Mister Baileys started the first colts' Classic at relatively long odds. It was absurd in hindsight, but back then? "I believe the important thing in looking at the form of a horse at Group level is what it did in its last run, and at what level," opines Johnston. "Look at that 1994 Guineas, and there were only two horses in that race that had won a Group race on their last start."

One was the Henry Cecil-trained, Mick Kinane-partnered King's Theatre, a son of that prolific sire of quality performers Sadler's Wells, who was the 9-2 favourite of the 23 participants. The other was the Johnston-trained, Jason Weaver-ridden Mister Baileys, who started at 16-1.

There could barely have been any greater contrast between the rival trainers. One had been ten times champion trainer (between 1976 and 1992), and was revered within and outside the industry. The other had made substantial strides, was regarded as manifestly blessed with potential, but this was only his seventh year as a licensed trainer.

Johnston adds: "I guarantee that if you had reversed the trainers, you would have reversed the odds. Mister Baileys had all the credentials. He'd won the Royal Lodge on his last start. In hindsight he should have won the Gimcrack. He was the best horse at York." He accepts that punters would have taken account of all the supposed negatives, but then adds, "16-1 was still a bit barmy."

He adds: "We thought we'd win. We certainly weren't going there to run down the field. I was supremely confident about it. The horse was there very much on merit."

There was just one element missing from the Johnstons' preparations. They had arrived at Newmarket unaware of the social etiquette for trainers and owners ahead of such a major racing event. So, rather than mixing with the great and good of the racing fraternity in one of the racecourse's pavilions, they sat and tucked into a Harrods picnic lunch, arranged by Johnston's business partner Brian Palmer, on the gravel of the NTF (National Trainers' Federation) car park. "Trainers were arriving, and looking at us as though we were mad, and thinking who are these upstarts come down from the North?" says a laughing Deirdre.

The Classic proved to be electrifying – though scarcely a backer's benefit, with the favourite soon out of contention. Instead, Weaver, belying his inexperience, produced his mount to forge into a lead three furlongs out on the far side, pursued by Dettori on Grand

Lodge. And it was the two 16-1 shots, both clear of the field, who thrust for the line, seemingly locked together.

Johnston was convinced that his charge *had* prevailed, though it was mighty close – just a short head separated him from Grand Lodge. He had indeed won – in a time of 1:35.08, a record for the 2,000 Guineas.

"Most people's eyes were on King's Theatre, and he was on the stand side. Then, just as they enter the dip, I see that not only is ours in front, but he's opened a gap, and the other jockeys are having to go for their whips.

"From two furlongs out, until they crossed the line, I had no doubt that we were going to win it – although as I was running down the steps to go to the winner's enclosure, I suddenly thought, 'Shit, *have* we won it?'

"Ironically it was William Jarvis, trainer of the runner-up – although I had no idea where his horse had been placed – who was the first to say 'well done'," remembers Johnston. "I just turned to him and said, 'He *did* win it, didn't he?'"

He adds: "It was a very typical Jason Weaver ride. It was something that you'd normally see Jason do in lower-grade fields where he'd coast up front, then kick with quite a way to go and get them all in trouble."

Today Weaver says that he had not planned such tactics. "It was more that he was going that well that I found myself in that position. Richard Quinn was leading [on outsider Star Selection] and he absolutely carted me into the race. It wouldn't matter how fast somebody was going, [with Mister Baileys] you would always feel like you were only in second gear. That's the kind of ability he had. I thought 'I'm getting a lead, we're on the right side of the track [the far side], I'm quite happy.' We passed the bushes, and I thought 'now it's time to push the button.'"

He adds: "I might have been the villain if Dettori had come and got me on Grand Lodge. But typically, in a Johnston-horse fashion, he was challenged really hard, but he would not be denied. As we cross the line, it's all a little bit of a blur, but Dettori slaps me on the back and tells me 'well done.'"

There had been a certain irony in the fact that before the Guineas, Weaver had been invited to Dettori's house – they'd both been Luca Cumani apprentices, were close friends, and still are – and viewed tapes of previous Guineas.

"I'd been riding work in Newmarket and bumped into Frankie. He was going home for a coffee – he had the best espresso coffee machine. We chatted about the race and the shape of the Classic. Even at that stage, he had so much more experience than I did in bigger races."

He adds: "Honestly, that sort of thing so early in your career, trying to understand the enormity of it all is pretty tough. You can't take it in mentally straight away. You haven't been in that situation before."

The same applied to the trainer.

At Kingsley House, there is a photo of an unusually animated Johnston, fist in the air – the one he was able to use, that is; the other arm was encased in plaster, his wrist having been broken in two places after being kicked by a horse – acclaiming victory.

Yet, in essence, this image encapsulated every emotion that surged through him at that moment: euphoria, relief, vindication. That is why he insists: "For all that Attraction would achieve, and Double Trigger and others did, nothing will ever surpass Mister Baileys' win. We won another later race as well, with Double Blue, but I was almost oblivious to that."

Fortunately, Deirdre hadn't been similarly distracted. "I had to do all the saddling because Mark had a broken wrist," she recalls.

"So, for me, Mister Baileys' victory meant: you saddle it, you win it; Mark and the owner go and collect the prizes. I just had the next one to saddle for the handicap, Double Blue. That was normal for me."

She laughs and adds. "It was the same with our horses at Royal Ascot. But I didn't mind. I liked something to focus on straight afterwards. Sure, I get excited, and still do, but I don't need to be in the limelight. I don't need to be on the podium. I'd much rather be back with the horses. I love that bit. I love thinking I've actually made my contribution."

And, on this occasion, she had played her part in the yard's first Group 1 winner. "It was like we'd really won a big, proper race. We lived on it for weeks afterward – just kept watching the video."

She adds: "Before then, the big races we'd won had been handicaps, and the odd Group race. It was strange how people's attitudes changed. Sir Michael Stoute had never spoken to me before, but I went to Lingfield a few days later, and I remember he said: 'Congratulations on winning the Guineas.' I thought, 'Wow! He didn't even know who I was the week before.' We felt we'd climbed one huge rung up the ladder."

And the belief of her husband – as powerful as Billy Graham's at the lectern, right from those early days – that he could win Classics, had been validated. "I was pleased most for Mark," she says. "When we'd come to Middleham, here was this guy who told everyone he'd train Classic winners, and everyone laughed. Not anymore. Now it was, 'Oh, gosh. He's actually done it.'"

It was a pivotal moment. Thereafter, Johnston became regarded as an authentic threat to the training hierarchy; moreover, here was a man prepared to ignore conventional thinking in his search for major prizes. "It really did change people's attitudes," Deirdre continues. "But there were several things that made us a bit different

– not just because it was a smallish trainer doing it, but that we'd done it with a cheap horse. We'd also done it with a first-time-out horse [in a Classic], which was breaking the trend. In those days, most people still gave them a prep run. It made it more of a training performance."

That victory also enhanced the profile, and career prospects, of Weaver, who would proceed to ride over 200 winners that season. He reflects: "Thousands and thousands of jockeys, and probably many of them better than me, never get to win a Classic. So, from a selfish point of view it was absolutely tremendous. But for the Johnston point of view, the wheels had really started to turn. Everything had started to roll along."

As for Paul Venner, it was appropriate reward for the sustained faith of the stable's first owner who had supported Johnston all those years, ostensibly with a principal view to gaining publicity for his company, Baileys Horse Feeds. He would not have dared to imagine this day. Yet here he was, owner of a 2,000 Guineas winner.

He had first encountered Johnston when the Scot, then a vet in Braintree, had been called out to look at a broken-down racehorse in a paddock. Venner has recalled Johnston telling him that he was determined to train thoroughbreds. "I told him, 'for God's sake, don't be so bloody stupid...'"

It would be fair to say that, not for the first time in his life, Johnston did not heed such advice. "Paul will always be one of the most important owners we've ever had, or ever will have," insists Johnston. "He was the only one who backed us from the start, from day one." He adds, not entirely flippantly, "In fact, when we first started, I think he was the only one paying us any money!"

* * *

But what next for Mister Baileys? It has long been a conundrum for any 2,000 Guineas-winning trainer: do they head for Epsom, or maybe The Curragh, to contest the 12 furlongs of the Derby or its Irish equivalent, or because of doubts regarding the horse's stamina, do they restrict it to one mile or maybe 10 furlongs?

The ensuing developments in the career of Mister Baileys, in which it was decided to adopt the Dante Stakes-Derby route, will always prompt his trainer towards a degree of self-admonishment. "Originally, we thought he was a mile-and-a-half horse, though the fact that he was by Robellino out of an unraced Sharpen Up mare called Thimblerigger should, maybe in hindsight, have told us that he wasn't," Johnston reflects.

Johnston admits that, if he could book a ticket for H.G. Wells' time machine and return to 1994, Mister Baileys' programme would have been different. "I'm sure now that he wouldn't have gone for the Derby. He probably wouldn't have run in the Dante [over 1m 2f, and a major trial for the Derby, run at York] either."

In the Dante, Mister Baileys started favourite, but finished third of nine behind the John Dunlop-trained Erhaab. Apparently cruising three furlongs out, the fuel tank warning was flashing red by the final furlong.

In the 1994 Epsom showpiece event itself, in front of 103,406 racegoers, Weaver opted for an audacious strategy, bursting clear four furlongs out in a catch-me-if-you-can tactic designed to outmanoeuvre the opposition.

Willie Carson, then 51 and participating in his 26th Derby, on the favourite Erhaab, was wise to the move and, under his urgings, the John Dunlop-trained colt came with a sustained run. It prevailed by a length and a quarter from King's Theatre, followed home by Colonel Collins – that pair had finished respectively 13th and third in the 2,000 Guineas. Finishing a highly respectable fourth was Mister Baileys, who had faded in the final furlong.

Johnston admits: "Paul [Venner] probably enjoyed the race more than I did. He thought for a long way that we were going to win. But he had no regrets. He's very good at making the most of things, and Mister Baileys certainly did him no harm from a business point of view. It was great publicity for his company."

Venner certainly concurs. "He did everything for the business," he would tell the *Racing Post* in 2019, though he revealed that he and partner George Knowles "owed a small fortune" in acquiring it, and when Mister Baileys came along he saw him "as an opportunity to get rid of some of the debt." He said: "After his two-year-old career we were offered money [reportedly offers of £250,000 and £400,000], I turned that down, I thought we may as well ride him the whole way."

The Derby proved to be virtually the end of Mister Baileys' spectacular but all-too-brief racing career. "After that, he got a tendon injury," Johnston explains. "We patched him up and ran him in the [one mile] Sussex Stakes [at Goodwood], where he finished fifth." The colt was then retired to stud, with the honour of being Middleham's first Classic winner since 1945.

He stood for several seasons in Kentucky, before returning to England in 2000. He died in 2009, at the age of 18, having sired the winners of more than 100 races.

Returning to 1994, could it be argued that the same radical thinking that had brought Mister Baileys home first in the 2,000 Guineas without a preparatory run, just a racecourse gallop, was also justifiably applied to the conclusion that he could stay the Derby distance? "No," Johnston states firmly. "It was an error. It was my inexperience."

He adds: "You know, I wrote a long letter to Paul Venner, stating all the reasons why the horse *should* run in the Derby. He didn't want him to run."

Maybe the trainer had been influenced, albeit unconsciously, you contend, by those photographs of equine legends he'd had pinned to his bedroom wall in his youth. Johnston doesn't demur. "I suppose I was dreaming of Nijinsky and Triple Crowns, and the Derby being the most important thing in the world. It wasn't. Maybe going to the Dante as a Derby trial *was* a sensible move, but I should have seen the writing on the wall at York. I really should have learned from that."

Johnston also has his doubts about whether it did Mister Baileys any favours being asked to go for home so early, and even Weaver admits ruefully: "To this day, every time the Derby comes around, I get Matt Chapman, or one of those [racing presenters] saying: 'So, Jason, when did you think the Derby was a mile?!' I get constant ribbing about it."

He adds: "He ran so hard that day, he'd gone clear around Tattenham Corner, which is an awfully long way from home. Looking back, was it the right thing? Of course, it wasn't the right thing, but he was in my hands, galloping, there was a tunnel of noise and colour, and people screaming. I thought 'away you go' and, sure enough, away he went. But the problem was he came up for air with two furlongs to run."

That all said, first in the Guineas, fourth in the Derby could scarcely be regarded as failure. "He ran a brilliant race," says Weaver, before adding: "Was it the greatest ride in the world? Probably not. But what I will say is that he ran so hard that day, I don't think he was ever the same."

Returning to the drama of Mister Baileys' Guineas triumph, some observers couldn't find it in their hearts to bestow any plaudits, despite Johnston's charge establishing a new track record. Could his trainer give a damn? He certainly could.

Reflecting back in a *Racing Post* column, dated 5 May 2001, Johnston opined:

"That Guineas was rated by most 'experts' as the worst of the decade, but I have always felt that that was a very unfair assessment. It could not have been rated as poor on the basis of the time as Mister Baileys set, and still holds, the record for the 2,000 Guineas, and it could not, surely, be rated as poor based on the quality of the field: Mister Baileys beat the likes of Grand Lodge and Distant View. No, it was rated as poor for one reason and one reason only: because 16-1 shot Mister Baileys won it."

Johnston has long regarded comparing generations of racehorses as: "Nostalgic rubbish." He adds: "Sure, when I was young, I was talking about horses as being horses of the decade or century, whatever. But not now. It's nonsense. You cannot really have a bad year. It can't be the case that three-year-olds of one year are better than the next. You can argue, a bit, that the best ones don't compare. But not a whole year. Only if, at the end of the year, the Guineas winner is rated tenth can you say it was a bad Guineas."

Racing at its best is not about the Form Book and time. It is about theatre, about a twisting plot, about unpredictability, about characters and, in 1994, the Mister Baileys story was about the convergence of three men – Johnston, Venner and Weaver – whose lives would all be enhanced by their association with one horse.

Johnston recently rifled through his desk drawers, and discovered this, penned by his proud sister Lyn, the poet of the family, just after Mister Baileys' Guineas triumph. The final line encapsulates what it meant to her brother.

She wrote:

Mister Baileys! He did it! Isn't he grand?
Truly, he's one of the best in the land
Mark was delirious, quite 'over the moon'
Now we prepare for the big race in June
Bet you all wish you'd seen him that night
They danced on the floors, they danced on the tables
They danced with Gretas, with Anns, and with Mabels!
They laughed and they drank and they talked till quite late
And all, they agreed, said the horse he was great
But things settle down and it's back to the grind
There are races to win and entries to find
So it's up at first dawn and on with the fray
Of mucking out horses and carting the hay
So it's back to the yard and things carry on
But none of the glory will ever be gone.

MISTER BAILEYS TURBO-BOOSTS THE JOHNSTON PROJECT

If reservations were expressed in some quarters about the standing of Mister Baileys' 2,000 Guineas performance, in comparison with others that decade, there could be no questioning the talents of his jockey. That season, as his partnership with Johnston flourished, Jason Weaver became one of only seven jockeys in British racing history to ride a double century of winners, and finished runner-up to Frankie Dettori in the jockeys' championship.

Weaver would be at the zenith of his powers when partnering Johnston's much-loved Double Trigger to a famous triumph in the 1995 Ascot Gold Cup, and when claiming another Group 1 at Royal Ascot the following year, galvanising the stable's Bijou D'Inde to victory in the St James's Palace Stakes.

In the spring of that year, Bijou D'Inde had gone straight to the 2,000 Guineas, without a preparatory run, just as Mister Baileys had, two years earlier.

Again, the Johnston horse was relatively friendless in the betting market, starting at 14-1. Coincidentally, Weaver recalls once more bumping into his friend Frankie Dettori before the race: "I said 'Hey, I'll come round to yours for a coffee this morning'. He said 'No, you f******' won't.' I said: 'Why's that?' He said: 'you beat me a short head when you did that last time. You're not coming round!'"

Just jockeys' banter, but the rebuff clearly had its effect. This time, the Italian prevailed on Mark Of Esteem in a thrilling climax to the colts' Classic, with Weaver's Bijou D'Inde a neck behind in third.

But to return to his early months at Middleham, Weaver had discovered a very different environment to that he'd experienced in his years with Luca Cumani in Newmarket. "Mark's views were completely different from Luca's and what I had grown up with," he says. "At Middleham, I'm learning again from a different trainer. But I found working with him and Deirdre very easy. My biggest problem was trying to beat the scales." Weaver would eventually retire, aged only 30, in 2002 after a constant battle with the scales.

Weaver adds: "Luca was very old school. With him, you'd go first time out on a horse, and if they could win, maybe you could give him or her one back-hander. At Middleham, I'd come back in the morning after, and Mark would say: 'maybe you could have given him or her a bit more of an education, or a stronger ride when you're out there.' And I'd say, 'Luca would tell me not to hit them first time.' And Mark would say, 'maybe so, if you're beaten miles, but if you've half a chance, I don't mind them having one either side, just to let them know what it's about.'

"But it was also about backing horses up quickly. Mark's horses could win on a Monday, and I might think to myself, 'she's had a hard race there'. Of course, I'm not doing the entries, so I don't know, and then I look, and find I'm down to ride the same horse on the Thursday. Of course, you go out there confident you're going to win, though my initial thought is: 'She had a really tough time on that tough course at Pontefract on Monday and the ground is bad at Hamilton...', but it would go out and it would win. It would be as fresh as paint."

He adds: "Of course, he's driven, and he's opinionated, but for good reason. He didn't just fall in line with everything that should happen, or has happened before; how the horses should be trained or campaigned. All of that, for him, must have been a huge process as well. As you go up the grades and get better horses, you have to change as well."

Although Weaver feels blessed by his association with Double Trigger – "an absolute superstar, what a wonderful horse he was" – with Double Quick, an excellent sprinter who nearly broke the world record over the minimum at Epsom in a Listed event in 1995, and horses like Bijou D'Inde in the St James's Palace – "a wonderful horse" – he recalls how supposed lesser lights, transferred from other stables, could also flourish at Middleham.

Weaver particularly remembers riding work on two four-year-olds that had arrived in the yard from other stables. One was Star Rage, formerly with Mick Easterby. He had failed to win on the Flat or over hurdles; the other was Argyle Cavalier who, intriguingly, had been with the former Manchester City and England footballer and later trainer, Franny Lee, winning twice.

Weaver says: "At the time, the Low Moor was a very tricky, tough gallop to work anything on, let alone two big gangly horses. We worked them, myself and Bobby Elliott. I said to Bobby: 'What did you think of yours?' He said: 'Rubbish.' I said: 'Yeah – this as well.' Sure enough, Star Rage went and won nine that year, 1994 [running in no fewer than 29 races]. The other one won four. The Johnston method was proved correct again."

He adds: "Horses like Star Rage, a multiple handicap winner, a superstar, just kept on winning. Mark had horses like that who were just incredibly tough. They were so fun to ride, from a jockey's point of view."

Weaver believes his old guv'nor has thrived because he's watched and listened; he's questioned, and rejected some traditional thinking, but assimilated the best. "That's why the machine would get so much bigger, quicker, stronger in a short space of time. And he demands that everybody is focused – on going forward and getting better. It was like that for me as jockey, I had a pair of blinkers on. The outside world didn't matter; it was the yard, the horses and winning. That was it. That was Mark's attitude as well. I have a massive amount of respect for him."

That knock on the door of Kingsley House by Weaver in 1993 could not have come at a more apposite moment for both these upwardly-mobile characters. "He was a fantastic rider," says Johnston. "He wasn't around long enough to become recognised as one of the true greats. If he'd stayed around, I'd say he would probably – probably – have been champion several times."

Yet, for all they may be perceived as members of a mutual admiration society, it didn't stop the pair separating twice. Breaking up may be hard for lovers, but for jockeys and trainers it is an occupational hazard. "Of course, there were huge frustrations at times, but then you get that with all jockeys. In fact, you get it in every walk of life," says Johnston. "When you get a successful jockey–trainer partnership – and we'd had around 70 winners together that first season – you want it to continue. But he decided to go his own way, and I don't blame him for that."

He adds: "People have to think for themselves and make those decisions. But the second time, did he jump or was he pushed? I don't know. Probably there was something wrong on both sides."

It was September 1997, and Johnston planned to run the stable's high-class miler Fly To The Stars, in a Group 2 race in Turkey (the Topkapi Trophy at Veliefendi). That event coincided with Land Of Dreams running in the Flying Childers (a Group 2 two-year-old test at Doncaster) on the same day.

"I wanted Jason to go to Turkey, basically because there would be no problem getting another jockey for Doncaster, but we couldn't easily get one for Turkey. At least that was my official reason. It's always been my view that you pay a retainer so that the jockey is available to go where you want him to go. The jockeys, however, tend to see it differently. They see it as giving them the right to the best rides. Jason insisted he wanted to go to Doncaster. I told him: 'We pay a retainer so that you're available to go where we want to send you. You either go to Turkey or the deal's off.'"

Weaver balked at that request, and the deal was indeed off. In the event, the Peter Savill-owned Fly To The Stars finished third in Turkey, under the Irish-based rider Warren O'Connor, before the talented colt moved on to Godolphin, for whom his victories included the Group 1 Lockinge Stakes at Newbury.

Land Of Dreams captured the Flying Childers impressively, having been held up off the pace for a late run by Darryll Holland. "I think I was fully entitled to do what I did," says Johnston. "Having said that, I did have some underlying sympathy for Jason, but the truth was that I particularly wanted Darryll Holland to ride Land Of Dreams. She was a sprinter, but a hold-up horse, to an extent, and I believed that Darryll was a lot better at executing that. Rightly or wrongly, I always thought Jason was a better front-running jockey than coming from behind. Maybe that's unfair. But in principle I thought 'I pay the retainer – I'll decide where you go.' He didn't agree with that."

Johnston adds: "It was a shame, though I suppose his career was limited after that through weight, anyway. Maybe if it hadn't been, he'd have come back again.

"When we went to Royal Ascot with Bijou D'Inde or Double Trigger, we weren't thinking: 'We wish we had Frankie Dettori,' we thought we had as good a jockey as anyone. At the time he was riding for us, I had more confidence in him then than I'd ever had in a jockey."

When Weaver surrendered to the inevitable and quit the saddle after a 14-year career, he had partnered five of Johnston's then six Group 1 winners. Weight was always liable to be his greatest adversary. The ex-jockey, who rode at 8st 9lbs in his later riding years, recalls: "To get into racing school when you were 16, you had to be a certain weight, so my mother put me on boiled rice and apples for six weeks so that I could make it. And that was before I'd even ridden a horse." It would lead to a daily regime of sweating and saunas. "It was a long time to be putting your body under that kind of pressure," he says.

When Jim Ramsey, a producer from what was then the Racing Channel, asked him to come for a trial, he had no hesitation. Weaver has since established himself as an engaging and professional pundit for Sky and ITV.

"There's no end of them, ex-jockeys on TV, and most of them aren't very good. But Jason's fantastic, one of the best," says Johnston. "Very knowledgeable and he's funny. He makes it light and entertaining, without being stupid, like some."

Weaver had been a crucial cog in the construction of the winning machine, or as he invariably describes it "the juggernaut from the north". As he says: "This was when people really started to sit up and take notice, and think 'this really is a bit of a game-changer we've got going on at the moment.'"

It was an accurate assessment. That year 1994 was, by every

judgement, a pivotal one for the stable. Apart from Mister Baileys' Guineas triumph, it was a season in which the yard amassed more than £1 million in prize money and the campaign also saw Johnston celebrate a century of domestic Flat victories for the first time, finishing with a tally of 117.

Johnston reflects: "It's incredible how fast the progression was. One winner in 1987, five in 1988, then 15, 28, 31, 53, 77, then 117...so clearly, we were getting there fast. But that one win [the 2,000 Guineas] enabled us to make another huge jump. We bought another yard on the back of that. There's been a lot of milestones along the way, but that was the most important."

Initially, Johnston had rented another 20 boxes from trainer Chris Thornton at Spigot Lodge in Wensley, some five miles from Kingsley House. "But by the end of 1994 we were in such demand that if we didn't get another site we were out of Middleham [and looking to relocate]." So, that year, Johnston bought Warwick House, the yard across the road from Kingsley House, from Patrick Haslam.

"We paid £240,000, I think. We were getting into further debt, but now it was not a problem. The situation had changed significantly in the two years which followed those financial problems, and we continued that expansion," he says.

It meant that, since arriving at Middleham, Johnston had spent more than £1.5 million on creating one of the most up-to-date yards in the country. It would be far from the extent of his empire-building.

For some, complacency could have set in, like dry rot, once a century of winners began to become an annual occurrence. Once distinguished houses of excellence have been known to decay and decline. But by 1999, just 11 years after moving to Kingsley House, Johnston had 147 horses under his care; sufficient to compete with the major players. And Middleham had once again become a significant contour on the equine landscape.

Never, after 1994, would the stable's annual score of winners worldwide be less than 100, with double that number becoming a regular feature after 2009. Johnston was training winners, but importantly he was he was becoming associated with star names, true characters with whom the public, and potential new owners, could identify.

DOUBLE TRIGGER: THE 'CLOWN' WHO BECAME A CUP KING

"There are two distinct branches of Clan Johnston, those from Caskieben in Aberdeenshire and those from the border reivers of Annandale in Dumfries and Galloway. I, personally, have not traced my ancestry beyond early twentieth century Glasgow, but I must assume that I am descended from the latter group: the desire to raid and plunder in England has never left me," Mark Johnston declared in 2000, in a regular column he then wrote in *The Times*.

And, it could be added, it is certainly the case when the incursion takes place at Royal Ascot.

Only the Druids, gathering at Stonehenge for the summer solstice, await June with more joyful expectation than the horseracing world. The Derby meeting at Epsom and especially the five days of Royal Ascot are what stimulate Johnston: they are what have him planning his regime weeks, months and even a year ahead.

There is no occasion when the Johnston tartan is more proudly donned than at Royal Ascot. A sartorial flying of the Saltire by this proud Scot, confronted by the Old Enemy? He relishes the week of competition. You suspect that every victory is another thrust from the loyalist's blade.

"By far the greatest race meeting in the world," was his description after the 1997 Royal Ascot meeting, as reported in the *Sporting Life*. "I love it. I can't stand the pressure in the preceding days, but once we are up and running, I love it."

For most of us, the Royal meeting represents a delicious combination of cultures which co-exist admirably: those who perceive themselves as connoisseurs of the equine elite, and those who arrive to make a fashion statement, more intent on promenading in chic and outlandish fashion on the turf catwalk.

Traditionally, Royal Ascot witnesses an all-out assault by Johnston. All troops are placed on alert, prepared for action. Anything with any chance of being involved is pencilled in. As he says, "That's what's different about this meeting. At any other, there's no way I'd declare so many of my horses to run against each other. We throw everything at this meeting."

It brings to mind a fairground coconut shy. Roll up, roll up! The more balls you hurl, the more chance you have of dislodging that hairy oval.

"It must make sense," Johnston declares. "You're giving yourself a far greater chance." He has been known to declare as many as five in some handicaps. The policy is easily justified. "It's huge prize money and every owner wants to win it."

Marina Park was Johnston's first Ascot victor, back in July 1992. But it would not be until 1995 that he would effect a breakthrough and claim that special badge of honour, a *Royal* Ascot winner.

"In between, I made many attempts at breaking my Royal duck, and I had Deirdre convinced that it was some crazy obsession which led me to take our best horses to the same meeting every year to get beaten," Johnston once said.

"It has been well reported that by Wednesday of the 1995 meeting we were close to requiring some marriage guidance after Gothenberg, Argyle Cavalier, Star Rage, Unconditional Love and Sweet Robin had been beaten.

"Double Eclipse's second in the Queen's Vase was the only ray of hope and I was losing our long-standing argument by five goals to one, and that was only by virtue of a place. The next day, however, I made a miraculous recovery and settled the score once and for all – now we were both hooked."

What a day that was. What a horse. What memories for both the Johnstons and owner Ron Huggins.

* * *

Ron Huggins' weekends had always been dominated by rugby and sailing. He was a fly-half and had played at Loughborough University and at county level, and later founded a small rugby club in Kent, called Linton.

When he turned 40, Huggins, who worked for Kimberly-Clark, the 'tissues-to-nappies' worldwide brand, gave up both rugby and sailing, and devoted his energies to a sport that was far more liable to bring despair than euphoria.

His interest in horses up to that point had been limited. He had ridden a little as a child and had followed eventing – his sister and her husband had event horses – but he had only been to the racetrack as an occasional racegoer.

That was until one Christmas when he'd watched a film about Desert Orchid, and how he was bred. "I said to my wife, 'I'd be interested in trying to breed a Desert Orchid.'" Huggins recalls. "So, I went off and bought a broodmare. Then I realised it was going to be quite a long process, getting her progeny to the track. So, I thought I'd better get something to run in the meantime."

He sought out a trainer. "I looked at both experienced ones and up-and-coming ones who had a good ratio of wins to horses. When I drove into the yard at Middleham we just got on very well. I just thought that this was the place to be. That was 1991. I was one of Mark's early owners. At the time he had 31 horses. I bought a horse out of a field, which was Better Be Bold, and split it between four of us. She ran a few times, and was absolutely useless." Not the most auspicious start, perhaps, but the new owner was unperturbed.

"Our second horse was Double Blue, and he won his first four races in 23 days." That was in April 1992. The sprinter would proceed to win 12 of his 68 races. One, incidentally, had been the handicap on the same card as Mister Baileys' 2,000 Guineas victory. "That's what got it going for us, and what got the 'Double' thing going as well."

Huggins and his fellow owners decided to invest some of the winnings. "I went to Goffs in Ireland with Mark. I earmarked Ela-Mana-Mou as a top-class stallion, even though he was unfashionable and his progeny were going a lot cheaper. But they were something I could afford. The horse that we would come to name Double Trigger was the one I really liked. Mark bid, and we got him for IR7,200gns. Incredible really."

The impression that he had purchased a talented bargain swiftly changed when the chestnut with film-star looks – a broad white blaze, four white socks and flaxen mane – went into training at Middleham. "I owned half, and two friends, Dick Moules and Julian Clopet, owned 25 per cent each," Huggins continues. "We all went up to see Trigger on the gallops, not long before his first race was planned. He came plodding up like an old jumper. I can still hear him today: p-dum, p-dum, p-dum. Not galloping at all, just cantering, really. After the gallop, Mark asked Bobby Elliott [then chief work-rider] what he thought. He said, 'He'd make a good circus horse.'

"We adjourned to the pub in Middleham, the Black Swan, to decide what we should do. There were options. Should we have him gelded? Should we send him eventing? Should we sell him without racing him? Should we run him? After we'd had a couple of pints, we said, 'Oh, let's run him.'"

It was an epoch-making decision, for the owners and for Johnston, who later would admit, "I think Ron was a bit annoyed with my attitude; that I had just written him off and kept saying, 'Oh, he shows nothing.'"

However, the trainer decided to leave the horse as an entire. "People do say some need gelding because of their behaviour as two-year-olds, but I like to run them first," he says. "It's amazing how a race can change their attitude."

That said, the trainer couldn't quite believe how badly the horse performed at home. "He spent more time on two legs than four," Johnston recalls. "He was just full of himself, always clowning around. In all the time we had him, he never did a good gallop."

He attributes much of that reluctance to perform at home as pure laziness. "Yet he was actually capable of doing a phenomenal amount of work. You could give him a five-furlong canter on the Low Moor, a seven-furlong canter on the High Moor, then turn him around and do a mile-and-a-half canter, and he'd still be bucking and kicking all the way home. He had incredible stamina." And he was certainly a character. "He wasn't the easiest horse in the world," adds Johnston. He could take a chunk out of you at times."

The date 25 September 1993, began as one of enormous expectation for the yard, though that had nothing to do with

Double Trigger, who had been despatched to Redcar for his debut in a nine-furlong event.

The explanation for this sense of anticipation was that Mister Baileys was entered for the Group 2 Royal Lodge Stakes that day at Ascot, while Branston Abby, Quick Ransom and Marina Park were the other runners at the Berkshire track. "We went off to Ascot; Trigger went off to Redcar, with Jason Weaver," recalls Johnston. "At the time, Jason got the odd ride, including this horse that day. As I recall, Ron didn't want to go to Redcar that day. He was a bit depressed about Double Trigger – that he appeared to be such a disappointment."

Trigger's owner was persuaded to meet up with Johnston at Ascot to watch the stable's runners in the big races and view Trigger's race on the course TV.

Johnston was understandably preoccupied with his Ascot runners. Mister Baileys had just fulfilled his initial promise with victory in the Royal Lodge when Huggins went off to view Double Trigger's debut, for which he was a 14-1 outsider.

"He was actually out the back at the start," Huggins recalls. "About a third of the way into the race, Jason started to ease him forward. Suddenly, he took off. It was the first time he'd ever galloped in his life. He beat the field by ten lengths and broke the track record. Jason had time to ease him down 100 yards from the line, put his stick away and give the horse a big pat, so he hardly knew he'd been in a race and loved every minute of it.

He adds: "I was absolutely amazed. While this was happening, Mark had gone off to have a glass of champagne after Mister Baileys' victory. When he came back to us in the Owners and Trainers Bar about two minutes after Trigger had won, I said, 'You won't believe this, but Trigger's just won by 20 lengths.'"

Johnston *didn't* believe it.

"I came into the bar and Ron Huggins and Richard Huckerby [a colleague of Huggins; he was then marketing director of Kimberly-Clark] were standing there with a bottle of champagne and glasses. They told me he'd won by 20 lengths. At first, I thought they were making a joke of it, with the champagne. I refused to believe it and went out to look for the results, and yes, he had won. He didn't actually win by 20 lengths, he won by ten lengths. But I had absolutely no idea he was a good horse."

Huggins admits he still frequently relives *that* race, a seemingly modest maiden, as much as the Cup triumphs which were to follow. "When your expectations are zero, to win by ten lengths and break the track record is incredible."

The Listed Zetland Stakes at Newmarket – that real stamina examination for two-year-olds, run over ten furlongs – was next, and Trigger seized that prize, too. But before that Huggins and Johnston were back at the sales to purchase, for IR17,500gns, Trigger's full brother, to be named Double Eclipse.

They could not have foreseen that, two years later, racegoers would experience the ultimate in equine sibling rivalry as the pair slugged it out to the line in the 1995 Goodwood Cup. Trigger would prevail by a neck, but there was no family honour lost by the kid brother. "I took huge pride in Trigger," says Johnston. "It was fantastic to have a horse that will go down in history. The fact that we had his brother as well made it all the more pleasurable. The 1995 race was one of the most thrilling I have ever been involved in."

In the space of five years, before he was retired to stud in 1998, Trigger won seven Cup races, and the devotion of the racing public. Those flying sprinters, milers and middle-distance horses have their disciples, but for many there is no finer spectacle than a scrap between the doughty warriors of the staying game.

Trigger's complete record of achievement was: 29 starts, resulting in 14 victories, two seconds and one third, with total earnings of £559,102. In his *annus mirabilis* of 1995, his haul included the Ascot Gold Cup, Goodwood Cup and Doncaster Cup. At the Yorkshire course, where he secured three Cups in his career, his memory is cherished. There is a bronze statue of him near the entrance and the Double Trigger Bar. The rail operator GNER also named an engine after him.

Maybe in Double Trigger, Mark Johnston sees something of himself; like him, the horse refused to be vanquished if he found himself on the wrong end of an argument – as Trigger so thrillingly did in 1998 after looking beaten in his third Goodwood Cup victory, which was his penultimate race.

His trainer is a fierce protector of Trigger's reputation, as he is with all his best horses. Certainly, the chestnut's defences were exposed on occasions, but when Johnston is asked to assess where Trigger stands on the pantheon of staying greats, he will say: "I never, ever allow anyone to belittle anything that Double Trigger did." And certainly not when he reflects on his feats of 1995.

Johnston adds: "In that year he won five races, all over two miles and above: the Sagaro, Henry II Stakes, Ascot Gold Cup, Goodwood Cup, Doncaster Cup. He was also fourth in the Group 1 Prix du Cadran [at Longchamp], when boxed in. Then he went to the Melbourne Cup, where he was beaten, as he had been in the Yorkshire Cup earlier in the season. He won five out of seven starts that year. It got to the stage where he was expected to do it. Frankly, in 1995 he was in a league of his own.

"We thought that Mister Baileys had been under-estimated after the Guineas. But I will never forgive them for Double Trigger not being champion stayer in 1995. There was not a horse even close to him. Yet Strategic Choice [trained by Paul Cole] was champion stayer, based on winning the Irish Leger and finishing third in the King George [and Queen Elizabeth Diamond Stakes at Ascot]. Nonsensical."

Yet, for all the exhilaration of that year, Johnston regards Trigger's penultimate race in the 1998 Goodwood Cup and valedictory performance in the Doncaster Cup as his most treasured moments. "The days of Trigger being favourite and there being huge pressure were probably gone by then," he explains. "It was probably one of the reasons why those wins were all the more pleasurable, because he was probably past his best. To do that was fantastic really. You couldn't have planned it better."

In five years, there were more gradients of emotion with this horse than the downlands of Goodwood, where Trigger won three Cups and was undefeated. Some would reflect that he wasn't always putting in 100 per cent. There have been comments over the years referring to Trigger's "quirks" and being "invariably very much in control of his own destiny". When we have discussed this suggested flaw over the years, Johnston has always contested the point. "Most days he did put everything in," he insists.

"The owners and the public have to accept that these horses that have long careers can't be expected to win every time. Trigger was a great, great horse. Of course, he had his defeats, but then we kept him going for so many years."

During that time Trigger was partnered by five different jockeys. Jason Weaver rode him 19 times, Michael Roberts four, Darryll Holland three, Frankie Dettori twice and Thierry Jarnet once. "The strange thing about Trigger was that though he had this front-running style, each jockey would give him a new lease of life," says Johnston. "He'd get in a rut, and maybe the jockey would lose confidence in him, and you'd change the jockey, and away you'd go again. They were so different in the way that they rode him."

So, what does that tell you about Trigger's character? Johnston is always extremely wary of anthropomorphism – endowing animals with human qualities and flaws. "People try to build characteristics into horses far too much," he says. "We're all guilty, though hopefully me less than most." Which is why he tends to refrain from employing terms like 'courageous' when describing a horse.

"Trigger's last Goodwood Cup was probably the most spectacular, when he led, fell away into midfield, met the rising ground, then came back again. If you analyse it, you'd probably actually find that the leaders slowed down, and he stayed on again," says Johnston, who insists that his words are not meant to diminish Trigger's prowess in any way.

However, he adds: "People talk about fighting spirit, and character, and fighting back against another horse, when the reality, sadly, is that the other horse is probably simply slowing down. It's not fighting spirit, it's just stamina."

Expanding that theory, he adds: "I believe there are leaders and followers. Horses learn how to win, and how to lose. If you put them all out in a field and let them run around, some are faster, some are braver, some are bullies. Generally, those tough leaders are going to lead the pack and push the others around. But it's not just a matter of being the strongest horse. Because they're flight animals, speed counts for a lot. They've got all those natural instincts, but life is not a race for them. Having said that, if you put two horses side by side on the gallops, they'll go faster than on their own. They will race with each other, and you can teach them to win. Similarly, I believe that if you deliberately get them beat, you'll teach them to lose. They become followers not leaders."

It had immediately become evident during that first race at Redcar that Trigger was in the latter group. The initial prognosis of Trigger as more of a Big Top performer, one who would provide laughs more than thrills, made the reality even more pleasurable for his owner.

"The Gold Cup was incredibly special, as were all the Goodwood Cups, and particularly the one against Double Eclipse," Huggins says. "It was amazing how the crowd really took to him. His third Goodwood Cup victory was an incredibly emotional experience. Even some of the journalists were in tears."

When Trigger bowed out in 1998 with a plethora of plaudits, the *Racing Post's* Alastair Down, one of the country's more perceptive and original observers, opined: "Dry old statisticians with minds like adding machines and hearts of granite will tell you that Double Trigger wasn't anything special. With meticulously prepared arguments, rooted in fact and figure, taking into consideration weight, age, going, the exchange rate with the dollar, the direction in which the grass was cut and the price of crude on the Rotterdam spot market, they will gently let you down with the fact that Trigger was not among the all-time great stayers; that while he was admirable he was not exceptional. They are right of course, but not as right as they are wrong. The point is that you cannot reduce a horse like Double Trigger to mere numbers – ratings are not the only means by which greatness is measured.

"There was a wonderful sense of his sheer bloody-mindedness. Sure, there were times when he wasn't having a going day, but that merely added to the allure because it made him fallible, just like the rest of us. But on those wind-behind, God-is-in-his-heaven afternoons when Trigger was in full cry, he could play a tune on the disparate souls who make up a race crowd like few other horses in recent years."

The curious element, of course, was that Trigger, who in a career which took him to Italy, France, Australia and Hong Kong as well as England's most prestigious racecourses, would overshadow the stable's Royal Rebel.

That gelding, sired by Robellino, as Mister Baileys had been, was owned by then British Horseracing Board[8] chairman Peter Savill. He not only lifted the Ascot Gold Cup in successive years, but was also involved in two heart-pounding finishes when overcoming David Elsworth's hugely popular Persian Punch by a head in 2001 and Dermot Weld's Vinnie Roe by a neck in 2002.

Royal Rebel won seven of 39 races overall, and Savill admitted after that second Gold Cup: "I was not at all optimistic. He has a good day about one day in seven."

But the Royal meeting seemed to induce the best from him. "He has the heart of a lion," said his exhausted jockey Johnny Murtagh, after his mount had appeared beaten, but rallied to get up in the last hundred yards. "He's possibly run the best race of his life," added Johnston.

Royal Rebel had also been triumphant in the Goodwood Cup in 2000, and was, according to his trainer, "the great unsung hero." Johnston adds: "People talk about the best stayers and they don't mention Royal Rebel. I was probably as guilty as anybody, because when he won his first Gold Cup all people wanted to talk about was comparisons with Double Trigger, and I said he didn't compare. But that wasn't fair. He won two Gold Cups. He was a really great horse."

Yet, with Trigger, it is evident that when Huggins came along it was a case of right owner at the right time for Johnston; just as Paul Venner had been with Mister Baileys. They were, as it is said, a great fit.

He recognised, right back in 1991, that here was a man with the drive to fulfil his own aspirations. "Absolutely", Huggins declared. "He was always amazingly ambitious, and very open about it. He was quite determined to get the top owners in the country into the yard. He's always reaching for the stars. And, as I say, if you do that, you won't come up with a handful of dirt."

Trigger was sent to stud at East Burrow Farm near Crediton, Devon, and died in 2020, an elderly gentleman in equine terms. When Johnston wrote in the *Kingsley Klarion*: "There was nothing tragic about Double Trigger's death," he was not being callous. As the trainer continued: "He was 29 years old and he died suddenly and without suffering. It was an opportunity for us all to be reminded of his wonderful racing career and the long, healthy and productive life he had afterwards at stud: the life that we dream of for every colt we bring into training."

He added: "He was a truly remarkable horse that gave me, Deirdre, and his owners more wonderful memories than we could get from a host of other top-class horses. From the day at Goffs sales when Ron Huggins came to me and said: 'I've seen a horse. I'm going to buy him and call him Trigger', to the day when he bowed out at Doncaster with his groom, Geordie Charlton – who never normally went racing with Trigger because he wasn't big enough or strong enough to handle the boisterous big horse – in floods of tears, Trigger gave us a roller-coaster ride."

CHAPTER 17

JOHNSTON GLOBETROTTERS RETURN WITH RICHES

By the mid-nineties, with a burgeoning reputation to sustain him, Mark Johnston's outlay at the yearling sales was on the increase, though he had still not breached the £50,000 mark.

However, in 1996, he was prepared to outlay the most he'd ever spent at the sales when he successfully bid IR75,000 for a horse that caught his eye at Goffs sales in Ireland. He was like a teenage boy besotted by the stunning girl across the dance floor.

It should be emphasised that though he admired its looks, its pedigree was paramount. "Pedigree is always the priority," he says. "If I haven't picked a horse on pedigree, I won't look at it. If you go and buy horses cheaply on how they look, you'll buy an awful lot of slow horses."

He adds: "If someone asks me to look at a horse because they think it looks beautiful, I look at the pedigree and say to them, 'you're wasting your time and mine.' If it hasn't made the list on pedigree, we're not going to buy it, at any price. Saying that, even when they've made the list, once we've looked at them, we might scroll them out."

Buying bloodstock had come naturally to him since he had witnessed his father's attempts when he was a teenager. "I'd always been into it, and at first I probably had my father's ideas about pedigrees, but I just thought about them, and realised they were wrong. When I started buying, I was probably doing what he did and was looking at three lines of pedigree. After a few years, I was looking at two. Now I only look at one." His main criteria, in terms of the dam, is that it must have a handicap rating of more than 90 at least, and/or have produced stock rated over 90.

He says: "I love the challenge of finding the value at all levels of the sales and get tremendous satisfaction when competing at the top level with horses bought cheaply for our owners."

Returning to that Goffs sale in 1996, he says: "Up until that point, the most I'd ever paid was £50,000 for Hinari Televideo in 1987, but that had an owner already in place. The most I'd ever paid on spec was £15,000 or £20,000. But I just loved this beautiful horse."

He was a half-brother to Mujadil, who was champion first season sire, and the sire was Hansel, who had won the final two legs of the U.S. Triple Crown races, the Preakness Stakes and the Belmont Stakes, in 1991. "The dam's side was fantastic. It was a Secretariat mare. And the yearling was magnificent-looking as well. I drooled over him, and thought 'I want this horse'.

He adds: "I thought it would make fortunes. What I hadn't realised was that Hansel was considered to be a bit of a flop [as a sire]. Also, I had no idea who I was buying him for, says Johnston. I simply didn't buy horses for 75 grand then on spec. And when he walked into the ring, I thought, 'I can't afford this. I can't buy this.'

"But then I decided to have a go. I'm not sure what was in

my head, but I was so taken by it I would have probably gone to £100,000. It was way, way beyond what I'd ever dreamt of spending on a horse. Anyway, he came into the ring at Goffs. I often stand down in what's called 'the pit', down the side, below the rostrum. A number of my owners would be there, too. I would normally have gone up to £50,000 maximum. Most of the time, my owners around me would know what I was doing, and how much I was prepared to go to. They were all a bit shocked when I kept going.

"Eventually he was knocked down to me. Almost immediately, Mick Doyle tapped me on the shoulder, as I was signing the ticket, and asked, 'Who's that for?' I said, 'I don't know.' He pointed at himself and said, 'Me.'"

Doyle, who owns a multi-million-pound super trawler and is managing director of a fish sales and processing plant based in County Donegal, named the yearling Fruits Of Love. The long-standing owner had fished deep financially and had netted what transpired to be an outstanding specimen.

The colt would proceed to win three Group 2s, the Princess of Wales's Stakes at Newmarket and two Hardwicke Stakes at Royal Ascot and the Dubai Turf Classic at Nad Al Sheba. When Fruits Of Love went off to stud, he'd by then also finished third behind Daylami in the King George and Queen Elizabeth Stakes, and was second in the Grade 1 Canadian International at Woodbine, both in 1999.

However, it was the return home from that Dubai success on 1 April 1999 that resulted in a mobile call to Johnston that no trainer wants to receive. It came from Robynne Watton, his travelling head lass, who in a call from the hard shoulder of the M25, said that Fruits Of Love had been spooked in the horsebox conveying him from Dubai to Middleham and was attempting to climb over the partition in the box.

The emotions of that night remain infused in Johnston's mind. He told me: "I was on the motorway ahead when I was called to be told he had jumped the partition in his stall and had his front legs in the air thrashing around. Now, as a rule, I don't panic when I have a problem with horses. I'm a vet, after all."

He added: "My first thought was 'What drugs do we have in the lorry to sedate the horse?' And I'm also thinking, 'Where is the nearest experienced equine vet who can get there?'"

By sheer good fortune, the fire brigade was able to advise them that the horsebox was only one junction away from the Royal Veterinary College at Potters Bar, just north of London. "Once at the college, a brave vet named Sarah Freeman, assisted by three colleagues, had to risk flying hooves to sit between Fruits Of Love's front legs and put a catheter in his jugular to give him a fluid anaesthetic. Then the fire brigade cut out the interior of the horsebox and winched him out."

He was moved to an operating theatre because there were concerns that the patient might have broken a bone in his pelvis or back, but he was unscathed apart from requiring a few stitches for cuts.

Johnston told the *Racing Post* at the time. "My thought was that there was little chance of him surviving. Even if he did, there were few chances of him having a stud career as the race in Dubai had no Group status. It never entered my head that he would race again. It also occurred to me that he was desperately underinsured."

Remarkably, Fruits Of Love was racing again by the beginning of June. Indeed, by the end of that year he had won the Hardwicke Stakes at Royal Ascot. A year later he repeated the feat. Between those victories he sustained a suspensory ligament injury in the Japan Cup, and again recovered. Johnston reflects: "He lived a charmed life, because he also fractured his pelvis at two."

A pleasing postscript to the whole drama is that Sarah Freeman, who was later made lecturer in equine surgery at the Royal Veterinary College, had her efforts recognised by being named Lanson Lady of the Year for 1999 for her contribution to the racing industry.

Johnston reflects on life with the worldwide adventurer Fruits Of Love, and says: "It's hard to say between him and Lucky Story the best horse I've had that didn't win a Group 1 race. I mean, Lucky Story was the champion three-year-old miler, without winning a Group 1 race. But Fruits Of Love is right up there, and he proved to be a very respectable stallion, too." He died, aged 23, in 2018.

Remarkably, the stablemate that Fruits Of Love defeated in the second of his Hardwicke Stakes triumphs, the enigmatic Yavana's Pace *would* become a Group 1 winner, as a *ten-year-old*.

Early in 1998, Johnston had received a phone call from owner-breeder John Keaney. The Irishman told him he wanted to send two geldings to his yard, both sired by Accordion: a four-year-old and a six-year-old. Accordion was a prolific sire of National Hunt horses. His progeny would include the 2002 Queen Mother Champion Chase victor Flagship Uberalles.

The trainer thanked him for the call but told him politely: "I don't train jump horses." Still, Johnston sought counsel from Michael Cunningham, who had been training the elder of the horses up to this point. He had vouched for Keaney and advised him to go ahead and train the horses.

Yavana's Pace, who had cost IR1,000, had won a maiden and three handicaps from 22 races in Ireland before arriving at Middleham. Johnston had received a message from John Keaney's father, Terence, who explained that the objective was to obtain 'black type'. As Johnston recalls: "I concluded that the whole Keaney family must be stone mad."

Nevertheless, he went ahead and accepted the duo. "In his second race for me, Yavana's Pace won, and then we ran him in the Hong Kong Jockey Club Trophy at Sandown – a valuable handicap."

His jockey was W. M. 'Eddie' Lai, a tiny Hong Kong apprentice who had been sent over by the Hong Kong Jockey Club to gain experience. That was his one ride of the day. Yavana's Pace was one of the outsiders of the 20-runner field, at 20-1. Rarely would Johnston offer guidance to a jockey, but he did here. "The instructions were to 'bury yourself in the pack, and then go for it at the last minute, when you can see the winning post.'" Johnston can barely stop laughing at the memory. "I don't think Eddie could understand what I was saying. He didn't speak much English.

"Anyway, he was stuck in against the rail, and was getting bounced around. I don't know how he even stayed on it. The horse was such a difficult ride. But in the straight he just went straight up the inside, headed for home, stick in the air, and won. After that Yavana's Pace just went from strength to strength, through the handicap ranks.

Johnston remembers the horse being: "very difficult to train, very temperamental. He wouldn't go on the gallops; he'd whip round and dump his jockey. He was also very temperamental on the racecourse until the stalls opened. He had to go down early. God knows how many jockeys fell off him on the way. John Carroll famously parted company from him on the occasion when Yavana's Pace cantered loose for a mile and a half, then buckled down to the task and won a Listed race. He was a horse full of quirks, but we had some fantastic days with him."

He did, though, have to accept second best when coming up against Fruits Of Love in the 2000 Hardwicke Stakes at Royal Ascot. The trainer relatively often runs two, or more, of his horses in the same race.

He will accept if you question this: "Owners can get upset if they are beaten by another horse in the yard. But it's not really logical. If Michael Stoute trained the horse, it would still beat theirs. Generally, if horse A's best chance is at Beverley and horse B's best chance is at Pontefract, I'll try to keep them apart, because I want to win two races. But if for both of them their best chance is in the Hardwicke, you'd be unfair to one owner not to run theirs."

That's decidedly what he was doing when he declared Fruits Of Love and Yavana's Pace to run in the 1m 4f Hardwicke Stakes at Royal Ascot. However, it proved to be a curiously excruciating spectacle for the trainer, despite the result.

"Yavana's Pace was not normally considered anything like a front-running horse, yet Darryll Holland went off in front on him," recalls Johnston. "I couldn't believe it. Fruits Of Love was known for coming from off the pace. So, I'm watching this race and cringing: 'What's the owner going to be thinking? Probably that we're using Yavana's Pace as a pacemaker!' Anyway, as they turn into the straight, all I can hear is John Keaney [owner of Yavana's Pace] screaming for his horse, and Deirdre, shouting even louder, standing in front of him, yelling for Fruits Of Love [she rode the horse out every day] to win. I thought, 'What is the guy going to think of this?'"

Fruits Of Love eventually seized control a furlong out, and maintained that advantage to the line, with Yavana's Pace runner-up. "When I turned round, John was hugging Deirdre. His reaction to coming second was one of the great things, for me, about that race." Indeed, Keaney, a house builder, was so magnanimous in defeat that he went out and commissioned for the Johnstons a painting of the finish of that Hardwicke Stakes. They bought the copyright and used it for that year's Christmas cards.

Yavana's Pace rewarded the Keaneys with an astonishing four

seasons under Johnston, who campaigned him in seven countries as well as Britain. He had been second in two German Group 1s, runner-up in the Irish St Leger, and had also contested the Melbourne Cup in 1999, finishing 12th of 24. When his 16th and final triumph came in a Group 1, under Keith Dalgleish, at Cologne, "Many locals told me that they had never seen a foreign winner given such a warm reception in Germany," says Johnston. "There were aspects to the character of the old horse that most people could identify with. No horse has given me so much pleasure and so little pain as Yavana's Pace." His jockeys, though, might qualify that statement ever so slightly.

When he was retired after failing to overcome recurring injuries, he was sent back to his owners John and Joan Keaney in Clonee, County Dublin. He had amply rewarded their faith, and provided sustenance to the belief of all owners. Here was a horse costing IR1,000 who had contested 74 races worldwide, and been retired having garnered 16 wins and 25 places, earning more than £740,000 in total.

There were attempts to dislodge Yavana's Pace from his pedestal in the aftermath of his Cologne victory. The *Racing Post*'s John Randall, referring to the horse becoming "the oldest horse to win a Group 1 race in Europe", contended, "in terms of absolute merit, his performance on Sunday was probably no better than when this supremely tough and genuine gelding carried 9st 10lb to victory in the November Handicap (at Doncaster) in 1998".

A wounded Johnston brought out the heavy weaponry in his veteran's defence in his column in the same paper, but in truth, it was unnecessary. The horse had stirred the soul, and the calculator of the form-fixated could not detract from the sheer poignancy of the moment: a Group 1 victory at the age of ten.

Yavana's Pace also evokes memories for Hayley Kelly, who

arrived at the yard in 1994, the year of Johnston's first Classic triumph, and was pitched into a world of route-planning and notching up air miles as travelling manager. Kelly was only 21 when she was despatched to Melbourne with Yavana's Pace in 1999. "He always has been, always will be, my favourite – Mark will tell you that – because I used to ride him at home a lot," says Kelly, who is now an assistant trainer at the yard. "Not that he was a Double Trigger or Attraction. He could be quite a difficult horse, to ride and to take racing. It's funny, he used to run in Germany a lot [nine times], and he had his own fan club. They love English horses going over there and winning. They'd want their picture taken with him."

She adds: "A lot of the staff do get too attached to the horses. I try not to. But I used to go and see him on his winter holidays in Ireland. I got on well with the owner. Sadly, after he retired, he got cast in his box one day and the owner rang me, and basically, he'd snapped his leg, getting up and thrashing about. He had to be put down. He was still going, at 18, I nearly cried that day. I was devastated."

Johnston is a firm advocate of international racing, but admits: "We travelled far more in those days than we do now. There was one year when we raced in 17 countries in one year. All we were interested in was prize money. We went where the prize money was best; we didn't care where it was. I'm ashamed to say in some ways that is not always the case now. Winning black type races has become a bigger priority than the prize money. It's a shame. It's one of the things that's wrong with British racing. We race for prestige more than we race for prize money. We have to, otherwise we wouldn't be in business."

He adds: "Another year, in the mid-nineties, when Gothenberg was around, and he was a big money-earner abroad, we had

100 winners in Britain who earned just over £1 million and ten winners abroad who brought in half a million in prize money. We used to run a lot more, and were right up there at the top of the international table every year."

Gothenberg, whose two-year-old victories included the Listed Woodcote Stakes at Epsom, never won a Group 1 event, but the bay, who cost only 5,700gns as a yearling, did claim three Group 2 prizes abroad: the International Stakes at The Curragh, Premio Emilio Turati at San Siro, and the Berlin-Brandenberg Trophy at Hoppegarten.

CHAPTER 18

THE BARGAIN BIJOU WHO BECAME A PRECIOUS GEM

For much of the century, as each year draws to a close, a hundred or more yearlings have arrived at Mark Johnston's Middleham yard, many purchased by him, some consigned by patrons. They will emerge in the early months of the following year as spirited two-year olds.

How do you assess these precocious athletes, assembled from a variety of sources? And, crucially, when will they be ready to run?

You imagine it's akin to surveying a school hall of new pupils, and trying to determine which are going to be the smartest, the sportiest; which will be the grafters, the slothful, the little terrors.

With racehorses it's easier. Much depends on breeding, which isn't the case with humans – well it is, but perhaps not to such a great extent – but also date of birth and conformation.

Johnston once explained to me how he and Deirdre would approach this evaluation process. "We try to sort them into four groups for each quarter of the season, when they're likely to start their racing careers. Those in group one are those suspected to be the earliest runners. Group fours will be those who will mature more steadily. The two-year-olds are then worked against one another within their groups."

Today, Charlie plays a significant part in this evaluation process. Indeed, Johnston says "He has a bigger input now than Deirdre and I put together."

However, Johnston stresses that this stage of assessment of his juveniles "is just a preliminary stab at it". After that, the yard managers who look after the two-year-olds are asked to go through the same process.

Yard managers, it should be explained, were introduced by Johnston early this century as staff numbers increased. They are the equivalent of department heads in an office environment and are like mini-trainers, responsible for everything in their yard. Currently Johnston has seven. It is a subject to which I will return.

"If a horse matches my assessment, that's fine. If not, we have a debate about where it should be. The yard managers could have more feedback from the work-riders, which means they may try to push a horse forward to an earlier group."

So, in general, the few in group one are earmarked to run early, based on pedigree, conformation and value. "But even a group four horse will get some fast work now, or if not early on," Johnston emphasised. "We still give them work in case something bounces out of it. Horses can jump from one group to another. Once you've got your first winner, everything starts falling into place."

However, he added: "I have to say that value comes into it as well. To be quite honest, you're not going to put a horse costing 150,000gns in group one, and send it out to Redcar or wherever, in the early weeks. You're not going to use it to test the water of how good your group is. You're going to send out one or two cheaper ones. Over the years we've had very few March and April two-year-old runners. If they're no good this May, they're not going to be any good next May."

Johnston recalled that the earliest he has ever galloped a two-year-old was four days into the new year, 1989, the aforementioned Starstreak. He did not win a race until August but the following season he progressed to capture the White Rose Stakes at Ascot, then finished a close second in a Group 3 event at Longchamp, before going hurdling for National Hunt trainers. "He was a big, scopey, middle-distance horse and [starting him so early] didn't do any harm, but in later years I learned that there wasn't an awful lot to be gained from galloping them so early."

Johnston added: "So, as each year went by, our galloping of two-year-olds probably grew later and later. But the gap between doing a good gallop and running in a race got shorter and shorter. Everything they're doing in January, February and March is just education. You're not really trying to find out how good they are."

It was a crucial part of the development of the yard in the nineties and early in the 2000s that Johnston could identify quality at basement prices. Apart from Quick Ransom (6,000gns), his buys included Spirit Of Love (IR1,000) who progressed to win Listed events, and Bandari, who set the trainer back a little more, at 40,000gns, and was fitted with ear-plugs two hours before his races to counter his pre-race nerves. Owned by Hamdan Al Maktoum after previous owner Abdullah Al-Rostamani had gifted the colt to him – Sheikh Hamdan's first connection with the stable – the horse was retired to stud as a seven-year-old, having won eleven races, including six at Group level.

Does Johnston concede the sales can be as exciting as running the horses? "Yes, there are all the possibilities and dreams." However, he adds: "I put my neck on the line at the sales. There have been times when I've been £500,000 down on purchases and have to find buyers."

One acquisition was particular testament to Johnston's astute judgement. "The year we won the Guineas with Mister Baileys, I bought maybe 25 yearlings, mostly on spec for a total of 200,000gns, which was a lot of money for us then. But an owner Stuart Morrison had given me an order for a £20,000 purchase. I could just buy him a horse and tell him: 'This is it'.

"So, I bought a horse for him by Cadeaux Genereux out of Pushkar, for twenty grand. This mare Pushkar, none of her progeny had black type, but she had been to all the worst sires you could imagine, like Electric, who you've probably never heard of. But she had gone to him and produced his best son.

"Three stallions she'd been to, she'd produced the best, and had now gone to Cadeaux Genereux [the flying sprinter, the best in Europe in 1989] who was in a different league to anything she'd been to before.

"His pedigree had no black type in the first dam, and she'd had several foals. Yet, I did my research and I discovered that three or more of these foals were rated over 100 and deserved to have black type. Two or three were the best sons of their sire. She'd been to moderate sires, and here she was going to Cadeaux Genereux."

The first signs hadn't been encouraging. "It was a big heavy thing. We had another horse by Cadeaux Genereux, owned by the Duke of Roxburghe. And it was a great brute of a thing as well, but two years older. And dead slow. This thing looked just like it. And all through the winter, Deirdre would say: 'that Cadeaux Genereux colt you bought – his half-brother's just won again over hurdles.' I thought: 'What have I bought here?' But from the first time he galloped I knew he was the business."

The colt, named Bijou D'Inde (Jewel of India), was narrowly

Below: Under the media spotlight…Mark and Deirdre Johnston with Poet's Society, who became the stable's 4,194th winner when successful at York on 23 August 2018. It set a new record for winners in Britain. (Credit: Mikaelle Lebreton)

Below: Mark Johnston's first Classic winner Mister Baileys – he of the white blaze and three white socks – ridden by Jason Weaver. The partnership won the 1994 2,000 Guineas. (Credit: Alamy/Allstar Picture Library Ltd)

Top: Mark Johnston with his Double Trigger after victory in the 1998 Doncaster Cup. This was the final race of a glorious career for the grand stayer, who that day was partnered by Darryll Holland. Double Trigger is led in by his emotional lad Geordie Charlton who was in floods of tears, according to the trainer, and Robynne Watton, now senior travelling manager at the yard. (Credit: Racing Post/Mirrorpix)

Above: The star Attraction poses for the cameras...Mark and jockey Kevin Darley with the stable's extraordinary Classic-winning filly after her victory in the 2004 Sun Chariot Stakes at Newmarket. (Credit: Mark Johnston)

Top: A long-serving trio...three assistant trainers at Kingsley Park: Jock Bennett (left), Hayley Kelly and Andrew Bottomley. (Credit: Mikaelle Lebreton)

Above: A deal is sealed on a lifelong partnership...Mark Johnston and Deirdre Ferguson are married on 8 June 1985 at a church on the shore of Loch Achray. (Credit: Mark Johnston)

Top: Charlie Johnston (right) riding work on Road To Love in 2006. In a TV interview he had tipped the horse to win at Ascot – and he did, easily. (Credit: Mikaelle Lebreton)

Above: Deirdre Johnston on her homebred eventer Lucky Libra at Floors Castle, the home of the Duke of Roxburghe, owner-breeder of the magnificent Attraction. (Credit: Mikaelle Lebreton)

Above: An ebullient Frankie Dettori embraces trainer Mark Johnston after partnering Poet's Society to victory at York in 2018 – in the process establishing a record of 4,194 British winners for the trainer. (Credit: Racing Post/Cranhamphoto.com)

Top: Pure Gold…Joe Fanning returns to the winner's enclosure on Subjectivist after their triumph in the 2021 Ascot Gold Cup. They are led in by a jubilant groom David Hickin. (Credit: Getty Images/Harry Trump/Stringer)

Above: The Johnston family – Angus, Mark, Deirdre and Charlie – celebrate a winning return to Royal Ascot in June 2021. (Credit: Mikaelle Lebreton)

Top: A family affair...Mark Johnston with wife Deirdre, and sons Charlie, one of his assistants (left) and Angus pictured in the office of Kingsley Park stables. (Credit: Mikaelle Lebreton)

Above: Watching the horses work...Mark Johnston and son and assistant Charlie on the viewing platform above their Middleham gallops. (Credit: Racing Post/ Grossick Photography)

defeated in his first two outings, in maidens at Newcastle and Goodwood, "but we had undying faith in him," Johnston recalled of his charge who claimed the Acomb Stakes at York and a Group 3 event at The Curragh, before, the following season, going straight to the 2,000 Guineas, as Mister Baileys had done two years earlier, finishing third in a freeze-frame of nodding heads, behind the Frankie Dettori-ridden Mark Of Esteem.

"A lot of the time we don't know how good they actually are before they've won, but with him and Mister Baileys we were pretty sure they were decent horses," says Johnston.

The trainer then saw his miler finish fourth in the Irish Guineas, after losing a shoe. Victory in the Group 1 St James's Palace Stakes at Royal Ascot was handsome consolation, followed by a narrow second place to Halling in the Group 1 Eclipse Stakes at Sandown.

Bijou D'Inde never won again, but he saw the world in the hands of his travel agents, Kingsley House Globetrotters, travelling to Dubai (where he was brought down in the Dubai World Cup but was unscathed), Longchamp and Sha Tin.

"I always say that, at the beginning of 1995, if I could have given one back it would have been him [Bijou D'Inde]. You see, when you come from the yearling sales, every year you feel: 'this is the best horse I've bought. I was really smart there. I got a bargain'. But there's others, even when you're bidding, you're thinking: 'I'm paying too much for this. I wish someone else would bid', and afterwards you're thinking: 'I wish I hadn't bought that.'" He paused, and added: "In hindsight, though, I was very proud of buying him."

There are others in the same category. "In more recent times, Dark Vision cost 15,000gns. Ugliest brute. And every time I saw him without the saddle on, if I could have given one back it would have been him. He won the Group 2 Vintage Stakes at Goodwood before being sold to Godolphin. We sold him for £1.2 million, I think."

Johnston also paid 20,000gns for a horse named Austrian School, a son of Teofilo. "I was really pleased with myself. I thought: 'this is fantastic'. Then people kept saying to me: 'I didn't know you were going into training jumpers!' The horse is a half-brother to the dual Grand National winner Tiger Roll, through the mare Swiss Roll. He would go on to win or be placed in 15 of his 21 runs, including third behind our Dee Ex Bee in the Group 3 Henry II Stakes at Sandown."

Johnston admits that, once in work, even after all these years he is still stirred by the prospect of a star in the making. "The ones that excite me, jump out at me, are the ones that get a bit behind in the gallop, then they just pick up, lengthen, and they're there. It's as if their stride's one and a half times more than the stride of the horse next to them, without putting in more work. But then the gallops don't always tell you which is the exciting horse. It's racing them that tells you that."

One thing that irks Johnston is anyone within the yard assessing the current crop of two-year-olds, and suggesting they are collectively below par. The trainer has an anecdote which he often tells to remind people of how a handful of early runners can damn a whole season's intake.

"He's sick of me reminding him, but at the start of one season we made a very slow start with the two-year-olds. Jock Bennett had remarked on more than one occasion, 'I don't think they're a very good bunch.' Well, I jumped down his throat.

"I said, 'Jock, you can have ten who are not a good bunch, even 20 who are not a good bunch, but you *cannot* have 100 who are not a good bunch.' It's surely not possible for a whole generation of two-year-olds to be inferior to the previous year's. It just can't be the case."

He adds: "The best one may be inferior to last year's best, and the worst one may be too. But the average of 3,000 horses has to be the same. It's the same with us. If we have 100 two-year-olds, they can't all be bad. Neither can they all be superstars. The question we have to answer is: are we running the right ones?"

"What I always try to drum into the yard managers is this: good horses don't win more races than bad horses. It's completely ridiculous to think that. It's actually quite the contrary. So, all those small struggling trainers out there who are blaming the fact that that's what they are – because I've got better horses – are talking absolute crap. What makes a good trainer is making the most of what he's got.

"As I said to you before, this job is not rocket science. It's not particularly clever to be a good racehorse trainer. But at other times I remind myself that it's blatantly obvious some are more successful than others. We are one of the best set-ups, and that has proved that it's not all from having the best opportunities. Because we didn't have the best opportunities. You can't start any lower than we did."

SIZE MATTERS: EXPANSION OF THE JOHNSTON EMPIRE

M oving into the new millennium, the equine population at Kingsley House had continued to expand rapidly, and with it the team of staff who devoted their working lives to them.

By this time, Johnston had bought out his original backer Brian Palmer, and instead set up a business advisory board. Members included, and still do, Richard Huckerby, who had been marketing director for Kimberly-Clark, and had had an interest in the stable's 1,000th winner Double Honour (at Hamilton on 4 September 2000), amongst others over the years.

Johnston knew he had to adapt the organisation to handle his growing horse numbers, and introduced yard managers. "When we first came to Middleham, the structure was me, Deirdre, a head lad, who was Declan Condell, and an assistant head lad," he explained. "Everybody was answerable to the person above him. Then we went to head lad, two assistant head lads, and two enormous teams of people beneath them.

"At one time we had a vet-cum-assistant trainer, James Given,

179

a head lad, and two assistant head lads. But, in reality, it was just an opportunity for folk to pass the buck. Anything that was wrong was always somebody else's fault. It took me a while to realise it just didn't work."

Also, as much as Johnston instinctively believed he should have knowledge of all his charges, increasingly he realised that was impractical. That fact was confirmed one day when he was at the sales with John Warren, the Queen's racing manager and a director of Highclere Stud, who formerly managed for Lord Hartington and the Duke Of Roxburghe.

"John kept asking me questions, like 'How did they gallop last week?' I had to phone somebody to check that out. 'What weight was he [a certain horse] today?' I had to phone somebody else to check that out. It ended up with me having to phone three or four different people. I realised that one person should know the answer to all those questions, and not one person who's got 150 horses under him. It should be one person who's got 30 horses." (Today, as stated earlier, the trainer also has up-to-date information on all the yard's horses immediately available on his smartphone.)

Initially, Johnston split the operation into four yards, and over the years that has increased to seven, operating under Johnston (managing director & trainer) and Deirdre (director & assistant trainer), together with four other assistant trainers: Charlie Johnston, Jock Bennett, Andrew Bottomley and Hayley Kelly.

Each yard manager is like a mini-trainer; responsible for everything in his or her yard. "There's no way the yard manager can say, 'Oh, the groom did that; I didn't know about it'," Johnston once explained to me. "The yard manager cannot say, 'The vet's dealing with that.' They are responsible for whether a horse has been wormed or vaccinated. They cannot pass the buck. If the vet is called because a horse is injured and he diagnoses it and treats it, it is still the yard manager's job to know what he did, what he gave it and what he's got to do with it."

Also records of attendance, sickness and holidays were maintained in various colours on a board – for everyone to see. That has changed, though staff still clock in, as they did then. "We no longer have a board up, but we do have a points system and we have bonuses associated to good timekeeping and reliability," says the trainer.

"Our staff structure is pretty much the same as it was back in the early 2000s," he says. "It's evolved, of course, over the years, but essentially it's the same." Johnston admits it has all been a continual process of trial and error and changing systems, but his principal aim has always been to increase everyone's degree of responsibility. "I want to improve the business by pushing that responsibility further down the line. That's the hardest thing to do."

In 2002, Johnston wrote in a *Racing Post* column that he had his biggest ever string with, at peak, 178 horses:

"And I have decided never again to apologise for this fact or play down the size of our squad. Some trainers with smaller teams… have questioned the ability of trainers like myself to offer individual attention to the horses. It is a fair question, but for me my stable is easier to run now than ever before.

"Management systems and a team of yard managers and staff that put them into practice have evolved to a point where they run like clockwork. Our results, based on individual winners to runners and individual winners to horses in the yard, stand up to closest scrutiny, even before you consider the prize money in relation to capital outlay. Size matters."

And yet, as owners and winners continued, gratifyingly, to

increase, an element of the operation still troubled Johnston – his own role. "Back in 2003 [when the yard enjoyed a summer of saturation when it came to winners], I remember thinking there was no limit to the number of horses we could train," Johnston recalled. "We'd just added another yard manager. No problem at all. Then 2004 was arguably our best-ever season. Even better." He paused before adding: "Yet it was driving me mad."

He explained: "I planned all the horses' work, all their entries, what they're going to eat…my belief had always been that the day I stop doing that is the day I stop holding the licence. I had to do the list [of proposed work for each horse] at night. I used to say, 'I haven't got anyone good enough to delegate the list to.'"

'The list' was the bane of his life, and things came to a head at the end of 2004. Johnston was discussing his concerns with Ian Harland, one of his owners, who was also head of a major accountancy practice. Harland had handled the buy-out of Brian Palmer in 2001. "Ian came in to do an official review, not just of the business but of our whole lifestyle and plans for the future.

"He asked me, 'What is the worst thing about your job?' I said, 'Doing the list.' At that stage we had around 180 horses, and I'd get my vet diaries at seven o'clock at night, read them over dinner, then go straight out into the tack room [where work for each rider is displayed on a board]. I wouldn't be finished until midnight. Everyone else had gone to bed. If I'd been racing, I might be there until one in the morning. It was like that day in, day out. I said to Ian, 'You can't delegate this job.' Yet at the same time I also realised that was the limiting factor. The more horses you have, the longer the list takes.

"Ian gave me a little lecture about McDonald's. He said, 'If you go to them anywhere in the world, the standard of food is exactly the same. Do they employ brilliant, capable people or

16-year-old spotty kids who can't get a job anywhere else, and pay them the minimum wage?' I said, 'The latter.' He said, 'That's because the systems are so good, they can't get it wrong. If you think you can't delegate things, the system you've put in is not right. Go back and re-design the system so that you can delegate and still have the input you want.' That gave me a new lease of life. I realised that was what I enjoyed about the business, as well – designing the system."

Johnston did radically alter things. Amongst other changes, he promoted Jock Bennett, who had formerly worked for Bill Watts for 25 years, from yard manager to be his assistant. "His one and only job in the afternoon was to do that list," says Johnston, although an admission followed: "I still kept tabs on it all."

Deirdre recalls: "Mark's never lost that drive to succeed. The year we got more horses, it got really tough. He was just out there all hours, doing the list. He never came to bed, hardly. We both felt we couldn't work any more hours, and we still felt we weren't doing things as well as we wanted to do them. Once we made the change in the system, we got all our drive and enthusiasm back. There was a little bit of breathing space."

Today, Charlie Johnston has responsibility for 'the list', a subject which will be broached later.

It must be stated that such matters as HR, wages, working conditions and organising of staff efficiently were, if not totally alien to Johnston, not his forte. He was a racehorse trainer; not a businessman.

Indeed, if there's one description apt to rile the trainer it's being described as a businessman. Put it to him that he is as much a businessman as a horseman and the eyes glint as he responds: "People say that about me, and I have to say that it annoys me a wee bit at times. I would say it's a fairly common misconception: that the reason we are so successful is because I'm so good at running the business. That's absolute nonsense."

Johnston elucidates: "I didn't do a business degree. I did a veterinary degree, and vets are notoriously bad at running a business. It's a very narrow degree. I had no training whatsoever in how to run a business when I was at vet school. Luckily, in the first 12 years, I had a business partner who taught me a lot about how to run the business."

Johnston reflects briefly on Brian Palmer, boss of Hinari, and a crucial component in the Johnston machine. "When he was trying to persuade me to go in with him in 1988, he told me: 'I can't make you a better horse trainer than you're going to be…but I'll move you on ten years.' I think he did."

That said, the trainer adds: "People often say, 'what would have happened if you'd never met Brian Palmer?' and I say, 'I'd have found someone else.' He's almost certainly correct. His dynamism and enterprise, even in those early days, were seductive qualities. Paul Venner of Baileys Horse Feeds had been highly influential, too. "Paul was the first person to send me a horse, and the company still has them with us [five in 2021]," says Johnston, before adding: "It will be interesting to see how Charlie gets on with this, going forward. I didn't come into this wanting to be a big employer. I always say I wanted to train horses, not people. It didn't occur to me that so much of it was about employing people, motivating people. It hadn't occurred to me that it's so labour-intensive and that managing the staff is a bigger job than managing the horses.

"I had to learn, like everybody else. I've never run another business. I've taught myself as I've gone along. With all due respect [my success] is not because I know more about running a business than other trainers. It's because I know more about horses.

"That's the difference between Charlie and me. Overall, there's very few jobs in this business that I haven't done myself. When I started, I was the rider, I was the mucker-outer, the vet. I did the VAT return, did the wages. I wrote the invoices out by hand. I did every aspect of the business. I couldn't do it now because it's different from the little cottage business that I started. But I have done it at some stage.

"That's what's different for Charlie. He's going into a business where there's a big business side to it that employs a lot of people, doing jobs that he has never done, and he has never had the opportunity to do because it's gone beyond that.

"This business is not built on me being good at managing staff, or good at finances. It's not even built on me being a good vet, and being able to keep horses healthy. It's entirely built on having winners. Right back at the start here, we were winning races, and climbing the trainers' table quickly. Everything was snowballing.

"There comes a point in the year where you've had enough winners and enough spread of winners across all the owners, that you know next year's going to be good – financially. You know all those existing owners are happy, and they're going to spend their money next year. That's entirely about winners.

"What gets you *new* customers is big winners. New customers come because you've won big races. Unfortunately, you can have a fantastic year, and no high-profile horses. A lot of people won't notice you've had a fantastic year."

I refer him back to the early years when, as he said, they could have gone bust, and ask if that had been a valuable lesson? "Absolutely," he replies, "and we do well now. We don't pretend otherwise. But we haven't built it from money that came from anyone else. It's all been from racing. I could see off my life living off our assets, but Charlie couldn't. The business has got to continue to make a profit. We can't just be selling off bits of the property to keep it afloat."

* * *

The expansion of the Johnston operation at Middleham continues apace, even today. Late one afternoon in early May 2021, Johnston summons me to his Range Rover, and we drive out of the gates of Kingsley House to make the short journey to Kingsley Park, the operational centre of the business for more than a decade.

To return to the Fleetwood Mac line at the start of this book, Johnston simply can't stop thinking about tomorrow; he never has. In 1988 he had arrived at Kingsley House, with its 39-box yard. He extended that to 67 and, in 1994, in the wake of Mister Baileys' 2,000 Guineas triumph, bought Warwick House to bring the complement of boxes up to 142.

Today, Warwick House is the main yard stabling two-year-olds, with the house itself used for staff accommodation, and a canteen on the ground floor. "A large majority of the staff that we accommodate live in Warwick House – together with 70 two-year-olds."

As we enter the Kingsley Park estate, Johnston declares – not for the first time: "If I see a space, I need to fill it." He points out where Charlie lives nearby. "He only moved out of the house when I got Covid. He lived in the cottage opposite the house. But then an owner came to stay. That was the only way we got him out!"

Just as an aside, it could be observed that if there's a pause in a conversation, Johnston feels obliged to fill it, too. He abhors a verbal vacuum, though, that said, he is not a man for idle chit-chat.

Warwick House was a substantial addition, but Johnston still did not possess the capacity to accommodate his aspirations. So, in 2003, he made his third property purchase when he bought the 260-acre Park Farm from brothers Peter and Tony Walton. At the time, it was a dairy farm.

It was renamed Kingsley Park, and it has its own gallops. "We'd looked at it for years and dreamed about where we could build gallops," he says. "But it was some time before we moved the office there – around 2009. Now it's very much the hub. The gallops were built in 2008, and we moved permanently to them and off Middleham Moor in 2009."

There was a reason for that move: a dispute over sheep grazing. Though the saga has a somewhat comedic edge, there was a serious side to it.

As the *Darlington and Stockton Times* reported in 2007: "The dispute involves gaitowners, who have ancient grazing rights on the moor, and the Middleham Trainers' Association, which put up a fence on the moor to prevent sheep straying into the path of horses during training on the gallops. Top trainer Mark Johnston threatened to pull his horses from training on the moor and is having all-weather gallops constructed in the grounds of his Park Farm. Last year, a horse owned by Mr Johnston and its rider were injured in a fall after sheep crossed in front of them.

"The fence was erected in May and retrospective planning permission is being sought. Middleham Town Council, which receives £30,000 a year from the trainers for use of the moor, said that the fence should be taken down until the application was determined. The issue was passed to Defra."

Johnston says: "It simply wasn't safe to train the horses with sheep running all over the place, and I thought: 'This could go the wrong way, and if it does, we could be without gallops.' So, while it was going on, I applied for planning permission to build an all-weather gallop for Park Farm."

He adds: "Michael Dickinson [the trainer, whose feats include training the first five home in the 1983 Cheltenham Gold Cup and later, as a Flat trainer in the U.S., winning the Breeders' Cup Mile twice with Da Hoss] who had developed the Tapeta surface[9], told me he had been making it for Godolphin and if we wanted it, to buy it then. So, we did. Building that gallop cost around £600,000. In mid-2009, we came off the moor completely."

Today, his facilities include three separate grass gallops, two of which are uphill, plus the uphill all-weather ten-furlong Tapeta gallop.

Johnston has also established a breeding sideline to the training operation, though he insists: "It's just a hobby. You need really good mares, and you need to spend silly money on stallion fees. We have Friar Ings [Stud]. We keep some cows there – that's another hobby – and half a dozen broodmares that we have."

He explains further: "It all happened after Mister Baileys was retired and went to stud, and we had a breeding right to him, so we bought a mare, and the same with Double Trigger – we bought another mare. We also had one nomination every year to Shamardal and that was at the level that we started buying better mares." He adds: "We have bred a Group 1 winner, Sheikha Reika. We sold her as a yearling. She was with Roger Varian, and won a Grade 1 event at Woodbine [in Canada] in 2018."

At Kingsley Park, the equine athletes are pampered. No doubt about that. There is an indoor equine pool and a water-walker at Kingsley Park, as well as an equine swimming pool at Kingsley House. Swimming is acknowledged to be an excellent way for horses to build stamina and improve overall fitness, particularly when returning from injury.

---

[9] Tapeta is an artificial surface, with a combined upper layer of sand, fibre, rubber and wax, installed on top of either porous asphalt or a geotextile membrane.

You survey the facilities. It resembles an equine version of a gym-cum-therapy health spa like Champneys. You do not require a horseman's eye to recognise the scale or excellence of the entire Johnston enterprise, on which the trainer estimates he has lavished around £8million since his arrival at Middleham in late 1988.

It is late afternoon and Charlie Johnston is still here – on what is notionally his day off – allocating the following day's work for the stable's staff. He has his own form of treadmill, one from which he rarely steps off – as will become apparent later.

The scene takes you back to his father's observation in the previous chapter, that "managing the staff is a bigger job than managing the horses", and how Johnston introduced innovations which often ran counter to the traditional thinking he encountered when he arrived in Middleham.

It is an area in which he has invested much time and energy over his career – which helps to explain his antipathy for a crusade on this very issue run by the industry's trade paper.

CHAPTER 20

AN EXPLOSIVE FALL-OUT OVER STABLE STAFF CAMPAIGN

The late racing writer Paul Haigh once opined, in inimitable fashion, in the *Racing Post* that "the structure of racing is so steadfastly anachronistic...with owners at the top, trainers who are little gods, jockeys who are lionised but regarded as social inferiors by many, and then at the bottom the mass of stable staff, whom we never really register, who get up before dawn has cracked to work for weekly wages that wouldn't pay a poshie's dinner bill."

It was a pretty brutal assault, but like so many issues – including animal welfare and the whip specifically, to which I will return – it is a subject often energised by perception rather than reality. But what can be said is that horseracing, a labour-intensive sport, has traditionally found its shortcomings, in employment terms, difficult to escape the searchlight of exposure if anyone has set out to illuminate them.

In 2003, that subject was given prominence by the sport's own trade paper when the *Racing Post* ran a campaign against the perceived poor wages and conditions in racing. Mark Johnston, who was writing a weekly column for the paper at the time, resigned on principle.

It had been inevitable that his upwards career trajectory would be accompanied by a demand by the print and broadcast media for this provocateur, armed with trenchant opinions, to become horse-racing's articulate, questioning voice on a whole gamut of issues.

Bombastic. Arrogant. Analytical. Contrary. Trenchant. Such adjectives have all been used to describe him, and there are many more. He has 230 horses in his yard. He also has as big a stable of hobby-horses. And he gallops them frequently. It can rarely be said about Mark Johnston that "he preferred to maintain his own counsel".

As he once wrote in the *Racing Post*: "I could never resist an argument, I don't really care what the subject is. I can even, quite often, argue for either side. I've always fancied myself as the devil's number one advocate." For the print media, prominent figures espousing controversial views, and who can argue them coherently, are a highly-prized breed.

Traditionally, the racing trade press, originally in the shape of the *Sporting Life* was principally, though not solely, a broadsheet chronicle of record, with the form easy to study on high-street bookmakers' walls.

But then the *Racing Post* appeared, founded in 1986 by Sheikh Mohammed, and set up as a rival to the *Sporting Life*, which had been the UK's main sporting paper since 1859.

The *Sporting Life* was owned by Mirror Group Newspapers and in 1998 they purchased the licence to run the *Racing Post* from Sheikh Mohammed for £1. The last edition of the *Sporting Life* was printed in 1998, as the two newspapers merged together. The *Racing Post* is now under different ownership, though Sheikh Mohammed continues to hold the trademark.

The tone of the two newspapers was markedly different. The *Racing Post* has been a more campaigning publication and, on occasions, been a scimitar of excoriation over certain issues.

Few in racing will forget the edition of the *Racing Post* which damned Peter Savill, the former BHB chairman, a precursor to the BHA and whose trainers included Johnston, for having the temerity to run his Lady Herries-trained Celtic Swing in the French Derby (the Prix Du Jockey Club) rather than the English Derby. "Sad. Mad. Bad." was the extraordinary front-page headline. That was back in 1995.

Johnston, who had written a bi-weekly column in the *Sporting Life* since 1994, moved over to the *Racing Post* when they merged. They appeared to be natural bedfellows. He was offered space to deliver his acerbic views, and his column made essential reading in a newspaper that was also blessed with the writing of such eloquent writers as Haigh and Alastair Down.

Granted such freedom of expression, Johnston was as content as the proverbial porker in a field of clover. They lived in harmony for three years. Johnston spoke about his runners but also aired grievances, in the process raising temperatures and hackles.

Consider this extract, taken from a column just before his Fruits Of Love was due to contest the Breeders' Cup Turf at Churchill Downs in November 2000. In his column, he defended the use of Lasix, which is used to prevent respiratory bleeding in racehorses. Its use on race days is banned in Britain, but permitted in the US.

Declaring that "those who shout loudest on the subject are probably doing so from a position of relative ignorance," Johnston stated: "Fruits Of Love will be on medication tonight in the Breeders' Cup Turf. I have never made any secret of the fact and I don't feel any need to offer excuses. I admit that, to some extent and particularly in the case of Lasix, we are giving him drugs to level the playing field with the other competitors."

It was a provocative stance; one that would be anathema to many of his counterparts and readers generally; yet, as in all of Johnston's views, there is a rationale about his argument.

The man who would become president of the National Trainers' Federation in 2003 inspired support and provoked controversy in equal measure – until that fateful day when the *Racing Post* announced its 'A Fair Deal for Stable Staff' campaign. So much for bedfellows after that. Johnston hurled his breakfast tray on the floor as he leaped from the covers.

This crusade, which was spearheaded by *Racing Post* writer David Ashforth, attempted to identify the reasons why racing suffered a persistent shortage of suitably qualified staff, and how the situation could be resolved. Ashforth wrote: "They are issues to do with pay, including overtime pay; with hours, particularly a lack of time off; with facilities and treatment at racecourses; and with a common perception that they and their skills are not sufficiently respected or considered."

The *Post*'s front page claimed that a survey "has revealed many stories of low pay and ridiculously long hours. Racing is lucky to be able to rely on such a skilled workforce. The *Racing Post* believes that, as a matter of urgency, stable staff must be promoted from the bottom to the top of racing's priorities."

There was an inevitable polarisation of positions. Stable staff reportedly backed the campaign, and, according to the *Racing Post* its 'hotline' received many callers with tales of long hours and poor wages, which were duly published. Johnston was among trainers who took exception.

The Scot summed up his opposition in his final *Racing Post* column on 6 June 2003, describing what had appeared in the *Post* as "drivel". He added: "This 'campaign' is very bad for racing. It is bad for all of us: trainers, owners, stable staff and, maybe, ultimately, racing journalists."

He asked: "What message is it sending to potential investors? How many sponsors will be looking to get involved with a training yard this week if they have believed even half of what David Ashforth has written? How many less recruits will we have now, thanks to this 'campaign', to help us with the seemingly ever-expanding fixture list?"

While he conceded that there were issues and he and many of his counterparts were trying to address them, "this ill-conceived, poorly researched and thoroughly biased 'campaign' has not helped one iota and, frankly, I don't think it will."

He wrote of his staff training initiatives, and wages, which he said were in excess of the national minimum, and which he regarded as only a safety net. He also addressed the problem of unsociable working hours. However, his main issue with the newspaper was a lack of "any constructive or sensible ideas in these areas; only pointless and unhelpful criticism."

Ashforth responded by contending there were "trainers, hope-fully a small minority, who have been damaging the industry for years by alienating staff and harming racing's public image."

This, to an outsider, appeared to be the crux of the matter. Do you sully the name of a whole industry for the perceived sins of a few? Nevertheless, the campaign had an effect. The following month, the *Post* claimed a victory when the British Horseracing Board set up an independent commission under former government minister Lord Donoughue to investigate problems for stable and stud staff.

The commission made a raft of recommendations, referring to "antiquated overtime arrangements", lack of proper pension cover, recruitment strategy, accommodation for staff, the "wasteful exodus" of graduates who had attended the racing schools, on-the-job training, and better facilities for stable staff at racecourses. It also called for a change in the culture of racing "to eliminate bullying and harassment and create a modern work environment". It advocated training for trainers and stud managers to help them deal with staff issues.

When we spoke about this a few years later, Johnston, whose sense of outrage was in part because he had worked tirelessly to enhance standards within his own establishment, remained unconvinced by the campaign and what it actually achieved.

"What makes me so bitter against the *Racing Post* is that, like any industry, you've got no choice but to move with the times and progress. Like all labour-intensive manual industries, we had staffing problems here. We had recruitment problems and retention problems. We had problems which the *Racing Post* maybe highlighted. But these were things that I'd been looking to do something about for as long as I'd been a trainer."

Asserting that the *Racing Post*'s campaign contributed nothing except negative PR about horseracing, he added: "It basically said to people: 'If you want to work with horses, don't work in racing.' They were basically saying: 'Low wages, bad hours, come and get treated like shit.' How dare they?"

Today, as Johnston nears the end of his first 34 years as a racehorse trainer, and prepares to join his son in partnership for the remainder of it, he declares: "I don't think I'm talking out of turn in saying that I've probably done more than anybody in modernising the way training businesses are structured and run, and the way staff are employed. Right at the beginning, I separated out yard staff and riding staff when everybody else was doing three lots and mucking them out."

He adds: "Imitation, as they say, is the best form of flattery.

Things like the 'Always Trying' branding. There are so many things…when we moved to Middleham, everybody went out six days a week, and everyone had Sunday off, and every horse had Sunday off. Now every stable sends their horses out on a Sunday.

"So many things we've changed and others have followed. It's one of the things I'm most proud of. That's my legacy, is it not? It's one of the reasons why I won't just play the game. It's why I can't keep my mouth shut when I think they [the BHA and its forerunners] are cocking it up."

In fact, that policy of not being able to keep his mouth shut was rather turned on its head three years after the 'Fair deal for stable staff' row when he refused to speak to either of the two racing television channels, then called ATR (At The Races) and Racing UK, over an issue which, outside the glasshouse of horseracing politics, may not have been exactly exotica, but inside definitely was: the introduction of 48-hour declaration of runners; an innovation he blamed largely on the influence exerted by the bosses of those two stations.

It had been said that this change would enhance opportunities to sell British racing abroad – to the advantage of the industry. His objection was that it made race-planning for trainers more complex and would result in more non-runners.

Johnston's boycott of ATR and Racing UK lasted three years, before he grudging relented, as the *Daily Mail*'s Marcus Townend reported in July 2009:

"Stressing this week that his opinion remains as strong as ever (and that money has not been delivered anywhere near the level to cover the increased costs he says trainers and owners are having to bear because of the system), Johnston had been persuaded to speak to ATR by owner Ron Huggins, of Double Trigger fame, and when approached by RUK's Nick Luck this week said he was 'pushed forward' by wife Dierdre.

Maybe Mark, whose profile was hardly helped by his stance, had been reminded of the value of reaching out to the public at large by another family member.

Writing on his website, he revealed how son Angus has fulfilled his ambition to become a busker and it has been a profitable one. Setting out with a guitar and a stool borrowed from the kitchen to play to the folk of Richmondshire, Angus made £82 for two-hours work."

By then, by his own admission: "My media profile had taken a dive and it was beginning to hit us. People were talking more about Richard Fahey, and he was the fastest-growing trainer in the north. We decided we needed a re-branding exercise, one that's going to say 'we're not dead.'"

That *Racing Post* campaign continued to rankle Johnston. He insisted there remains a basic lack of understanding about how racing stables function. He feels there is a lack of knowledge about how much of a team sport this is, with a win bonus system that applied to all staff; not just those responsible on a day-to-day basis for horses.

To illustrate this point, there was an occasion in the mid-2000s, when the yard was about to take on a new tractor driver. The basic salary at that time was £14,220.

"So, I asked our then HR manager what he actually got paid in the past year. It turned out he received £18,106 in total pay, including overtime. Then he also got £1,440 compensation for the loss of Shamardal [from Sheikh Mohammed when the colt was transferred to Godolphin], pool money, £720 in owners' bonuses, £1,430 in winners' bonuses, £400 pension and £418 clothing allowance, totalling £23,814."

When I told Johnston many would find it surprising that bonuses should apply to a tractor driver, who never went near a horse, he swiftly retorted: "It may sound strange. There's obviously a lot of difference between driving a tractor and riding a horse. But it's been a gradual thing over the years. In one sense it's crazy; yet they're all part of the team. It's very difficult to say where you should draw the line. If you draw the line above tractor driver, what about the guy who mucks out the yard but doesn't actually touch the horses?"

Today, Johnston will reveal: "Up until not that long ago, Darley or Sheikh Mohammed always gave bonuses to the staff at Christmas time, and sometimes if they took a horse from us. In their heyday, when they had a hundred horses with us, it was often six figures. They were very generous to staff."

He adds: "I remember there were two outstanding bonuses. One was when Mastery left us and went on to win the [2009] St Leger, and he gave all the staff a week's wages. You're probably talking a couple of hundred thousand. Then Monterosso won the [2012] Dubai World Cup, and he gave the staff a month's wages – despite the fact that the horse had left us 18 months before."

Teamwork is absolutely paramount. Yes, it's become a *mot a la mode*. But it is authentic here. If you were to list Johnston's aims, right back to his earliest years here, his absolute priority has been to create a team ethic for everyone – from the youngest lad or lass who mucks out to the most experienced yard manager. They must all feel they have contributed to producing a winner.

It is a structure designed to encourage staff to identify runners capable of winning a race. They can be senior people, right down to the yard man.

To demonstrate his point, Johnston once told me the story of

Winged Cupid during the 2005 season. "Winged Cupid was a very backward yearling, very small, and by In The Wings, who was known to be a backward sire," he said. "I could easily have left him a lot longer, could easily have run him less times. But his yard manager kept saying at meetings under 'Horses Fit to Run', 'Winged Cupid.' And I kept thinking: 'I can't run that thing.' And she'd say: 'Winged Cupid. You've got to run Winged Cupid.'

"As a result, he ran in races he wouldn't have run in otherwise. He was second in a Group 1 and then sold to Godolphin for a huge amount of money. I might not have spotted that if I hadn't got feedback from the yard manager saying: 'This horse is bouncing out of his skin.' All I could see was that he was small, he was backward and his pedigree screamed at me: 'Don't run him.'"

Johnston also told me of an elderly yard man who mucked out the stable of an exceptional filly with whom the yard will always be inextricably linked.

"He didn't look after her, didn't groom her or anything, just mucked out her box. Because of all her leg problems the first thing that happened in the morning was that he'd put her on the horse-walker for an hour.

"Once a month, this guy might come to me and say: 'She was a bit stiff this morning when she walked out,' or: 'I wasn't 100 per cent happy with her,' or: 'She's not eating her food.' One time, we had an annual review meeting for all the staff. I said to them that if everybody treated every horse like he had this filly then we'd win more races. Far more races."

That character who just 'mucked out' would play a minor but important role as a member of the team responsible for one of racing's truly romantic tales. But those involving damsels in distress, a Duke and a commoner, and ancient castles usually are, aren't they? The filly's name was Attraction.

THE 'COMMONER' WHO BECAME RACING ROYALTY

A ttraction was extraordinary; both in what she achieved on the racetrack, given her relatively 'humble' birth and her physical impediments, and because of what she represented in Mark Johnston's career.

If Master Baileys was the drum-roll for the stable in 1994, and Double Trigger the fanfare in the mid- to late-nineties, then the filly who, as a yearling was not even dispatched to the sales by her breeder, the Duke of Roxburghe, because there was no likelihood of anyone buying her, was the official proclamation and five-gun salute that her trainer was ready to consort with the masters of the turf.

Not that by the new millennium Johnston required any further witness to his prowess as one of the nation's leading trainers. By the time Attraction entered his life, the adjective 'powerful' would automatically preface any mention of his yard.

It was not just that he was the fortuitous recipient of a filly blessed with such awesome raw speed but who could also stay a mile; it was that the Middleham trainer achieved so much with a charge that the Duke of Roxburghe once described to me as "fairly commonly bred but who turned out to be one of the best fillies of the century."

The 10th Duke of Roxburghe, one of Scotland's wealthiest landowners, who inherited his title and Floors Castle, the largest residence in Scotland, in 1974, was said to be a confidant of the Royal Family and it was at Floors Castle that Prince Andrew proposed to Sarah Ferguson. Apart from his stud he also owned a golf course, 65,600 acres of land and Kelso racecourse.

It did not appear a particularly auspicious mating when the Duke sent his mare Flirtation, by the high class sprinter-miler Pursuit Of Love, to Efisio, a Group 3-winning sprinter in England and a champion miler in Italy. As he explained: "we were looking for an inexpensive sire to get the mare started." That mating cost around £6,000.

The Duke told me of his memories of the filly's early days. "When she was a yearling, she was pretty incorrect in front," he said. "One knee, probably both knees, were off-set. So, as a sales prospect she was not a runner at all. I never considered taking her to the sales. Well, actually, I did show her to one of the sales agencies, and they said, 'Don't even think of selling her. She'll make nothing.'"

Suggesting that, had she been human she would quite possibly have qualified for a disability allowance, may be a slight overstating of her flaws. Nevertheless, she appeared to have scant future on the racetrack. "It came to the end of the sales season and I thought, 'What are we going to do with her?' The filly – she was still unnamed then – went up to Mark in January 2003, having been broken at John Hills' [Lambourn yard]." Johnston had trained for the Duke for around a decade by this time. "I simply told Mark: 'Look, I'm sending you this filly. She's pretty crooked. See if you can win a race with her – but I'm not sure she'll stand training.'"

Deirdre Johnston takes up the story. "Mark said to me: 'You ride her and tell me whether she's OK.' The minute I sat on her, I thought, 'Wow!' I told him: 'Find a race for that horse.' The feeling she gave me was just incredible. It was clear from very early on that she had an engine."

Johnston phoned the Duke in March 2003. "I told him: 'You'd better name this horse because she's going quite well.' He hadn't expected that. He'd sent her here with a target – win a race. He thought that was maybe quite a tall target in itself."

Attraction's debut was at Nottingham, in the lowest class of five-furlong maiden. She led over one furlong out, and won by five lengths. After another victory, at Thirsk, both her owner and trainer believed she was capable of acquiring some black type, and she headed for Beverley and the Hilary Needler Trophy, a race for juvenile fillies.

"The first time she ran, I don't think I had any particular expectations," recalled the Duke. "Mark just told me, 'She's going quite nicely, she's got a bit of ability. I haven't done an enormous amount with her. I don't want to stress her because of her legs'. Although she won that first race very easily, it was a pretty crap event. I didn't get too excited. Her breeding didn't suggest anything special. The dam was a non-winning mare [Flirtation had been unplaced in her only start at three], and although Efisio was a successful stallion, he was not one that was particularly well known."

The Duke did, however, start to allow himself rather more fanciful notions after the Hilary Needler. "It's a Listed race, and she absolutely hacked up," Johnston recalls. "It's normally regarded as a good Queen Mary trial. That was the first point when we knew we had something quite special."

There was one sour note about that victory. Attraction had been partnered by Keith Dalgleish, who had also ridden the filly on her debut. "Keith hit her when well clear," says her trainer. "But there's no question that the horse had been abused or it had done it any harm. The Duke of Roxburghe said to me: 'He's showing his inexperience – so I don't want him to ride her in the Queen Mary.' He was replaced by Kevin Darley, who kept the ride in her remaining 12 races.

The Duke had never had a Royal Ascot winner at that point. When I told him that Johnston did not envisage her getting beaten that day at the Royal meeting, the Duke laughed. "I don't think I was so certain," he said. "She started favourite, although there were some well-bred and expensive fillies in opposition."

The 'commoner' put those equine blue bloods in their place, scorching home by three lengths in the Group 3 test. She then won the Group 2 Cherry Hinton at Newmarket, stepping up to six furlongs in the process.

What was extraordinary was that the filly raced three times in just over a month, in a Listed and two Group races, and won them all. Through it all she had been kept sound, but such providence couldn't last. Attraction went lame. "The vets inspected her X-rays, compared them to earlier in the season, and found marked changes," the Duke recalled. "The advice was that she shouldn't run again; that we should retire her."

He added: "I actually got as far as starting to draft a press release to that effect. But Mark was brilliant. He said, 'Hang on a minute. Why don't we try to get her sound again and run her in the Cheveley Park [the Group 1 race at Newmarket in September]?' The idea was to coax her there by swimming her and keeping the stress off her legs."

But then she had an unrelated problem: The filly fractured her pedal-bone (the area where the foot joins the limb). With the wonderful benefit of hindsight, that was probably the best thing that could have happened to her. Attraction returned to the Duke's stud for eight weeks' box rest.

It all meant that Attraction had been off the track for nine months when she flew from the stalls at Newmarket on 2 May 2004 to lead the field of 16 in the 1,000 Guineas. It was an audacious strategy by her trainer. Again, one of his Guineas contenders had had no preparatory race. On those problematic front legs, she was also attempting two furlongs further than she'd raced as a two-year-old.

Now, for the first time, her rivals asked her serious questions. Under Kevin Darley's urgings, the filly answered them, with the 11-2 shot prevailing by half a length from runner-up Sundrop, one of Godolphin's three horses in the race. The sum of searing speed and a powerful gallop equalled a sixth straight win.

Johnston concedes: "The 1,000 Guineas at Newmarket was an incredible race and the culmination of a lot of heartache and worry during that winter. Jock Bennett, who had the filly in his yard from three, recalls "the trauma we had with her, trying to get her to the Guineas after that fracture to her pedal bone. Also, because she was so fast over six, I remember there was a long winter debate: 'Would she get the Guineas trip?' One lad used to ride her out, and he said, 'she'll get the trip all right', and she did." He adds of her character: "She was almost like a colt. She was tough. If I went into her box to feel her legs, and she didn't want me to…well, I didn't feel her legs. I just said to myself, 'you'll be fine'. She was a good eater, and always got to her racing weight, certainly between her two-year-old and three-year-old career."

Three weeks later Attraction completed a then unique double on an even more exacting track than Newmarket, defeating Alexander Goldrun in the Irish equivalent at The Curragh.

For Deirdre, though, it was the 2004 English Guineas that remains a gloriously colourful page in her mental scrapbook. "Although she'd not run after July the previous year, Attraction had finished her two-year-old season on such a high," she says. "There was all the worry about her knees through the winter. Then she fractured her pedal-bone. Was she going to run again, or wasn't she?

"We went through all that and just took her straight to the Guineas. Then it was: 'Is the ground going to be OK? Was it going to be fast enough for her? Was she going to be the horse she was before? Would she train on? Would she stay a mile, or should she stay at six furlongs?' It was all exciting. There were so many ifs and buts."

Deirdre adds: "Mark, Charlie and I were walking the course on the morning of the race, and picking the ground for her, and Charlie was saying: 'This is where she's going to win.' All those things I look back on and think, 'That's what makes it really special.' It was complete elation. The Irish Guineas was fantastic too, but the pressure was off because she'd already won the English one."

Her husband had never harboured anything but complete faith in the filly. "The Queen Mary was by far the biggest pressure," Johnston recalls. "I put it on myself. I really went there thinking: 'I'll be devastated if she gets beat.' But after that it was plain sailing. At the Guineas I went there believing that if she stays, she wins.

"You just looked down the racecard and this horse had five 1s next to its name, the last one being in the Cherry Hinton. And there's no question: if she stays a mile, she wins. There was nothing in the race with the class to beat her."

The same was true of the Coronation Stakes at Royal Ascot, an eighth successive triumph, and scintillating performance. The *Racing Post* form summary of the race said it all: "Made all, quickened clear 2f out, in no danger after, ridden out, impressive."

Even rival trainers eulogised over her achievements. Mick Channon, trainer of Majestic Desert, who finished runner-up to Attraction at Royal Ascot, placed her achievements in context with the words: "You probably won't see another horse like her in your lifetime." Johnston could only concur. "She wins her races by having an incredible cruising speed. She is really a very relaxed filly and I am not actually certain you can fire her up."

The trainer was considering the Breeders' Cup, at Lone Star Park, Texas in October as a possible target for his filly when two defeats by the James Fanshawe-trained Soviet Song, between which she finished last of ten at Deauville, caused a rethink of those plans.

But Attraction possessed supreme "bouncebackability", as one of our football managers once described his squad, and which has become a term frequently associated with the Johnston team, too, over the years. Before her three-year-old season was out she had secured another Group 1, the Sun Chariot Stakes at Newmarket.

The Group 1 Lockinge Stakes at Newbury might have been many trainers' option for the filly's first run as a four-year-old, but why should Johnston start to bow to convention now? He harboured the notion that the Champions Mile at Sha Tin should be her destination, not least because second place there was worth as much as victory in the Newbury race.

Attraction's remarkable story preceded her there. She had been deemed a 'freak' by the local media in Hong Kong, but in hot and humid conditions the Johnston filly never struck a blow and finished 11th of 13.

The omens were hardly portentous when the filly disappointed again in the Group 3 Hungerford Stakes at Newbury. One concert too many for the diva of the turf? With almost a sense of mischief her response was victory in what would transpire to be her valedictory performance, in the Group 1 Matron Stakes at Leopardstown. It was 10 September 2005, and she had made her final bow.

As Johnston had been preparing Attraction for another tilt at the Sun Chariot Stakes, Attraction was found to be very marginally lame. "But you can't be going into a Group 1 race with any sort of problems," her owner told the media. "We have taken a decision that the logical thing is to say we are not going to run and therefore retire her. It's nothing to do with her much-fabled action in front. She's just marginally lame behind."

This time, the press communiqué from the Duke Of Roxburghe went ahead. It included the words: "That is the end of her career, I'm afraid. Obviously, it's very sad, but maybe in some ways I'm rather relieved."

Costing 6,000gns, Attraction's career concluded with ten victories, including five Group 1s, from 15 starts and lifetime earnings of just under £900,000 – and far, far more in terms of what it meant to her owner-breeder, both in future breeding terms, and the emotional impact of those three exhilarating years. They would have been nothing less than life-transforming for the majority of us. But did they mean quite the same to the owner of a Scottish pile?

The Duke swiftly disabuses you of such a notion. "I think it probably was a life-changing event for me too," he told me. "Not too many people have a horse that is champion two-year-old filly in Europe, and then to go out and win three Group 1s on the trot, including two Classics."

He added: "Don't forget, it has been an era of fantastic fillies, too: Ouija Board, Alexander Goldrun, Soviet Song. Those three fillies and Attraction have won 21 Group 1s between them. Three of them are from the same generation."

What made it all the more remarkable was that she defied all equine physiological logic to achieve what she did. Which begged the question: could anyone but Johnston have achieved it, given the circumstances? Not just because of his veterinary expertise, but his perseverance.

"I'm not sure the veterinary factor was anything to do with it," reflected the Duke, who, throughout, had accepted triumph with appreciation and defeat with stoicism. "But I think, without any shadow of doubt, that what she achieved in her first season and latterly achieved in her second season was, in huge measure, down to him. He has a very cavalier – perhaps that's a bit too strong a word, but you understand what I mean – attitude to training. He gets his horses very fit. Once they're fit, he wants them at the racecourse as often as they can."

He added: "I think it's his ability as a trainer rather than his veterinary experience. I think the fact that he was a vet probably was quite useful when it came to the dramas we had with her between two and three. He was able to take a more sanguine attitude than maybe another trainer, who would possibly have taken the straightforward view of the vets and accepted it. To win the Guineas after nine months off was quite fantastic. That was the most exciting day of my life. It's a great testament to him and his staff."

Johnston analyses it all in purely rational terms. "When you get one with questionable front legs, your job as a trainer is just to keep her sound," he says. "But it did surprise us all that she stayed sound so long. She had plenty of problems with them. Her legs obviously hurt her at times. But she was the sort of horse that coped with it.

"We had many excuses not to run her, on many occasions, like just before the Coronation Stakes. She could be lame on the Thursday and run on Saturday. It's the main difference between a good and a bad racehorse, and the same with human athletes, probably. They don't stop when they're tired; don't stop when it hurts. There was an element of throwing caution to the wind in those early days. But then we learned that she could cope with it. In many ways, she was an incredibly easy horse to train."

Deirdre adds: "I rode her at two. I rode her before she ever ran, and saddled her for her first race. I rode her, on and off, through all her career, although I was actually relieved not to be riding her out all through her Group 1 wins, because there's quite a lot of pressure on you when you're riding a horse like that.

"But I would often sit on her when they thought she had a problem. I often do that when somebody's not happy with them, when they can't make them trot or they're worried whether they're sound or lame, or whatever. And we had that a few times with Attraction.

"She was a real character. She wouldn't let anyone catch her in the box. She had her own mind and she knew exactly what she liked and what she didn't like. Yet, she was brilliant when she went to the races. She was so laid back. You never had to worry about her in parades or anything. Before the race she'd just have a good snooze, then she'd get up and go. Anyone could get near her when you were saddling her. The kids would come in and pat her and she'd just stand there. The only time to watch her, though, was when you put the jockey up. Then she might kick you. But that's great – I like attitude like that!"

It must be said that trainers aren't always blessed with such owners as The Duke of Roxburghe, who died in 2019, aged 64.

Black type and the prospect of mega-money, in prizes and later in parenthood, have been known to persuade owners to cash in and sell their asset – not a decision, as will be seen later, Johnston decries in any way.

Johnston and Deirdre were always slightly surprised that there was never a serious approach for Attraction, though that's probably because after she won the Queen Mary she was never for sale.

The trainer recalls: "Before virtually every race the Duke would say: 'It's just another race. Let's not worry about it. This is everything we've dreamt of. This would be a bonus.' He took any defeat on the chin and just got on with it."

There were mixed emotions when Attraction left the yard for good. "She lived across from our bedroom window," says Deirdre. "First thing in the morning and last thing at night when I went to bed, I could see her. When she went to stud, fit and well, without having an injury, there was great relief. She had done all that racing yet she was in great condition. I was both sad and happy."

She adds: "We didn't really want a big send-off because we would have found it very hard. We just wanted her to go quietly; almost not know she was going."

Following her retirement, there would be thorns among the bouquets of plaudits. It wasn't the first occasion that the reputation of one of Johnston's outstanding horses was diminished in some quarters.

The *Racing Post's* "Flat Horses of 2005" suggested that "even in her Classic season she did not hit the heights sometimes claimed for her. Hers was not a vintage generation of fillies."

As has already been stressed, Johnston has long grown weary of comparisons between horses of different generations, and instead restricts himself to the following: "What she achieved was more than we could have imagined for any horse, let alone one with dodgy legs. It was fantastic that Shamardal came along while Attraction was still here. To have two horses like that at the same time, both free-running and front-running, was remarkable."

He adds: "Between 1994 and 1997 we had five Group 1 winners; Attraction did that by herself. She did what all those horses did rolled into one."

She left behind a trainer's wife who has seen thousands of horses come and go through the gates of Kingsley House, but who can still become moist-eyed at mention of an equine 'Special One'.

* * *

Attraction departed Kingsley House in 2005 for a liaison with Ouija Board's sire, Cape Cross. It was a moment imbued with both sadness and pride for the trainer and his family.

Not that it was the last Deirdre saw of Attraction. "I was desperately keen to compete at the Duke's horse trials, at Floors Castle," says a woman whose equine interests extend far beyond riding out. "When I went up, she'd just come back from stud, where she'd been covered by Cape Cross, and there she was, galloping around the field. It was just fantastic to see her looking so well, ready to have her first foal the following year."

That foal was a filly named Elation, who remained in the ownership of the Duke Of Roxburghe, and won a maiden at Lingfield easily for Johnston, but succumbed to grass sickness and died.

The longer-term postscript to Attraction's departure to her new life as a broodmare was that she was introduced to some exalted male company.

Three times her progeny have been sold for prices in excess of £1m; twice when the sire was the undefeated, prodigiously-gifted Frankel. On the other occasion, she was covered by Dubawi, a Godolphin colt, undefeated as a two-year-old and the 2005 Irish 2,000 Guineas winner, who has proved an exceptional sire.

The first of these sons of Frankel was named Elarqam by the buyers Sheikh Hamdan's Shadwell Estate, who had paid 1.6m guineas for the privilege. He was consigned to Middleham. For the Johnston yard, it could be said to be heaven-sent, manna from Hamdan.

Expectations of Classic potential had been heightened as a juvenile when Elarqam's first two races in September 2017 produced two facile victories. The latter, the Group 3 Tattersalls Stakes at Newmarket, had propelled the colt to second favourite for the 2,000 Guineas.

When we spoke in April 2018, Johnston could barely conceal his sense of anticipation, though he conceded: "Every time I say things like 'imagine what a stallion this would be?' Deidre tells me to 'shut up! Stop tempting fate.'"

He added: "He doesn't have the racecourse form, but he's bred for it – by a Guineas winner out of a Guineas winner. It's a pedigree amongst pedigrees. They simply don't come better. I've never had a horse bred like this that cost this sort of money. To get him was just fantastic. There was no horse in the world that I'd rather have had to train. He was clearly number one.

"Win or lose [in the Guineas], there'll be a lot more races to come from him, hopefully. All the indications are that he's better than last year. He's grown brilliantly, he's shown more speed and versatility.

"Attraction's had a lot of winners, had a previous Group winner, before this, and is already a very good mare, but people are very hard on champion race mares. They expect them to produce champions overnight. Of course, that rarely happens. Odds against it are so great. For her to get a Group 1 winner – that would be a crowning glory." And, understandably, provide an emotion-charged moment for the Johnston family.

Dreams turned to reality, albeit a very decent reality. Deirdre had been quite correct to remain circumspect. Elarqam would not emulate his father and mother, both Guineas victors. The colt finished fourth in the 2,000 Guineas, and sixth in the Irish equivalent, though he would proceed to secure Group 2 and 3 victories and be placed in the Group 1 International Stakes at York before going off to stud. He covered his first mares in 2021.

"CASH OUT WHEN YOU CAN" ON TALENTED HORSES

O ver the years, the yearling consignments from the Maktoum family and their operations have been a boon to the Johnston operation. But there can be a downside. If a horse performs with distinction, they can be transferred to the Godolphin fold. Shamardal would not be the only horse to depart Middleham for the Newmarket stable of Godolphin trainer Saeed bin Suroor after an undefeated sequence of three victories as a juvenile, culminating in his Group 1 Dewhurst Stakes triumph, but he is manifestly unparalleled in sheer quality that Johnston has trained.

Shamardal had been one of the horses consigned by Gainsborough Stud Management in 2003, having cost 50,000gns. One of Johnston's assistants, Andrew Bottomley, a 'lifer' as he wryly terms his near 20-year career at the stables, during which time he was a yard manager, views Shamardal as "the best horse in my time." And he should know. "He was in my yard. From his first gallop, to his first run, to winning the Dewhurst, you just knew he was something special."

He adds: "I saw him do a gallop on the High Moor. People in racing talk about Nashwan working [a gallop at West Ilsley ahead of his 2,000 Guineas triumph which had the work-watchers running to back him, and the bookies running for cover] and this was one of those gallops of a lifetime, too. It was unbelievable.

"When they jumped off, I thought 'Jesus, he's going far too fast'. All of a sudden, you saw this horse forge about ten clear in the space of two strides, and the lad that rode him that day, Joe O'Gorman [now assistant to Middleham trainer Karl Burke], told me that when the horse kicked off, he nearly did a somersault backwards off it – with the force of it going forward.' And from going flat out, he kicked again." By all accounts, it was like a Formula 1 driver operating DRS to aid overtaking.

"He went to Ayr about two weeks later, and won by, what, eight lengths before winning the Vintage Stakes and Dewhurst. He went to Godolphin after that, and he was a superstar there, but we nurtured him here."

The move to Godolphin hadn't been exactly a bolt to the boys in blue, so to speak, but it had still been a critical loss for Johnston. Instead of being readied for the 2,000 Guineas at Middleham – for which he was at one stage 3-1 favourite – the colt wintered in the United Arab Emirates, in preparation for the UAE Derby at Nad Al Sheba, a stopover before the onward flight to the ultimate destination: Bluegrass Country and a tilt at the Kentucky Derby.

In the event, the latter never occurred because the Frankie Dettori-partnered Shamardal took a pummelling from the opposition at Nad Al Sheba, causing plans to be reviewed. However, Shamardal went on to claim the Poule D'Essai Des Poulains (French 2,000 Guineas), Prix Du Jockey Club (French Derby) and St James's Palace Stakes before being retired to stud. He died in 2020, aged 18.

It must be added there had been handsome compensation for Johnston's staff when Shamardal departed. "There was a big bonus, a hundred grand, shared between everybody in the yard," Bottomley recalls.

Though it was a significant loss for Johnston, he is far from being the only trainer to have potential glory seized from his grasp, and he is phlegmatic about such moments. You could view it as the price of training them just too well? "Nobody wants to lose such a grand horse, but we all know that's the name of the game," he says.

There have also been horses owned by his other patrons sold out of the yard to join Sheikh Mohammed's battalion. The previously-mentioned Winged Cupid, who cost 9,000gns, was bought by Godolphin after finishing runner-up in a Group 1 event at Doncaster.

At the time, he had high expectations for the colt, and told me: "Winged Cupid would be the horse I regret losing more than anything this season. He's my Derby favourite at the moment. On the other hand, you have to advise the owners to sell. Bids often come in for our good horses. I negotiate them."

In fact, Winged Cupid raced only four more times, winning a Listed race at Windsor, and died at the age of five. Such decisions can be finely balanced.

"Mister Baileys was nearly sold at the end of his two-year-old career," Johnston once told me. "Thank goodness he wasn't. Double Trigger was also nearly sold at one stage. But for every one like that, there's two that could have been sold for far more than they're worth now. As soon as the offer gets to the stage of what it's going to be worth after it wins its next race, if they're giving you its potential value, then you *have* to take it."

He adds: "Once you get over a million, you're into stallion value.

That's what the horse is going to be worth at the end of his career; so, if you get those sorts of figures for any horse during its racing career, you've *got* to sell."

The trainer emphasises his point further: "You have to ask your owner of a good horse: 'What's your dream? To win the Guineas or the Derby?' But even if he does that, it won't be worth any more than it is now. And if he doesn't, it'll be worth a tenth of what it's worth now. We're going back a few years now, but Mister Baileys was eventually sold for £1.4 million. Bijou D'Inde, our 2,000 Guineas third and St James's Palace Stakes winner, was going to be sold for a million. But the deal fell through, and he was later sold for less after a brief career at stud."

Johnston adds: "But if you've bought a horse for ten grand and won the Guineas with him, you'd probably be lucky to get a million. So, if you can get a million for him when he's won his maiden and a Listed or a Group race, then for God's sake take it. The danger is, if you don't, he's going to be worth twenty grand again one day."

For Johnston, 'cashing out' is a no-brainer for the small owner of a talented horse attracting interest from the moneyed bloodstock elite – particularly in Britain where the rewards for winning races, for all but the most prestigious contests, are still relatively modest compared with the costs involved. The trainer encourages his owners not to be seduced by romantic possibilities of what may be around the corner.

It's rather reminiscent of *Take Your Pick*, the first UK TV gameshow to offer cash prizes. At the climax, winning contestants could either 'take the money' or 'open the box'. They could keep their winnings or take the chance of winning a holiday – or possibly the booby prize, like a mousetrap or bag of sweets. With horses, you seize the moment and take the money – or open the box. It could turn out to be Group 1 class. The chances are that it won't.

Celtic Silence was another horse that left the stable to join the Godolphin elite corps, after just two races. Seemingly with a propitious future ahead, having won the 2000 Chesham at Royal Ascot for Peter Savill, when trained by Johnston. He moved to Godolphin and finished second to Dilshaan in the Dante Stakes, but failed to make the Derby because of injury. He spent the remainder of his career racing in Dubai, but never won another race.

"A lot of people were trying to wind me up and get me to criticise Peter Savill for selling that horse. They were saying, 'Peter Savill doesn't need the money. He shouldn't sell the horse. He should leave it with you.' But he was right to sell it."

Johnston believes that the best analogy is a small football club under pressure to sell its star player. "We are only 'the managers'," he once told me. "Better to sell that one superstar and upgrade the other ten. That gives them a better chance of continuing to compete at the highest level."

He added: "Racing's not sensible in Britain any other way. Some people are so rich they can afford to take multi-million-pound racehorses and race them for five-figure prize money. But most people can't, and shouldn't, be doing that. If a horse acquires a seven-figure value, for the owner to say 'I'm going to keep it and race it for five-figure prize money' is just plain stupid. You must sell it to someone who can really afford to do it. British owners are not racing for prize money. British owners are racing for re-sell value.

"I haven't ever had an owner sell a horse for big money and regret it, regardless of what the horse goes on to do afterwards. I've had plenty not sell and regret it. I'd say 90 per cent are now not worth what they were sold for.

"There are loads of them. There was Love You Always, a horse of Mick Doyle's, which won unbelievably impressively at Hamilton.

Sheikh Mohammed bought it after one run. That turned out to be disappointing. Inevitably, Godolphin have had their failures too. Sheikh Mohammed knows when he buys a horse that has run, it is like buying yearlings. There are no guarantees."

WHEN EXPECTATION
TURNS TO DESPAIR

"There are no guarantees" – not when it comes to racehorse ownership. That phrase couldn't help but return to me when, in 2006, I visited Johnston shortly after the death of his Classic-placed colt Shalapour, who had collapsed and died on the gallops.

How swiftly can the thrill of witnessing the majesty of a racehorse at work or at full speed on the racecourse, turn to distress. The four-year-old had been third in the Irish Derby the previous year, having been bred and owned by the Aga Khan and trained by John Oxx.

He had only recently made his debut for his new yard, having been bought by owner Markus Graff but, disconcertingly, had been beaten at 6-1 on at Southwell a few days previously.

"He just cantered up, walked off the gallops, went 50 or 100 yards, started to stagger and keeled over," Johnston told the media. "It was one of those things, no drama, and it could have happened at any time. Kevin Dalgleish was on him – Keith's brother. He jumped off before the horse went down. We haven't had the result of the post-mortem yet, but it's most likely a heart problem or a ruptured aorta."

A sudden death like that, or a horse having to be put down after injury is a rare, but inescapable fact of stable life. Not just on the National Hunt fields of conflict, but on the Flat racecourse too, and on the gallops.

The power of a half-ton thoroughbred is transmitted through limbs that are rendered remarkably frail if they encounter a hazard. Sometimes the heart simply fails them, as it almost certainly did in the case of Shalapour.

According to the Form Book, the official explanation given after the Southwell race (a long odds-on shot being turned over would normally be considered suspicious, to say the least) by Johnston was this: "The trainer was unable to offer any explanation for poor form shown."

Trainers must report anything which might have adversely affected the race performance of any horse they train. "So, slightly tongue in cheek," said Johnston, and with a touch of gallows humour. "After Shalapour died, we did phone the Jockey Club and told them, 'We were asked if there was anything to explain its poor performance when it got beat at Southwell when it was 6-1 on. Well, there is. It's dead.' The fellow who answered told me drily, 'We don't need to know that.'"

"You actually phoned to tell them that?" you ask him with an expression of faux outrage. "You're supposed to," he said. "If something comes to light, at the time or afterwards, that might explain the bad run."

On a more serious note, even for a veterinarian and experienced trainer who has witnessed such moments before, it can be a devastating experience. Indeed, one of Johnston's worst memories surrounds the death of his horse Eldorado at Leopardstown in August 1997.

He wrote in his *Horse & Hound* column at the time:

"I remember the delight of winning my first Group 1 race in Ireland and my first Group 1 ever with a two-year-old when Princely Heir landed the Heinz 57 Phoenix Stakes. And I will remember the horror of losing Eldorado, my only Classic hope for this year.

Eldorado had completely ruptured his superficial flexor tendon and the suspensory apparatus (the system of tendons and ligaments which allows the limb to bear weight) was collapsing. Repair is impossible and the degree of pain and suffering involved could not be justified. Eldorado was put down very soon after the race.

Thankfully such injuries are extremely rare. The vast majority of injuries that we see are minor, and fatalities are few and far between. Injuries will always occur in this sport where highly tuned equine athletes compete with an inherent desire to run that human athletes could never emulate."

In more recent times, Johnston witnessed his talented Mister Monet having to be put down after Kevin Darley pulled him up six furlongs out in the 2004 Champion Stakes at Newmarket.

The reality is that most racehorses still have an easier death than most humans, I contended, recalling that tears had flowed, understandably, after the death of Best Mate, the triple Cheltenham Gold Cup winner and, arguably the most popular national hunt horse since Desert Orchid, in November 2005. Yet, there was no prolonged agony when he collapsed at Exeter. The light was extinguished quickly.

The trainer returned to my observation, comparing the death of humans with horses. "My father died, aged sixty-five. Snap. Just like that. You think at times, 'What a waste, what an age to go at, what a way to go.'"

He recalls that day in 1993 because it was the day his first Arab-owned horse, Pearl Kite, won at York. "He saw us win the Ebor, and have our first Group winners. He missed out on Mister Baileys' Guineas and the meteoric rise, although it was a pretty big rise from '87 to '93. By '93 this place was full and we had ten horses up the road in another stables. So, we had 80 horses."

He adds: "My mother, on the other hand, was in hospital, dying for maybe two or three weeks, mostly unconscious, with a morphine pump. You think, 'Rather his unexpected death.' The same applies to racehorses. They drop dead, doing their job." He asks rhetorically "That's fine, isn't it?"

Or are put down, after a leg fracture. It is an act which many of those not involved in the sport cannot always comprehend and, indeed, in these times of social media, they tweet often uninformed and, at their worst, ignorant, views.

This would be exemplified in 2017, after his outstanding colt Permian, winner of the Dante Stakes and King Edward VII Stakes after starting out in handicaps, was put down after he shattered his left foreleg after crossing the line in the Secretariat Stakes at Arlington Park, Illinois, USA. Charlie, representing his father, took the decision quickly and had no other option.

It was an horrific incident which left Mark and Charlie being trolled on social media; the father for having "over-raced" the Sheikh Mohammed-owned Permian, who was having his eighth race of the year; and his son for being quoted that he had spent "30 seconds" with the stricken horse before he was put to sleep – the implication being that it was callous to have spent so little time with him, rather than merciful to have made the decision so quickly.

Charlie later explained in the *Kingsley Klarion*: "I was quoted as having said I was 'with him for 30 seconds' when in fact I had said I was there '*within* 30 seconds'." He added that this was a moot point, anyway. "As soon as I saw the horse, I knew there was only one option. There was no decision to be made, no grey area. I phoned Dad and said: 'he has to go, and he has to go now' [rather than remove him to the stables]. It was the only humane thing we could do for the horse.

"It is always a distressing situation when a horse suffers a catastrophic injury and, in this case, it was horrible to see a horse that we had all become so fond of, and grown so attached to, over the previous 18 months, end his career like that. But I had no problem in standing there as he was put down as I knew it was the best and only option for Permian.

"I am upset that the negative comments on Twitter gained more coverage than the fact Permian had been a fantastic racehorse. He rose from mediocrity this season with his ability, courage and thirst for racing capturing the imagination of many. I will remember him for the very special days he gave us this year, and not for the irrelevant things said after his death."

His father was quoted in the *Racing Post* as saying: "Social media was fantastic for seeing all of the condolences coming in but there were also bastards blaming us for giving him one run too many. Aidan O'Brien's horse who finished second [Taj Mahal, who would race 11 times in 2017] had more runs than Permian, as Aidan's commonly do, because he, like me, believes in racing them."

This is an area, veterinary ethics, if you like, in which Johnston maintains a profoundly held belief: that you cannot repair or treat equines with irreparable injuries and untreatable conditions, or provide them with a life worth living, as you would with humans, and the swifter they are despatched the better.

He once told me of shooting one of his sons' ponies: "I'd heard them talking about how it was ill, and had this and that. Deirdre and I debated what we were going to do with it. We were going to get the knacker-man. But I said: 'I'll deal with it.' I drove up the road and I could see it from about 200 yards away, and there it was, grazing. Standing there eating grass, looking as happy as Larry. I thought: 'What am I doing, coming to kill this wee boy?'

"But then I went towards it, and he had a big, bowed tendon. It had Cushing's Disease, big hairy legs and it had hair falling out on its face. I had no problem with it. None whatsoever. Like all the others, I just thought, 'Best thing.' I didn't miss a moment's sleep over it."

He adds: "When I look back at my career, when I was in vet practice, I got a jokey reputation among friends of being a bit trigger-happy. I got accused at times of playing God. It's a fine line, but I think it's part of the vet's job to take responsibility away from the owner.

"People talk about giving a pet, a semi-pet like a horse, 'its best chance'. But so long as the vet keeps telling them there's a chance, even if it's only 25 per cent, 40, 50 per cent, that owner continues to feel obliged to give that animal 'that chance'. What is not weighed up against it is the pain it will have to go through.

Johnston, who has a firearm certificate and owns a humane killer pistol designed for euthanasia of horses but says he has not used it for over ten years, adds: "The owner suffers along with their animal, and there is such relief when someone comes along and says, 'The best thing you can do for your animal is put it out of its misery.' If you've got an animal suffering, you get a fantastic sense of relief from ending it. The faster you can do it the better.

A thing with a leg hanging off or something – it's such a relief to hear the bang."

It becomes apparent such beliefs were formed almost as a reaction to his parents' attitudes. "It goes back to when I was seven or eight," Johnston says. "My parents weren't like that. My father definitely wasn't like that. He was desperately emotional about his animals, to a fault. He was very much one of these people that, as a vet, I certainly didn't like working with: people who would keep animals through thick and thin, trying to keep them alive, thinking they were doing them some wonderful service. I don't approve of that. If an animal died, he'd go off on a bender and literally drink for two or three days because he was so upset."

He adds: "I was maybe so influenced by that; that I reacted against it. Like every farmer and commercial animal keeper, you have to understand that where there's life, there's death. If you hide yourself from it, you're not going to be good at keeping animals."

Once on the subject of animal welfare, there's no restraining the Scot. He told me a few years ago: "To me, one of the most misguided people in public life who talks about animal welfare is Paul McCartney. I mean, can you believe he sings songs about wanting to see sheep in the field?"

The advocacy of McCartney and his late wife Linda of vegetarianism and animal rights meant that the animals on his sheep farm died a 'natural' death. "We shear the sheep, but they die of old age," the former Beatle declared on BBC Radio 4 in 2013. "But it can be embarrassing. People say, 'Look at the state of your sheep!' And I say, 'Yes, they're very old. There's only one alternative – to send them off to the knacker's yard. They just die like we do. It's life, it's death, it's what happens. We just give them a good life and I take the wool from them."

Johnston has told me: "I've got no problem with people having pets. They're doing a job. A cat or dog is being a companion for its owner, and it's usually well looked after, too. But I cannot go along with the Paul McCartney school of thought which teaches about having sheep or cows in a field but not for a purpose.

"My feeling is that cruelty mostly exists wherever you have animals kept without any purpose. Cruelty in Britain is 99.9 per cent ignorance or lack of money. I don't like to see animals kept by people who are ignorant of their needs or who can't afford them."

* * *

Animal welfare was again at the fore just before the completion of this book when the BBC broadcast a *Panorama* programme, titled: 'The Dark Side of Horseracing'.

It claimed that around 4,000 thoroughbreds had been slaughtered in abattoirs since 2019, and brought into focus the fate of horses when they are retired from racing or injured. The programme included harrowing scenes captured by hidden cameras set up by campaign group Animal Aid at an abattoir in Wiltshire.

Johnston has developed a scepticism towards television 'exposes' of horseracing and, indeed of other subjects. In his 'Bletherings' (his comment section on the Johnston Racing website) he opined: "It was only through having some inside knowledge of the subjects being covered that I came to realise how inaccurate and sensationalist many television documentaries are."

Notably, back in 1991, and just as Johnston was in the gestation period of his own career at Middleham, *The Cook Report* (presented by investigative journalist Roger Cook) broadcast its programme on another renowned record-breaker and a man the Scot greatly admires, Martin Pipe.

The *Racing Post*'s Steve Dennis wrote in a feature article on Pipe in 2017: "With success, inevitably, came suspicion. Who was this hick from the sticks winning all these races? ITV made a programme in its *Cook Report* strand that basically accused Pipe of every dodgy practice short of witchcraft, and although there was no foundation to the insinuations they wounded Pipe deeply."

The Times's Rob Wright, reflecting on the west country trainer in 2020, wrote: "Pipe was subjected to a savaging by the *Cook Report* on ITV in 1991, in which he was accused of cruelty to his horses, along with much insinuation as to the ethics of his training techniques. The truth, though, was that Pipe was just getting his horses fitter than anyone else, knew precisely when they were healthy enough to do themselves justice, and ran them in the right races."

So, when I raised this latest 'expose' of the sport, it came as no great surprise to discover that Johnston had viewed it as "another sensationalist documentary" and "an issue that basically had nothing to do with horseracing." He added: "It was an exposé of illegal and unacceptable practices in a single abattoir, where a very small percentage of the horses are thoroughbreds." I put it to him that the programme's concentration on thoroughbreds was not entirely coincidental, given the involvement of Animal Aid, a group whose objectives include: "We want to see an end to all horse racing, because it is an intrinsically cruel and exploitative industry."

Admitting he found scenes captured by cameras installed by Animal Aid as "abhorrent", Johnston added: "Their focus on retired thoroughbreds, and who had previously owned and trained them, rather than shires or Shetland ponies, was completely ludicrous."

Later, discussing what happens to his horses when they move on, Johnston told the *Racing Post*: "The vast, vast majority are sold on to do another job, many of them remaining in racing. Nowadays, a high percentage of the females are going into the breeding industry. The majority of ours go to the sales if they're not retired to the breeding industry and an awful lot do enter other jobs." He added: "I think we're blowing this out of proportion. There is not a major animal welfare issue in the UK and of the issues there are, horses would be a small percentage. Of the animal welfare issues in horses, thoroughbreds would be a tiny percentage but clearly it's good for selling tabloid newspapers and sensationalist TV programmes."

THE LAST LION ROARS FOR JOHNSTON AND FANNING

Horseracing and gambling are historic and necessary partners. The sport began with owners of thoroughbreds matching their best horses and wagering on the outcome.

Furthermore, betting revenue remains crucial to the sport and is part of its funding. Bookmakers pay a percentage of their gross profits on bets on British horseracing to the Levy, which the government reformed in 2017 to extend to operators based overseas who had previously not contributed. The bulk of Levy income is distributed as prize money.

But suspicion will always abound. Generations of readers of Dick Francis novels have been brought up with the belief that behind every well-backed victory, and, indeed, every high-profile defeat, there are nefarious minds at work – though such cases in question are a minute as a proportion of the number of races run annually under both codes.

The fact is that betting companies are quick to cry 'foul' at anything untoward they observe in betting patterns, and the BHA will also scrutinise anything appearing untoward.

It should be stressed that under the BHA's Rules of Racing, the trainer, owner and jockey of a horse must not lay a bet on it to lose – nor can they instruct another person to do so, or receive any proceeds from such a bet. Jockeys are completely banned from betting on horseracing; trainers can back horses, but not lay one in their charge. Owners can back their own horses, but not lay them.

Although that wouldn't deter anyone absolutely determined to breach those constraints, Mark Johnston will offer a derisive response to those who believe that those 'in the know' are amassing a fortune from gambling on racehorses. In a *Racing Post* article he wrote in 2000, Johnston quoted some lines from the Fleetwood Mac classic "Tell Me Lies".

"That was," he opined, "a great song that I used to listen to a lot. But I didn't think until just the other day that the composer may have had horseracing, and in particular punters, in mind when he wrote those lines, rather than cheating lovers. It seems that some people just don't want to hear the truth no matter how many times you tell them, and this affliction seems to affect those that follow horseracing more than other sections of the population.

"But, what the hell, here goes again. I'll try once more to explain some of the realities of training and placing horses and to dispel the myth that every trainer, jockey and stable lad has millions in ill-gotten gambling gains stashed under the bed and simply chooses to work a minimum of 12 hours a day in all sorts of weather out of some form of mass masochism.

"I have said before, and I'll say again, that if you want to be a successful punter, you must study the form. The vast majority of reliable form is established on the racecourse, not on the gallops, and the information is there in the *Racing Post* for you all to see."

Johnston has never been a gambling trainer. "It doesn't really interest me," he once told me. "It doesn't give me much of a thrill.

I have the occasional bet – mostly when I'm insulted by the odds offered against my horse!"

Another popular belief is that gambling is the major source of racing income. Not so, according to Johnston. "The punter likes to think he pays my wages, but he doesn't. Three-quarters (76 per cent) of my wages come from my owners. Their return, on average in Britain, is 24 per cent, not counting the capital they've put into the horses. That's simply prize money against running costs."

Johnston has long been insistent that prize money should be increased, and is not alone in that conviction amongst his counterparts. Should that come from punters? "No, I don't think we should take more off them," he told me. "But I do think a greater percentage of the bookies' deduction should come to make sure the sport survives, as it does in most other major racing nations. When it comes to prize money, we're still languishing way down at the bottom of the scale."

Prize money is an age-old issue which ricochets around any discussion of horseracing like a pinball. Johnston may be correct in his assertion, but you can hardly visualise the storming of No. 10 Downing Street by a concerned public on behalf of poor, impecunious racehorse owners.

The reality is that, no matter what the prize money, there will always be prospective owners, you contend. "Thankfully," said Johnston, adding: "For people who have been very successful and can seemingly have everything they want, who can buy success, it gives them competition. They can buy success in certain areas but they can't buy it in horseracing. It gives them a new challenge. An uncertainty. They think they've got a lot of money and can spend a hundred grand on a horse, and then they find there's a guy out there who can spend £1.6million." Or, in the case of Sheikh Mohammed, many millions. Two years ago, he spent 3.6m guineas at Tattersalls on a yearling by Dubawi out of the mare Alina, whose father is the great Galileo.

Johnston adds: "Some of them do [place bets] because they enjoy backing their horses, but quite honestly, the vast majority of my owners did not come into it because of the betting. Some did. If you look at someone like Sir Alex Ferguson, he had an interest in betting before he had an interest in owning a racehorse. I do have a number of owners like that. But they're very much in the minority, and that's old money and new money.

"The Duke of Roxburghe [who owned Attraction] didn't come into it because he liked a bet; Sheikh Mohammed certainly didn't. Even a lot of owners who do like a bet came into it because they like racehorses and they like competition between racehorses. Brian Palmer came into it and ended up buying half a racing stable, yet he hardly had a bet. He had no interest whatsoever in that. He had reached a peak in his own business where he didn't get the same kick or thrill out of it. That's what horseracing gave him.

"You get people like Stuart Morrison, who owned Quick Ransom and Bijou D'Inde, who do come into it because their first interest is betting. But they lose all that interest. It's inevitable when you're taking Bijou D'Inde to race for two hundred and fifty grand in prize money, and five hundred grand up or down in the value of the horse.

"It's one of the reasons we've been successful. If you find a trainer where the majority of the owners' principal objective is betting, then he's probably not been very successful. I wouldn't for a second suggest that there are a lot of gambling yards, because there aren't. But when I first came to Middleham there were all these stories in the pub about horses being 'not off'. And then, when it is 'off', it gets beat. It's an absolute mug's game.

"There are a lot of myths about the amount of gambling there is behind the scenes among 'insiders' in the racing industry, whether they be trainers, owners or stable staff. It goes right up to the level of J. P. McManus and Michael Tabor. Maybe they bet huge amounts, I don't know. But I don't really think they make their living at it."

One of Johnston's owners, the former William Hill chairman John Brown, exemplifies his idea of the perfect patron. "He's a fantastic owner because he doesn't expect me to know how his horse is going to run," Johnston told me. "John made a fortune out of the fact that trainers don't know how their horses are going to run. And neither do jockeys, and neither do punters. All I know is that there's still a lot more bookmakers driving Rolls-Royces than stable hands."

It can be firmly stated that John Brown definitely hadn't expected his colt The Last Lion to add another Group 1 to the Johnston roll of honour when the 25-1 chance captured the 2016 Middle Park Stakes at Newmarket. It was a front-running performance into a headwind that had Robin Oakley, the former BBC political editor and *The Spectator*'s Turf writer commending in his column as "the training performance of the season."

He added: "They don't stock much cotton wool at Kingsley House Stables: what was remarkable was that this was the two-year-old's tenth race in a season that began with his victory in the Brocklesby Stakes at Doncaster, the first of the season's meaningful tests for quality two-year-olds." Only in two of those ten contests, when he was third, had The Last Lion finished out of the first two.

It was also a first Group 1 victory for jockey Joe Fanning, then aged 46. He has been attached to the stable since his apprentice days. In the summer of 1991, Fanning, who would become the stable stalwart, had ridden his first winner for Johnston in a selling race (the lowest class of event) at Catterick, but he was some years from assuming his later close relationship with the yard; one that has produced more than 1,350 winners from more than 8,300 rides, at the time of writing.

The Last Lion was something of a rarity for Johnston, whose name has seldom been synonymous with precocious Brocklesby-type juveniles. "I want big, imposing horses. If you go out there [in the yard], they're all big. Or the vast majority of them are." It is true. Almost without exception, Johnston horses have magnitude and, just as importantly, scope. As one television pundit expressed it excellently, "You always feel as though the Johnston horses have been standing in Gro-Bags."

The Last Lion never raced as a three-year-old and instead was retired to stud. He sired several winners, but in 2021 returned to Middleham as a seven-year-old. "He's infertile," explains Johnston. "He's been gelded and he's back in training."

ESTABLISHING A NEW WINNER RECORD

Since 2009, Mark Johnston has existed in a rarefied existence of statistical abundance, from which he has rarely descended. The stable has accumulated more than 200 winners a season in nine years; the only three exceptions being 2011, 2016 and 2020 (when a significant number of meetings were cancelled because of Covid restrictions).

Even five-times champion John Gosden has never achieved that with his British runners. Richard Hannon Snr achieved the feat in the last four years of his career, and son Richard Jnr did in his first year when he was champion. But Johnston stands apart in terms of prolificity.

He has also been consistently among the leaders in the trainers' table, but the championship has always eluded him because it is based on prize money won, not winners. Essentially, he does not receive the best horses consigned by Arab owners – and even if he did, he would still have to contend with Aidan O'Brien and the Coolmore operation in Ireland.

However, as the number of his winners continued to rise, Johnston was well aware as his horses contested Glorious Goodwood in 2018 that the all-time record for total British winners was tantalisingly close to his grasp.

This Glorious Goodwood provided further testament to his purchasing skills. The *Racing Post* reported: "Trainer Mark Johnston's renowned eye for a bargain was advertised to good effect again when Dark Vision – a colt he bought for just 15,000gns at Book 2 of last year's Tattersalls October Yearling Sale – stormed to victory in the Group 2 Vintage Stakes at Glorious Goodwood.

"Dark Vision, who came into the race unbeaten in two starts, was brought wide and late by jockey Silvestre De Sousa to defeat the Alan King-trained Dunkerron."

The article continued: "Dark Vision is far from the first two-year-old bought inexpensively by Johnston to shine this year. Victory Command, a son of War Command who took the Listed Pat Eddery Stakes at Ascot on Saturday, was bought by Johnston for a scarcely believable 6,000gns at the Tattersalls December Yearling Sale. Like Dark Vision, he carries the trainer's silks and races under the banner of Kingsley Park 10."

However, it was not until 23 August, in a £50,000 handicap at York, that Johnston's record-breaking day would arrive. Partnered by Frankie Dettori, 20-1 outsider Poet's Society held off 5-1 co-favourite (of 3) Kynren to win by a neck, the trainer's 4,194th victory in Britain.

The Italian celebrated the trainer's achievement with one of his trademark flying dismounts, normally reserved for Group winners, before cheekily suggesting: "Perhaps I'm going to make it into the Johnstons' downstairs loo for ever now with a picture of the winningmost trainer in British racing!"

It was "a landmark it is difficult to see anyone passing, not least because Johnston has years to add to his tally," reflected *The Times*'

Mark Souster, who added: "The manner of victory epitomised much of what Johnston stands for, employing front-running tactics with a horse running fit and frequently. Remarkably, this was Poet Society's 26th race of the year."

Johnston, the recipient of extended applause, much back-slapping and hand-shaking by colleagues as he entered the winners' enclosure, told the media: "It was getting very frustrating, the tension of it. I was saying beforehand if it was Frankie [riding] no one will ever forget it. It's a relief to get it out of the way and on to the next one. I've been wishing we could switch it all off and pretend it never happened. Sometimes I think, how important is it? At the same time, I do have to pinch myself and ask how I could get to 4,194 from where we started. It's unimaginable."

The Telegraph produced a spread on the feat, with racing writer Marcus Armytage observing: "While other trainers may have had more big race successes, his achievement remains epic." Under the headline "Proof an outsider can challenge the Establishment", the paper's chief sportswriter Paul Hayward described Johnston as "the numbers king", as "a vet and a thinker" and opined that: "it takes colossal willpower to rise from outside the racing Establishment to train so many winners. This is a family affair, and Johnston's record is a victory for meritocrats in racing."

Frank Keogh, of BBC Sport wrote: "'Always trying' – that's the motto which adorns the horse lorries of Mark Johnston, who is always trying to set the bar higher. For the last quarter of a century, the no-nonsense Scot – who grew up on an East Kilbride council estate – has been racking up winners with familiar regularity. He may not have enjoyed quite the star quality of horses trained by greats such as Sir Michael Stoute and the late Sir Henry Cecil, but he has more winners than them. To put it in perspective, his tally equates to having a victory every single day for more than 11 years."

Perhaps most rewarding for the Scot was this from Martin Pipe, a former record-breaking trainer himself and much admired by Johnston. "I read the other day that I was his inspiration, which is nice. He's obviously a brilliant trainer. It takes a lot of dedication and preparation and he has a wonderful team behind him."

When, in 2021, I ask Johnston to reflect back on becoming part of Turf history, he admits the reaction had rather taken him aback. Clearly, he hadn't anticipated such a display of approbation.

At the beginning of 2018, he'd even told John Scanlon, who writes for the *Kingsley Klarion*, to include nothing about the forthcoming achievement. "I wondered if the *Racing Post* would even notice – I honestly wondered if there'd be any reaction at all to us taking the record," he says.

"And then about six weeks before it happened, someone from GBR [Great British Racing, the BHA's marketing arm] contacted me saying 'we believe you're going to break the record for the number of winners this year', and asking to check that their figures corresponded to ours. They did. They went into gear, produced a press pack, and everything. There was a press day at the yard, a couple of weeks before. They put quite an effort into it."

He adds: "Maybe it was going a little bit on the defensive, defending our position, but I was very surprised by the reaction. I can't remember, but I'm fairly certain that there was nothing like the same reaction as when Richard Hannon [Snr] took the record off Martin Pipe [in 2013], or when Martin Pipe took the record off whoever it was before." Pipe had passed jumps trainer Arthur Stephenson, in 2000.

Johnston admits: "Sometimes you have to defend quantity versus quality because there are people who try to knock it and say 'it's just a factory, that place – it just turns out winners.'"

Johnston has never deviated from the philosophy that winners must be his priority. Always will be. That's what launched him into the premier league of trainers. Yet, he was not oblivious to the fact that he needed to not only continue converting many into Group winners, but conjure the Group 1 triumphs that had been eluding him.

"You can have 220 winners in a season, but nobody notices unless you have a star horse," he says, having come agonisingly close to producing another Classic victor when his Dee Ex Bee, owned by Sheikh Mohammed, had been a tenacious runner-up to the Charlie Appleby-trained Masar in the 2018 Derby. He would then finish fourth behind Aidan O'Brien's Kew Gardens in the St Leger.

Though a Derby triumph still eludes him, Johnston regards it as a "very winnable" race – in part due to an entry system which he believes weakens the quality. In essence, it will cost the owner of a horse entered eighteen months before runners line up at Epsom a total of £7,860, through stages, to run in the Blue Riband event. But there is a final chance to enter, the Monday before the event, and that will sting them with an £85,000 supplementary fee (this is said to be roughly equivalent to fourth place prizemoney).

He says: "Of course, if you have a 500,000gns Galileo yearling, you stick them in the Derby [eighteen months before], but when you're not operating in that league and buying cheaper horses, you don't want to spend that sort of money. It's a crazy system and shows a lack of understanding on the part of those who set the conditions, the racecourse."

As Johnston prepared for the 2019 Ascot Gold Cup, aiming for a fourth victory with a third horse, in the event's centrepiece, following Double Trigger and Royal Rebel twice, he described Dee Ex Bee as his "dream stayer". But then the colt and his trainer came across a seemingly insurmountable obstacle.

Like some intimidating bouncer, one formidable individual simply wouldn't allow Dee Ex Bee entrance to that exclusive Cup club; not at Royal Ascot, not at Glorious Goodwood, and not at York. That horse was Stradivarius.

As we discuss this, the strains of Noddy Holder distract the trainer as his mobile bursts into life, loudly. The name on the screen is Frankie Dettori – a jockey all-too-familiar with riding Group 1 horses, and notably the now-retired Enable and the still very-active Stradivarius – who was "wondering if he had a runner planned for the Derby Italiano [Italian Derby]." Johnston responds: "Yes, but I've got no idea what. Give me 24 hours to have a look at it."

A common occurrence? "No, but we got beaten by a nose in the Italian Derby last year. Frankie had ridden the horse [King's Caper], and he had said 'this could win the Italian Derby – and I'll ride it'. We went and we nearly did. There's a court case going on, because the winner [Tuscan Gaze] wasn't entered! We appealed against the result – us, and the second, third and fourth horses. The winner got thrown out. They appealed the decision, and it got reinstated. But the case is still continuing." He adds: "Frankie was saying, 'the Italians are trying to book me, but if you've got something we can win it with, let's go and win the Italian Derby…'

"It's worth a lot of money [more than £270,000 to the winner in 2020], but [to Dettori] it's not the money, it's because it's the Italian Derby." In the end, a Johnston runner didn't materialise in 2021. Yet, it was an illustration of Dettori's desire to pursue prestige victories, even at 50 years old.

The Italian has partnered more than a half-century of winners for the Middleham trainer. You suggest that if Frankie wants to win something, there's no better jockey? Johnston nods. "Poet's Society, our 4,194th winner, he lifted it over the line. When he's on song he's brilliant, absolutely brilliant. And he knows the Italian tracks well. There's nobody in the world you'd want more on your horse in a race like that than Frankie."

CHAPTER 26

FRUSTRATED BY A GOLD CUP COLOSSUS

There would be no luxuriating in the after-glow of 2018, a year when 'record-breaking' or 'winningmost' would be added to 'powerful' in any description of the Johnston stable. There was, however, further acclaim for the Middleham operation, now deemed 'The winning machine' in a *Racing Post* headline in 2019, a year that proved to be yet another record-breaking one for the yard. A total of 249 winners – including 50 in July when he broke his own record for a month of 47 – was the most any Flat trainer had accumulated over a season.

Pertinently, the *Racing Post's* Scott Burton emphasised: "It is clear that the monthly and seasonal records have not been built on mopping up minor or uncompetitive records. A whopping 198 of his successes came in the heart of the turf Flat campaign between April 1 and September 30, in the teeth of opposition from the other major yards. Put simply, Johnston and his team are operating at rarefied levels when it comes to both quantity and quality."

And yet it would end as a nearly-year, one of profound frustration.

The Last Lion's Middle Park triumph in 2016 had been the stable's last Group 1 success in three years. Never mind that between 2017 and 2019, the yard accumulated 28 winners in Group 2 and 3, one of which was the German 1,000 Guineas, with Main Edition, and had the runner-up in seven Group 1 races.

"People keep saying how wonderful a year it [2019] was, but I would swap a lot of those winners for a couple more inches in two of those Group 1 races," he reflected.

The principal 'culprit' was Stradivarius. Consider this: on three occasions that year, Dee Ex Bee, Johnston's Derby runner-up had been beaten into second place by Stradivarius: in the Ascot Gold Cup (by a length), the Goodwood Cup (a neck) and at York (1¼ lengths). In 2020, the stable's Nayef Road twice went down to the John Gosden horse (in the Ascot Gold Cup and Goodwood Cup).

If Antonio Stradivari produced the best violins the world has ever seen – and heard – it would be fair to say that, in its equine namesake, John Gosden has nurtured the best staying instrument the world has seen, certainly this century.

By 2019, the very mention of this plunderer of staying prizes must have been regarded almost as a curse in the Middleham yards. Within the Johnston set-up, you have to suppress the inclination to make the sign of the cross when his name is broached. How different the stable's Group 1 tally would look without the Gosden charge confounding their Cup assaults so often.

That absence of a Group 1 winner would be extended into 2020, a fourth calendar year. It didn't help Johnston's disposition that one prominent media observer, Lee Mottershead, in a comment piece titled "So how simple is training?" in the *Racing Post* in October 2020, wrote:

"This is a column full of questions – and here are a few more.

Mark Johnston has been more prolific than anyone in British racing history. Nevertheless, despite taking in a vast number of animals each year, including a significant percentage owned by members of the Maktoum family, he has not produced a Group 1 winner since October 2016. Does that indicate in some way Johnston has been doing something wrong over the barren four years? Or has he simply not had horses capable of scoring at the top level?

The journalist continued: "The likelihood is it's just one of those things." However, he then broached the trainers John Oxx (a name always associated with Sea The Stars), Guy Harwood (with Dancing Brave) and Sir Henry Cecil (Frankel), all of whose fortunes dipped during otherwise illustrious careers, and added:

"The very best trainers do something, know something and have something. Whether they could describe those somethings to the rest of us is debatable. It's often innate and inexplicable. When talking about Enable, John Gosden has repeatedly said he has let her tell him what to do and when to do it. Would anyone else have made sense of what she was saying?

"Therein may lie the real secret talent possessed by the sport's elite trainers. When their horses talk, they hear them."

Johnston would be justified in contending that his name and Attraction should be added to those luminaries and their celebrated charges. It would be fair to say that no other trainer could have extracted the extraordinary achievements he did from the filly. What he did take exception to in those observations were the opening lines which, he maintains, took no account of the quality of horses he was sent by the Maktoum family.

"The article by Lee Mottershead suggested that people like Mark Johnston get all these superbly bred horses from Sheikh Mohammed and yet he hasn't had a Group 1 winner in four years.

Well, I'd had God knows how many bloody seconds. And as for all these good horses from Sheikh Mohammed, we're fourth in the pecking order at best."

"He wants to look at the horses I get from the Arabs – and compare them to those that their other trainers have got and *I have got to run against*," he emphasises. "It's not as though they say: 'We won't run our Gosden-trained Dubawi to let you win with an Ifraaj." (Their respective stud fees, incidentally, are £250,000 and £20,000.)

"Yes, that annoyed me. They [media commentators] don't know how difficult it is to win a Group 1 race. You're not just racing against Gosden, but against [Aiden] O'Brien, [André] Fabre. In Group 1s, you're racing against everybody, racing against the world."

He adds: "Just look at Stradivarius's record – we came second to him in five Group 1s. In 2019, I think we were second in five or six Group 1s, including two photos."

It all provokes an intriguing question: how many potential Group winners will there be among his assigned number in any year and where is Johnston Racing in the pecking order of Arab consignments? Unfortunately, unlike the American Football system, you don't get to pick your own from Sheikh Mohammed's draft.

The trainer maintains there is a league table of quality consigned. "For a while, it's been Godolphin, Gosden, Fabre. Godolphin's getting more – and better. Gosden's getting more – and better."

It must be stressed that Johnston is a great admirer of the five-times champion. "John Gosden has far and away the biggest stable in Britain, and most successful stable in Britain. I had him to stay in September. When we had Rishi Sunak coming, we thought there was nobody better to be here. It's why we had him on site. Even the champion trainer has serious concerns about the finances of British racing. There's nobody better than John to give a proper considered view of it. The same applies to Rachel [Gosden's wife], of course. She's very astute about getting the message across."

In summary he adds: "You have to say that if you take all Sheikh Mohammed's operations as one, and he graded all his horses into divisions, I'm not going to get his division one horses. There's no possibility of that. They will go to Godolphin."

However, with a piquant sense of timing, just five days after that *Racing Post* article had questioned the absence of a Group 1 success for four years at Middleham, Johnston despatched two horses to Paris tracks, and both emerged with Group 1 victories.

Notably, a horse, bought by Johnston for 62,000gns, named Subjectivist, and owned by a Scottish economist, Dr Jim Walker, had been rising through the ranks, with one victory as a two-year-old, but exuding potential. That promise was fulfilled increasingly in his second season as he embraced staying distances. He won the Group 3 1m 6f March Stakes at Goodwood by 15 lengths, and though he finished seventh in the St Leger, after pulling too hard, Subjectivist became part of a romantic weekend in Paris for the Johnston team.

After his stablemate Gear Up had gutsily prevailed in the Criterium de Saint-Cloud on the Saturday, Subjectivist made it a double on the Sunday in the Prix Royal-Oak at Longchamp over 1m 7½f. On heavy going, he made all to account for the favourite Valia, trained by Alain de Royer-Dupré.

Under Joe Fanning's exhortations, the colt repelled all challenges, despite hanging to the left in the straight. It was later found that one of Subjectivist's front shoes had come loose. They were the stable's first Group 1 successes since The Last Lion in 2016. Talking of shoes, that weekend, it must have felt like a metaphorical stone had been removed from those of the collective Johnston team.

That triumph boded well for 2021, with the Ascot Gold Cup the principal target. The two caveats were that the victory had been on heavy ground, and the going on the Berkshire course in mid-summer would probably be fast; the other was that the competition at Longchamp had been minus a certain Stradivarius.

Nevertheless, the Johnston camp could dare to dream going into the new year.

"WHEN I BUY 50 YEARLINGS, THEY'RE NOT THE 50 YEARLINGS I WANTED MOST"

It was almost inevitable that Mark Johnston, the winner-wizard, should begin 2021, a final year operating under his own name before establishing a formal partnership with son Charlie, by creating a new record. His first three runners scored an across-the-card treble on 2 January, and that was followed by four doubles. Overall, in January, traditionally the quietest month of the year for Flat racing trainers, he boasted 21 winners from 53 runners.

The *Kingsley Klarion* celebrated the achievement, revealing the following stats: a 40 per cent winning strike rate; 71 per cent placed strike rate; 54 per cent individual winners – and a headline which proclaimed: "Red-hot run melts those winter blues!" It was the most successful January of Johnston's career.

With his team cutting loose in the early months, Johnston's perennial fear of failure appeared to have been expunged for another year.

"If I could bottle it – whatever it is that is making our horses run so well at the minute – and sell it, I would. But unfortunately, there is no magic potion and it is no easier to explain a phenomenally good run of form than it is to explain a string of losers," Johnston told the *Racing Post*.

He added, reflecting on the effects of the Covid restrictions on the industry as a whole: "It's got to help [the yard's early-year form] because there must be a lot of owners out there looking at the invoices and re-evaluating what they want to do for 2021."

During a visit I made to the yard in early May 2021, Johnston admits: "Some owners have cut back. But most of our reduction will be in Arab owners. We're down very dramatically in [horses consigned by] Sheikh Hamdan Bin Mohammed. Down from… well, at one time, we did have 100 from him alone. We have got maybe 30 Sheikh Mohammed horses, including 12 two-year-olds. Those 12 are by sires like Ifraaj. There's no Dubawis.

"Apart from that, Jaber Abdullah may be up a little bit, but overall Dubai-based owners are probably about half of what they were. But we've made them up from other owners."

He adds: "Our biggest owners, apart from the Middle East, would be Mick Doyle, with ten, and Dr Jim Walker with seven or eight. But we're still talking horses valued at fifty, sixty grand. And the Kingsley Park partnerships are flying – there are 30-odd Kingsley Park horses now."

However, he is anxious to stress the following point: "The whole model when we go out to buy for them [the Kingsley Park partnership horses] is a maximum average of 15,000. We can't spend more than 45,000 on the three, often considerably less. We're mostly spending 35,000 on the three. It's believed that syndicates replace big sole owners for British racing…they don't. And they don't replace them for us, either.

"We bought about 50 yearlings last year and, if you take out the ones that were home-bred and we'd bought in ourselves, the average price was 30,000. And we're competing against John Gosden and his average price is probably 250,000 or 300,000. We're still buying horses cheaply and we're still running in Group 1s with them. The fact is that I bought our two Group 1 winners of last year, at 60,000 and 62,000."

He pauses, conscious of what he's said, and places such an amount into perspective. "Yes, 60,000 is a lot of money to someone who's going to buy a Ford Escort. In relation to the horses we are running against in Group 1s, it is pennies."

The long-established law of the Turf says that financial big-hitters in the sales ring invariably tend to out-punch their rivals once they progress to the fight ring, the racecourse. The best yearlings will, in general, go to Godolphin and Coolmore, at six-figures, sometimes seven figures.

Occasionally this law is broken. In June 2021 a Johnston debutant, named Austrian Theory, owned, like Subjectivist, by Dr Jim Walker, contested a seven-furlong maiden at Doncaster. He had cost 30,000gns, and started at 14-1, but stayed on strongly under Joe Fanning's encouragement to overcome the favourite, the Godolphin-owned Private Signal, also a newcomer, but costing… 680,000gns. Austrian Theory later finished an admirable third in the Group 2 Vintage Stakes at Glorious Goodwood, beaten by less than two lengths.

It is such divergence from the norm that continues to feed belief within the Johnston camp. "I would say that the average cost of horses in this yard, well, in the first few years, it was under 10,000. It stuck at around 30,000 for some time, and it's probably still less than 50,000 – and we're trying to compete for the Group 1s against people where the average is well into the hundreds of thousands," he says, adding: "When you're buying some horses for 3,000, like Rose of Kildare, and 15,000, like Dark Vision, to win Group 2s and be placed in Group 1s, it's not easy. It's fantastic that we're getting these horses for the Kingsley Park partnerships. We've got Dancing King this year [costing only 18,000gns, and with four successive handicap victories as a three-year-old]. He's rapidly on the way up." In late August, the gelding won a Group 3 event at Goodwood.

Johnston's career-long response to the moneyed elite has been to identify quality at the sales, and with significant success, but he emphasises this point: "In the last two to three years, we have had tremendous success at the sales with our cheap horses. But remember, when I go home from the sales with 50 yearlings, they're *not* the 50 yearlings I wanted most. There are 200 that I wanted more than I wanted those ones. They're the 50 yearlings I could afford that I wanted. There are horses I can't dream of – because I can't afford them."

He adds: "There are owners out there that buy what they *want*. Obviously, one wins the bidding war. But at that top end they go for millions, whereas my 50 yearlings, I'll buy one in six figures en spec, and only when I sell it can I buy another one at six figures. Of those 50 yearlings, there's probably only two over 100,000.

"This season, we got more than 100 [yearlings] again in total. But the quality will be down as well. Despite saying there is a pecking order in terms of what we got from Darley, they were still good horses. When we were getting 50 yearlings from them, they were 50 of our best. They were well-bred horses. We're now getting a lot less, and the quality has dropped a bit. When we make up the numbers with the ones we've bought, they're still not as good as Darley's third string."

SUBJECTIVIST CONFIRMS HIS CREDENTIALS IN DUBAI

Meydan racecourse, the luxurious construction that arose from the rubble of the former Nad Al Sheba course in Dubai, has been as much a magnet for stars of pop and rock as those of horseracing.

On rare escapes from the day job, Mark Johnston may well have appreciated a ticket for concerts by Elton John, Lady Gaga, Santana and Kylie Minogue, all of whom have performed there. But on 27 March, 2021, he was there for a singular purpose: to confirm that Subjectivist was the potent Ascot Gold Cup contender the colt's display in the final outing of his three-year-old season at Longchamp had suggested. In addition, there was the not inconsequential matter of a little more than £328,000 in first-place prize money on offer.

Over the years, the headline acts contesting the Dubai Gold Cup tended to be the elite stayers on the Godolphin and the Aga Khan books, although the Michael Owen-owned ill-fated Brown Panther, trained by Tom Dascombe, did claim it in 2015.

Subjectivist certainly confirmed himself a star in the making on 27 March. To borrow from Sir Elton's performance here, you could perhaps have renamed him 'Rocket Man' as he continued his exhilarating upwards trajectory with a victory so convincing it demanded little injection of excitement from the commentator.

There was no blanket finish and no hyperbole was required. He'd put the race to bed turning out of the back straight. "He's going to run them ragged. Subjectivist wins, and wins easily," were the words accompanying a devastating front-running performance.

Sky Sports Racing presenter Mike Cattermole followed up with: "Take a bow Joe Fanning, Mark Johnston and Dr Jim Walker", before a discussion was launched on his Royal Ascot potential, which would continue until 17 June, the day of the Gold Cup.

It became the subject of intense debate in racing circles. Tom Segal, the *Racing Post* tipster, concluded: "Stradivarius has won 13 races with the word 'Cup' in the title and trying to get him beaten in his bid to win his fourth Gold Cup next month looks to be a thankless task. He looked as good as ever when winning the Sagaro on his comeback run and provided the ground isn't too soft, Stradivarius is going to be an extremely hard nut to crack at the Royal meeting."

Adding that, "there simply haven't been many better stayers than him in history…on the negative side he's a seven-year-old now and this has the potential to be as good a Gold Cup as he's ever run in. Next in the market is Subjectivist, who looked awesome in Dubai and has taken his form to a whole new level at two miles. He has the potential to be even better with another half a mile to contend with and, on what he showed at Meydan, he's still improving…But I'm loath to use Dubai form as gospel back in Europe."

Johnston, rarely less than bullish when it comes to assessing his participants, insisted of Subjectivist: "He has got all the credentials. He's a Group 1 winner over a mile and six, a Group 2 winner over 2 miles, breaking the track record. He's the right kind of horse to take him [Stradivarius] on."

Such a challenge is one on which Johnston thrives. But presumably his charge would travel to the Berkshire course more with hope than expectation? "He's got to weaken one day, hasn't he?" was his estimation of the Gosdens' supreme performer.

Subjectivist is a close relation of Sir Ron Priestley, another Johnston horse. Both are out of the mare Reckoning, a daughter of Danehill Dancer, who was successful over six and seven furlongs at Group 1 level. Reckoning won her maiden, and was placed in Listed company.

Johnston, the sage of the sales ring, explains how he had paid 70,000gns for Sir Ron Priestley (sired by Australia, the dual 2014 Derby winner) at the 2017 Tattersalls sales, and sold him to Paul Dean, a long-standing owner, who named the horse after a friend who had died.

"Though he'd only run twice and hadn't actually won when we went back to Tattersalls the next year and saw the three-parts brother [sired by Teofilo, the undefeated champion two-year-old of 2006], I wanted him as well, and paid 62,000gns."

He adds: "Dr Jim Walker had seen I'd bought Subjectivist and called me up, saying he'd like him. I said: 'Sorry, but when we train a half-brother or sister [of one of the stable's horses], we always offer it to that owner first.' I called Paul Dean and asked: 'Do you want a three-parts half-brother to Sir Ron Priestley?' and he said 'no'. So, I called Jim Walker back and he bought him."

The following year, Johnston paid 100,000gns for the filly Alba Rose (by the top-class sprinter Muhaarar), a younger half-sister to

Subjectivist and Sir Ron Priestley. "Jim Walker got first choice and bought that."

To complete a family quartet, Johnston also has a filly by Ulysses (whose victories included the Group 1 Eclipse and International Stakes), also out of Reckoning, sent to him by Susan Hearn, the wife of Barry Hearn (chairman of Matchroom Sport, World Snooker and the Professional Darts Corporation) who runs the Essex-based Mascalls Stud. She bought Reckoning for £160,000 in 2014, and maintains a keen eye on all her progeny's progress.

Johnston relishes training members of the same family. Like human families, you get to know their qualities and quirks, but just how much of a benefit is it? "It helps," he states. "Alba Rose is different from the other two, but it gives us confidence in her, and gives us confidence in the fact that she'll improve with age, and stay further. We presume she'll have inherited some of what the brothers have got."

Alba Rose had won a novice, and been third in the 2020 Group 2 Rockfel Stakes at Newmarket, but had been disappointing on her seasonal debut, finishing sixth of eight in the Oaks trial, the Listed Pretty Polly Stakes, at the same course.

Johnston told me that Susan Hearn – as her breeder, and therefore a keenly interested party – had sent him a text message following that run in the Pretty Polly, asking: "Any excuses or just not good enough?"

Johnston had explained to the stud owner that the filly had been "a bit too keen and didn't quite get home." He had added, "She had done no serious fast work at home, and was entitled to need the race." The trainer had followed up with his plans to run Alba Rose next back at one mile in the German 1,000 Guineas.

The message had come back, "I just love your ambition."

"That's not ambitious," Johnston said: "I think she'll win. She's not a bad filly. We've won the German 1,000 Guineas twice in the last three years. It's a Group 2 race, and [winning it is] worth fortunes for this horse with her pedigree."

The night before I stayed with Mark and Deirdre in their splendidly-appointed cottage, across from Kingsley House – normally reserved for visiting patrons – the couple's compatriot Dr Jim Walker, owner of Subjectivist, had been their guest. An economist with RBS in the late 1980s, he is the founder and chief economist at Aletheia Capital Limited, an independent research platform for the Asia Pacific region.

Politically, he and his trainer are closely aligned. Walker's return from Hong Kong wasn't purely business-related. In March, the investment strategist had announced plans to run for Alex Salmond's Alba Party at the forthcoming Holyrood elections. He had decided to stand for the Scottish Parliament on the Central Scotland list, declaring that the task of the next Scottish Parliament was to put the country on the road to prosperity through claiming national independence.

Subjectivist's owner had accepted the Johnstons' hospitality, having been offered a lift in one of their aircraft. It had become more than just a status symbol of the Scot's success. Expansionist though he is, it's not exactly Johnston-Air. Middleham isn't yet a transport hub – but this is an essential part of the business. Having had a Piper Cherokee for many years, Johnston, a qualified pilot, also invested in a Cessna Caravan in 2019. The airstrip is alongside the gallops.

That purchase reflects the amount of travelling he undertakes in order to supervise the running of his charges, and to attend sales. "Life-changing," declares Johnston of his aircraft. "Newmarket is 55 minutes; you land on the track. It saves 2½ hours – each way. We generally take passengers. Yesterday, Jim Walker was coming down from Edinburgh, so we took him, Joe Fanning, P.J. McDonald – who was not riding for us – and a member of staff, five of us in all."

Charlie flies to meetings as well, "but he takes a pilot – as I did for the first eight to nine years of having an aeroplane." The Johnston slogan may be: 'Always Trying'. Perhaps he should add: 'And Frequently Flying'.

PREPARING FOR A PARTNERSHIP WITH CHARLIE

B y the time of my visit to Middleham in May 2021, nothing is settled yet about Mark Johnston and Charlie applying for a joint training licence. With York's Dante meeting, The Derby and Royal Ascot on the horizon, it's not a crucial concern – for now.

It remains the likelihood that the pair will seek a dual licence by the start of the 2022 season, "and probably Charlie on his own in two or three years' time," according to his father.

It hardly seems of great concern for the moment, anyway. While some father and son business combinations can end up sparring like Harold and Albert Steptoe, all the evidence is that this is more a dream team as they prepare eventually to join the increasing number of trainers who have established such partnerships.

In terms of a transmission of responsibilities, there has been a gradual shifting of the power base. Having turned 60 in October 2019, Johnston is still very much the guiding force (according to his LinkedIn entry he is Dictator, Johnston Racing Ltd!), although with Charlie the de facto 'guv'nor'.

Johnston offers an example of the gradual transition of roles and responsibility. "For two or three years now, Jono Mills [Bloodstock Director for Godolphin and Darley] has visited to see Sheikh Hamdan's horses. He wants Charlie to be here – not me. He sits with Charlie, and goes through every horse, and discusses them. Not with me. I sometimes chip in and throw in my pennyworth. When I commented on this, Jono told me: 'I talk to Charlie about individual horses. I talk to you about policies.'" Johnston shrugs and confirms quietly: "That's fine."

This handover process has been a dilemma for some time. He explains: "What I didn't want to do is what I've seen other trainers do, is hand over a sinking ship. It always worried us that changing would give owners, like the Arab owners particularly, an excuse to move their horses. I'd be pretty certain that John Gosden hasn't lost any [after going into partnership with his son Thady]; nor has Simon Crisford [with Ed]; or Paul Cole [with Oliver]."

He adds: "That said, I think probably that Charlie's been more to the forefront, both with the media and the owners, than their sons were. Everybody knows now how much Charlie is involved with this business. Everybody will be aware that nothing will change except the name on the licence."

No son could have been more steeped in the family business as this heir apparent. As Deirdre would tell me later: "It would be fair to say that Charlie posted his job application at around the age of five!" He has never wavered in his obsessive desire to take over the family firm. "Charlie learnt to read, reading the *Racing Post*," says Johnston. "I joke about it, but it's absolutely true."

The trainer adds: "Even when he was seven years at vet school, when we thought he was in lectures, we'd get text messages immediately after a race saying 'what was the jockey doing there?' He must have been down the bookies [watching the race]..."

The only concern both parents harboured about their son's background is that he has not spent much time in other yards. "He had a little spell with Ted Walsh – but that was principally to improve his riding," says Johnston.

Charlie returned to the yard from vet school in 2015. "He qualified in June, and he hung around the place, talking about getting a job, and helping out, and we used to talk about him working 'Charlie time'. We wanted him to go away and work in vet practice," Johnston recalls, but Charlie stayed put. "Come the following January, I said if he was going to stay here, he was going to start work and work fixed hours, the same as everyone else. He started on 1 January, and immediately his role was assistant trainer."

Johnston adds: "The only aspect that Charlie doesn't take much involvement in is the non-horse side. "Planning a new building, a new gallop, buying a new property – there's a lot that's not connected with training horses. It's such a big business now. It's very different from me coming into it.

"Business structure-wise, nothing will change in the foreseeable future. Deirdre and I will still be the sole shareholders, and Charlie will be an employed trainer – to begin with. And I will still work in the business in pretty much the same capacity as I do now. I will probably take more of a back seat – definitely when I hand over the licence entirely. He does a huge amount of it now. He's been planning all the work for the horses for at least the last three years, maybe more.

"He has a huge input. In the last year, he has had a much bigger input to entries than I have. Entries and work – that's 90 per cent of training them. He's already been doing it. He's been back in the business more than five years. They've been five of our best years.

So, nobody can say that him planning the work or the entries has had any detrimental effect on the business whatsoever."

Charlie also attends sales, alone and with his father. "I had nothing whatsoever to do with buying Rose of Kildare [who progressed from a handicap winner to Group class], for example," says his father. "He bought her for €3,000. I wasn't at the sale. I never read the catalogue."

Having spoken to Charlie over the years, he has never come across as 'the big I am', or, indeed, a Mark Johnston mini-me. Yet, with both being strong, opinionated characters, there must be plenty of scope for them to clash? "Every morning!" declares Johnston Snr. "I sometimes say 'why did you put him [a certain jockey] on that?' and 'why are we running that [horse] there?' – and vice versa." He accepts ruefully, however: "It's probably more him criticising me than me criticising him."

Who has the ultimate decision? "The ultimate decision is mine, but I rarely now make any decision without consulting Charlie. He books all the jockeys, and has done so now for two or three years."

Back in late March 2021, Johnston had been at Meydan to oversee Subjectivist's triumph. He had arrived in Dubai three or four days before the race and, after it, had stayed in the Maldives for 12 days to avoid having to self-isolate in a Heathrow hotel. Then, back home, he had to self-isolate in the house for ten days because he'd been in contact with someone who had tested positive for Covid.

The reality was that the yard continued to despatch winners under Charlie's control. That surprised no one. "In all, for nearly four weeks, I was never out in the yard and during that time, Charlie did it all. From a horseracing point of view, I have absolutely no doubt he can run the whole show, and the number of winners will not alter," says Johnston, who had also been absent for three weeks in 2020 after contracting Covid.

The trainer talks briefly about that experience: "I felt terrible. At the peak, I had maybe seven days of really raging temperatures. I might have ended up in hospital – except that was the last place I wanted to go. I knew the trigger point was problems breathing. And I never had that. In that sense, it wasn't concerning. A month ago –[early April], I'd have said I'd not felt better for years. I'd lost two stone, and I was an awful lot better for it."

There was no racing at that time, but Johnston had no doubt his son could cope. "Charlie has an incredible memory for it. Of all those horses out there, you could ask him anything about their pedigree and form and he'll just reel it off to you."

He pauses before admitting: "I've got lazier. I don't need to do all that. He's got everything at his fingertips. He doesn't need to look it up. That's partly an age thing, but also he's always had that kind of mind."

Johnston chuckles and adds: "Charlie can sit and beat 'the Chaser' [on the TV gameshow *The Chase*]; he's an expert on *Countdown*. He did maths competitions for the school. He's also got a tremendous memory; he can remember things about horses who ran when he was at school better than I can."

Yet, why his absolute insistence, to the point of what one could describe as coercion, that his son should emulate him and go to 'vet school', a lengthy, highly demanding spell of intense academia? This wasn't three years of 'media studies' or 'social science'.

For Charlie, approaching 31, it's taken half a lifetime to even get this far; a gruelling 15 or so years since I witnessed him scanning the *Racing Post*, and his early TV appearances. It's difficult to imagine anyone having to leap through more hoops to secure his perfect job.

And was it pure mischief that provoked his father to muse a few years ago? "You know, there's a side to me which thinks in ten or whatever years' time I should look for the best successor; not Charlie Johnston." In truth, you suspect it was more of a verbal boot up the backside to Charlie; a reminder that he could take nothing for granted, and not to get ahead of himself, clearly a concern for his father at the time.

I take Johnston back to what he told me at the time. "You're exceptionally demanding," I had commented. "Damn right I am," he had retorted. "But it's a very demanding business to run."

Going back 15 years, Charlie had appeared on Channel 4's *The Morning Line* to discuss the stable's Linas Selection, winner of the 2006 King George V Handicap at Royal Ascot. The three-year-old had developed through handicap company, and was due next to contest a one-mile-six-furlong Listed handicap at York on John Smith's Day.

Not every parent would necessarily desire their teenage son to be exposed to such TV scrutiny, but Charlie's father had no such misgivings, not initially, anyway. "I'm often asked to be on TV preview programmes," Mark told me at the time. "The day before John Smith's Day, Jim McGrath [the racing pundit and broadcaster] rang and asked me about appearing on the following day's *The Morning Line*. I was at Newmarket and I just wanted to get home. I said no. Then I had a thought, rang back and said, 'What about Charlie?' They thought that was a good idea. He did it, and it was fantastic. He was far better than I'll ever be…although I'm not sure about his tipping of Linas Selection to win at York."

Charlie remembers the moment only too well. He recalls, with a wry smile: "I was only 15, and 'Big Mac' [the late broadcaster John McCririck who was interviewing him] was saying: 'he's gone from 6-4 to 5-4 – what should we do?' And I said: 'Keep backing it!'"

Whether it was his advice that punters should plunge on the horse or merely that after his Ascot triumph he still looked a handicap 'good thing' despite rising nearly a stone in the weights, backers took the hint.

"I believe that was the most-traded horse or race of the entire season that year," recalls Charlie. "It went from something like 15-8 the night before and was returned definitely odds-on [11-8 on to be precise]."

His opinion was confirmed when Linas Selection won comfortably, easing down, under Kevin Darley. At least one firm would claim it was their worst result of the season.

Later the same month, Johnston Jnr became 'Nostradamus' once more, advising the At The Races TV channel viewers that Road To Love *would* win a one-mile-two-furlong handicap, also at Ascot.

His judgement was again sound, although this information was based on particularly close scrutiny: he had partnered the horse in work the previous week. Road To Love, sired by Johnston's old campaigner Fruits Of Love, was an impressive seven lengths too good for the remainder of the field.

By this point, it had become apparent that Charlie was becoming the stable's 'go-to' man for interviews, and Johnston began to be concerned about his son's over-exposure. "Charlie appeared again on TV after the race, and by Glorious Goodwood all the media had latched on to this," Johnston told me at the time. "I felt I had to put a bit of a halt to it. Newspapers wanted to interview him, but I said no by that time. It has got a little bit out of hand. I want him to keep his feet on the ground. He's got to go back to school and concentrate on his exams."

The Scot added, with mock exasperation: "It's got to the stage where At The Races was ringing up for *him*. Charlie was in France at the time, so they couldn't have had him anyway. So, as an afterthought, they asked me!"

What Johnston was at pains to emphasise to his elder son

back then was that succeeding him as trainer here "will not come that easy." By that easy, he meant Charlie studying 'equine science' at university.

I well recall the horror on Mark's features at the suggestion by Charlie's careers teacher that this could be a suitable option. Johnston grimaces at the words 'equine science', as if it was something nasty stuck to his boot. "I know it's rather insulting to those who are doing that course, but I just think that, by comparison [with becoming a vet], it's a Mickey Mouse degree," was his verdict.

The fact that Charlie would probably have studied that course at what Johnston regarded as a former poly added to his dissatis-faction. "When Charlie suggests a degree which you get at [what was once] a polytechnic, I throw up my hands in horror and say, 'What a waste!'"

I recalled advising him at the time that he was guilty of being just a touch elitist. "It's true. I am a believer in education for education's sake. I suppose I'm a bit of an education snob. I'd much rather see him go and study stuffy law, mathematics, physics, French or chemistry at an old established university than I would see him go and study animal science at Worcester."

He added: "I get applications from these people with degrees like those [animal or equine science] once a month at least and they don't get the job because they haven't got the practical experience that makes them of value to me," he stated firmly. "They don't want to come and work as stable hands; and neither would Charlie. They don't have the experience to come and do Andrew Bottomley's job or Jock's."

Purely as an aside, I had questioned whether it is right for him to be handing down a business like this to his son, anyway. It is the kind of nepotism he would surely object to on principle if he observed it elsewhere.

"You're absolutely right to ask that," Johnston agreed at the time. "As I've said, there's no way I'm just going to hand it to him. But I have to stress, nor do I think that would be morally wrong. As I say on many issues, *I didn't write the rules.* I'm not in a position to do something for everybody else. So, for my own kids I am, one, trying to get them the best education they can get – although that doesn't mean I'm paying to send them to private school. And two, yes, I want to give them both opportunities and advantages. Maybe if I was to start with a blank sheet of paper, I'd say that the State takes everything and we all start from scratch, that we all get the same education and the same chances in life, which everybody doesn't get."

It would not be the end of the family debate regarding Johnston Jnr's intended participation in the racing game. When Charlie was 17, he announced he wanted to be a National Hunt jockey. His father had been incredulous. "He's got size 11 feet, weighs ten and a half stone and he's only 15 – and he wants to be a jump jockey!"

Johnston added: "I said to him 'Don't be ridiculous.' I remember James Tate was our vet at the time. I said to Charlie, 'why would I hire you as assistant if I could have James Tate? He's also an amateur jump jockey, his father [Tom] is a trainer, his uncle was a champion trainer [Michael Dickinson, mentioned earlier]. *And* [here comes the crucial bit] *James is a vet.* Why would I have you if I could have James Tate?'" Johnston's faith in James Tate, now a successful trainer, incidentally, would be far from misplaced.

Charlie did as he had been advised and won a place at Glasgow University's School of Veterinary Medicine, just as his father had three decades earlier. So, what does Johnston say now about his 'guidance' to a teenage Charlie that he should obtain a veterinary degree? "I feel that I pushed him into vet school," he concurs with my earlier question on how much pressure Charlie had been under.

"He definitely doesn't have the same interest in it as I did. When he was at school, he sailed through his 'A' levels. He was a model student at school, but went to a university and was a bit of a disaster of a student. It was something I worried about a lot when he was at vet school. He was there for seven years!"

It sounds rather a case of like father, like son. Johnston adds: "Look, I was a terrible student. I took six years to go through. I had re-sits every year except the final year. But I still came to it from a different angle than Charlie.

"On our farm, there's sheep, and we've got a few pigs now. I'm interested in the animals. If I didn't train horses, I'd still work in horses. If I didn't work in horses, I'd work in cattle. If I didn't work with cattle, I'd work with dogs."

And still be a vet? "Probably, yes. If I'd never got to train horses, I still think being a vet is a great job. I wouldn't say I was happy doing it. I was never happy, because I was never content. I wasn't a very good employee, either, in the sense that I had three vet jobs in three and a half years. I didn't stay very long because I was always looking to do something else."

Returning to the family business, Johnston has long taken the rather radical standpoint that the rules should be changed so that limited companies could hold a trainer's licence. He believes it's an anachronism of horseracing that, though yards are run as businesses, they all have to be run under the name of a trainer – although Britain's most powerful operation comes close to being an exception.

"The public think of Godolphin. "They don't say, 'Oh, Saeed Bin Suroor's just trained that winner!'"

Johnston believes there is no reason why training businesses shouldn't have a corporate identity rather than a personal one. "Staff would get more of a kick out of it," he has told me. "They'd feel more a part of a team. Also, the business would have some value, and you'd be able to pass it on. It wouldn't just be bricks and mortar." Significantly, the business name was changed some years ago from Mark Johnston Racing to just Johnston Racing.

We discussed the timing of the transition from father to son a number of times over the years before finally, in 2020, the BHA introduced a sensible innovation, allowing training partnerships. As mentioned, certain fathers and sons swiftly seized the opportunity – but not the Johnstons. Not for the moment. The task of despatching winners took priority.

"WE'RE PUNCHING WELL ABOVE OUR WEIGHT"

It had been at Goodwood two decades ago that the stable's redoubtable stayer, Double Trigger, registered the third of his Goodwood Cups. It is one of Charlie Johnston's most striking childhood recollections. Around that time, he would ride his pony out on the gallops, and watch the first lot before he went to school.

By around 12 years old, he was riding out in the string. Later, he rode in point-to-points and hunter chases. Then came veterinary school, though he concedes his father's observation that he wasn't absolutely devoted to the curriculum was essentially correct. "I was always planning on coming back here – and as a result my motivation for lectures on pig transport and poultry were slightly lacking!" he concedes, with faux remorse. "On a few afternoons, I might have been spotted at Ayr or Musselburgh rather than lectures…"

In his holidays from vet school, Charlie would represent the stable, but confesses: "Looking back on it, I was something of a fraud really. I was just going and putting a saddle on the back, congratulating the owner, collecting the prize, and doing the interview afterwards. I'd played little part in getting the horse to that point."

He adds: "It's what goes on behind the scenes that really counts. I certainly feel now that I contribute a lot more to end results by what I do at home. I've probably got more respect from the staff now because they see me here, day in, day out, and not just turn up at the races and collecting the prizes."

It's no simple matter to drag Charlie Johnston away from the organisational coal-face, to discuss how he sees own future, but he had strolled in to the Johnston house just in time to watch on TV as one of the stable's horses, Ellade scores on her debut at Lingfield, under an excellent ride by Franny Norton.

"Running for her new owner [Ali Abdulla Saeed]," Charlie enthuses. "I bought her for £9,000. He'd just seen that she'd been knocked down to us, and phoned us out of the blue, to take her."

Charlie takes a call from the winning owner, or his representative. One of life's pleasures for a trainer, or in this case, his assistant. "Everyone enjoys those phone calls," he says. "They're easy. There's plenty of times I watch the horse fall out of the back of the TV [as he puts it], and literally just sit there for five minutes and you have to collect your thoughts, take a deep breath and click dial," he says.

Charlie is acutely aware of the downside of training. "We're having a phenomenal season so far, and still three in every four get beat. In a bad year, six in every seven get beat. That means a lot of bad phone calls, for every good one, but that comes with the territory."

He adds: "But we're very fortunate in that we've a very knowledgeable bunch of owners on the whole. We've got a whole lot of owners who've been with us since Dad started training, so they're well versed in how the game is."

He pauses, considers what he's about to say, but continues anyway: "I guess there's a slight negative to it when I say they've all been in the game a long time. That means, from my point of view, they've got an average age certainly a lot older than me. That's something I'll have to try and bring down over the next few years, and introduce some new blood."

I suggest that hand-me-down businesses hadn't done much harm to the Hannons and Baldings. He nods and adds: "Closer to home, I've become quite friendly with Ed Bethell, and he's just taken over from his dad [James, who trained at nearby Coverham from 1992 and retired in 2020, aged 68]. He's actually found he's attracting more owners now, simply because they like a bit of youth, and someone with fresh ideas, a bit more oomph, maybe. Whether that would be replicated in a yard of our size and scale is hard to say."

Charlie adds with a wry smile: "You know the sharks will be out there the first season [training under his name alone] who'd be quick to say standards have dropped. That's the reality of a yard of our size, with our results, in that the room for improvement is miniscule and the room for failure is huge. Any slight dip in form or standards, and people will attribute that to the change in name – although I take some confidence in the fact that each of the last two or three years have been a PB [personal best] in many ways."

Ideally, winning statistics apart, he'd like a Classic, or at least one Group 1 horse in his first couple of seasons, once training on his own, "to set everything in stone, and make sure there aren't any doubters."

Charlie adds: "I'm very fortunate, at the moment, that the reality is that he [Johnston] does all the mundane, horrible jobs that no-one wants to do that come when you're running a business of this size. Although I work very hard, and very long hours, 95 per cent of what I do is just horses and owners. I don't deal with planning permission, councils and a lot of staff matters – or the millions of other things that need to be dealt with."

I put it to Charlie that his parents will remain a crucial part of the business for many years, God willing? "Yes, it'll be interesting to see when the time comes. He's always been very much that, 'I'm going to retire and I want to get out of it. There's so many things I want to do', and, 'I don't want to do this, as some trainers have done, until their dying days', essentially. But when it comes to letting go, that might prove easier said than done!"

That support, from both parents, will be vital; not so much on the training side, but with the acquisition of bloodstock and maintaining ownership levels. "I guess because I've been here so long, and it's been an incremental increase, the numbers don't really overawe me," he says. "That's one place that I'm probably better equipped than Dad in many ways, just being younger and being able to process and keep track of the large number of horses. If someone said tomorrow, they wanted to send us 50 more, I'd say 'fine'. That doesn't daunt me in the slightest."

I put it to him that doing 'the list', was the one aspect that got to his father in the early noughties. He smiles ruefully, and nods: "Yes, I'm at risk of going down the same route. Once a week, usually Tuesday or Wednesday, I spend the whole evening, essentially going through every horse in the yard and plan what work they're going to do for the next seven days; deciding all the galloping, all the upsides, all the stalls work for the rest of the week.

"One night last week, I was doing the board at half past three, four in the morning. That probably happens at least once a week." However, he swiftly adds: "I'm 30, I'm single, I've no dependents. For the last 18 months, there's been no social life. So, I've no other commitments, as such. But I'm sure I'll want to get out of that habit, and use my time more efficiently."

Suggest to Charlie that he doesn't appear to have inherited all of his father's most distinctive genes, and he agrees: "I have a short-enough fuse, but I'm certainly a lot more laid back than he is, and I'm not one for confrontation."

In the work environment, up at Kingsley Park, it appears that their personalities also differ. "Dad's very sociable in his own way – they love hosting dinner parties – but he's not particularly forthcoming out on the gallops. He walks around just staring at his phone, doesn't sort of engage with people. I would know all the staff and engage with people, and would certainly know them better than he does, and communicate with them more frequently."

That said, he quickly adds: "They all respect him, a little bit out of – I hate to use the word 'fear' because it's not a very nice word [he laughs] – but there is an element of 'he's the big boss' up in the office, and if you have to go and see him, it's trouble. I think they respect us slightly differently. There's always a danger that some of them, though they might not quite view me as a friend, I'm sure they certainly do and say things in front of me that they wouldn't do and say in front of him…"

What Charlie will do is to fully acknowledge his father's virtues. "He always leads by example," he says. "If a horse can't be broken, he'll go and break it. If the horse won't go into the stalls, he'll go and put it in the stalls. His principle is that there's no job in the business that he can't do – and I'm certainly not in that position yet. There's so many other things that I need to learn before I'm in a similar position."

I refer Charlie back to his comments in the family's professionally-made home video, mentioned early on, of his astonishment at how his father had progressed from the Lincolnshire bombing range to this.

"We can all be a bit guilty of, when we go up to Kingsley Park every single day – I live there! – and it's not a case of talking it for granted, but I do get a bit blasé in some ways about what it is. It's only when you look back at where it came from, or every now and again, you think 'bloody hell, that's impressive, isn't it?' So, yes, when you look back at where it came from to where it is now, it's phenomenal, absolutely extraordinary. There'll be very few examples of a yard that's made such a huge progression and transformation."

Charlie adds: "We're in the position now where the target every year is to have more winners than anyone else, and the target is probably to be in the top three in prize money – which considering the average yearling price of the people we're competing against, we're punching well above our weight.

"I only want to do this to be champion trainer and to train more winners than everybody else. If I don't, I've got no ambition of simply making the numbers up. I'm not doing it to make a living – I'm sure there's plenty of easier ways of making a living."

He adds: "If I go out for dinner, or out to the pub in the week, you're still on call. My phone's gone four times in the time we've been sat here." There is a reason for that. Jockeys or their agents."

At least Johnston Jnr does have one distraction from the pressures of racing. He plays rugby union for Wensleydale between November and March. "A million miles from racing. It's where I feel comfortable," he explains, though because of Covid restrictions, he last played in mid-March 2020.

"It's really the only release I have from this…" He gestures at the stables and acres outside. "In the winter from about midday, I'm out of here, phone's off, I'm gone, playing rugby. We play in the Yorkshire League so that can be anywhere from Goole to Skipton, to Durham. They wouldn't know if we'd won a seller at Southwell or The Derby. We play rugby for an hour and a half, knock seven bells out of each other, and then have five pints afterwards. I want to keep that going for as long as I can."

Another text message appears on his phone. "That's a jockey asking me if I want him to ride work tomorrow," Charlie says. "It's the bane of my bloody life, in all honesty. I seem to have got myself into a situation where every agent in the country has my mobile number. I'm often sat in the office in the small hours of the morning, booking jockeys." However, he swiftly adds: "No, it's nice that we're on the front foot now that we've got three jockeys who essentially put us first.

"As we've just seen, Franny's riding as well as ever. Joe [Fanning] had the big winner in Dubai. We're a yard that when we get going in the summer, we'll have runners at five or six meetings, and there'll be a lot of big handicaps where we'll have three, four, five runners. So, it's good to have a good relationship with a lot of jockeys."

He adds: "We're fortunate in that a lot of them want to ride for us. Part of that is that 99 times out of 100 they know the horses are going to be well schooled, they're going to be well drilled, they're going to be straightforward rides. And they're not going to be tied down to an essay of instructions. They're just going to be told to go out and do their job. A lot of jockeys find it quite refreshing riding for us – people who don't ride for us often find it quite a nice change to get on a horse and get told 'go out and do your best.'"

On the subject of jockeys, recently there has been movement in the stable's hierarchy.

CURTIS RIDING HIGH IN NEW STABLE ROLE

Joe Fanning, the battle-hardened Irishman, who has partnered more Mark Johnston runners and winners than any other jockey – but relatively few Group 1s – had partnered Subjectivist in the last seven of his 16 races, including the Dubai Gold Cup. Under the stable policy of a jockey successful on a runner keeping the ride in the horse's next race, the 51-year-old knew the saddle would be his at the Royal meeting.

Contrary to most sports, the middle-aged can still thrive in the race-riding game. "Kevin Manning won this year's [2021] 2,000 Guineas, aged 54 – interestingly, the oldest since Lester [Piggott] won it at 56," says Johnston.

Modern fitness regimes partly explain this. Yet, even in the last century Scobie Breasley had won the Derby at 52 years old (on Charlottown in 1966). Both Charlie Smirke (on Hard Ridden in 1958) and Willie Carson (on the previously mentioned Erhaab in 1994) had both been 51 when capturing the Blue Riband of the Turf. However, even the indefatigable Lester Piggott had to yield to his advancing years, finally retiring at the age of 59. And he was something of a freak in terms of longevity.

As for Frankie Dettori – remember that young livewire who went through a seven-race card at Ascot a quarter of a century ago, winning every race? – he also turned 50 in 2020.

In a 34-year career, Johnston has sent out over 35,000 runners in Britain, partnered by 374 jockeys. But when it comes to statistics, no-one can remotely compare with the record of Fanning, who has ridden for the yard since 1991. At the time of writing he was heading for 1,400 winners for the stable, with Franny Norton, also 51, boasting the next highest tally, with more than 400 winners.

However, at the start of 2021, the talented Irishman Ben Curtis, in his early thirties, had arrived, with Johnston revealing in January that he would be riding "more and more" for the stable, though not on a formal basis.

The trainer explains: "Both Joe and Franny have turned 50, and they're riding, to my mind, as well as any time in their careers. But they can't go on for ever. And we can't have a situation where they just stop and we haven't got anyone else."

He adds: "We discussed whether it should be Ben Curtis or should it be Richard Kingscote. We certainly rate Richard Kingscote, but we were less sure that Richard would come and do it because of his association with Tom Dascombe [based at Malpas, in Cheshire]. He doesn't live here, or anywhere near here, whereas Ben Curtis lives in Thirsk which is handy. We spoke to Ben Curtis first, and he wanted to do it. We never got round to speaking to Richard."

However, Johnston is anxious to emphasise that Curtis, who was joint champion Irish apprentice, with Joseph O'Brien and Gary Carroll, in 2010 and moved to Britain three years later was "not on a retainer". Their arrangement is simply this: "We said to him 'we're not going to use somebody who keeps saying I'm not available to ride that one. We'll put you first, if you put us first.'"

The trainer adds: "We still haven't entirely done it. You've seen Franny on Sir Ron Priestley, and Joe on Subjectivist and Alba Rose. At Newmarket [at the Guineas meeting] we've used three jockeys. We stick with our policy that if a jockey has won on a horse last time, he stays on it. Ben was out with injury a bit through January, and we had a fantastic January. It meant that many of the horses early in the season, Franny and Joe had already won on them. We weren't going to jock them off and put him on."

Frankly, 'out with injury' scarcely does justice to the incident that caused Curtis's absence. He looked fortunate, indeed, to avoid a very serious injury, or worse, when in December, as *The Sun* put it, he had been "flung around the track like a rag doll in a sickening fall but miraculously managed to walk away" in an incident at Wolverhampton.

Curtis returned to reel off so many winners that, at one stage, he was forecast to be the 2021 champion jockey, including being tipped by Mick Kinane, champion jockey in Ireland 13 times. But if not this year, his time could well come. Unlike the trainers' championship, the riders' title is based on winners, but only those garnered between 1 May and 16 October.

"He could make it – absolutely could be champion," enthuses Johnston. "To be champion jockey, you need a yard that's going to give you a big chunk of winners. Obviously, we've done it before, not long ago, with Silvestre De Sousa. We made him champion; he was No.1, ahead of Joe and Franny – until he became champion jockey and other people snapped him up."

No-one can take anything for granted within the Johnston operation, though – even the highly-rated newcomer. The trainer admits to me when we talk in early May: "During the last few weeks, I've felt that Ben Curtis is not as good from the front as he is riding from behind as Joe Fanning is [admittedly an acknowledged master at making the pace]. I was wondering whether I needed to talk to him about it, and the way he rides horses from the front. But in the last few days, it's amazing how winners give confidence. Confidence is the most important thing in a jockey, and Ben's riding very well now."

How did Joe take what could be considered a demotion? "I did have Joe in, and explained to him about what we were going to do. Joe was fine. The press asked him about it, and he said, 'there's plenty of rides for everyone.' I'm not sure if he'll be thinking like that all the time because Ben Curtis is getting more rides than him now. But he still gets big ones, like Subjectivist."

Many other jockeys ride for the stable. At the time of writing, no fewer than 42 jockeys had partnered Johnston horses this year; ranging in experience from Ryan Moore, Aidan O'Brien's No.1 jockey for his Coolmore horses, to Jonny Peate, one of Johnston's three apprentices. Jonny rode a winner on his debut at Wolverhampton with Coupe De Champagne.

That was a sublime moment for the sixteen-year-old. However, in his *Kingsley Klarion* column in February, Johnston said: "Sadly, it will not be plain sailing from here. It will be difficult for me, despite the size of our team, to provide a reasonable number of good rides for Jonny. The BHA have done a horrendous disservice to young aspiring jockeys…they have removed all chance of a return for those of us who were willing to provide horses for them to ride and alienated the best trainers of apprentices in the country."

There has been what Johnston describes as "a bit of a war on" between trainers and the BHA and Professional Jockeys' Association. For many years, Flat trainers had retained up to 50 per cent of an apprentice's riding fee and prize-money yields, depending on their claim and regardless of who they rode for, in return for paying towards the jockey's expenses, such as travel and items of kit.

This changed in 2020, following claims that, in practice, some apprentices did not claim or receive the expenses owed to them. "They've cut it now to 20 per cent for the trainer, and 80 per cent for the rider," says Johnston, who objects, as he puts it, to trainers being portrayed in some quarters as money-grabbing abusers of vulnerable employees.

"My situation now is that I take nothing [from the apprentice fees and prize money] – but I'm not going to pay them [Peate, and his other two apprentices Andrew Breslin and Olli Stammers] when they're not working in the yard," Johnston says. "I've put them all on zero-hour contracts, which the BHA and PJA are upset about. It's a dirty word. But what would everyone else in the yard who would love to be apprentices think if they're being paid while they're away riding?"

Other leading trainers, including Andrew Balding, one of the most prolific producers of top-class riding talent in recent years, vehemently voiced their dissatisfaction at the new rules, believing they underestimate both the role trainers play in advancing the careers of apprentices and the cost to them financially.

We return to the subject of the stable's professional jockeys. Does he ever castigate them, even in private, afterwards? "I can't ever remember being upset enough [to have words afterwards]," he says. Or drop them? "I've dropped them from the next ride many times. On a regular basis. If someone makes a mess on a horse, we think they're not going to have confidence on the horse next time and we're not going to have confidence in them. So, we choose somebody we think will have confidence in the horse – somebody who's done better on it.

He adds: "So, many, many times we'll take them off because we don't think they've done a good job. Or maybe if they've won twice on a horse at Ascot, and next time it's going to Chester, and Franny Norton's a Chester specialist, so Franny will ride it. But we don't fall out with them over it."

And does he explain why they've been 'dropped'? "No, I probably should explain more. I don't tell 'em."

Clearly jockeys can get as piqued as footballers being demoted to the subs' bench. "I remember Joe Fanning got the huff with [owner] Mick Doyle because he got jocked off one of his best horses. I had a word with Joe and said 'just keep your mouth shut and get on with riding them.' On a couple of occasions, I've had to tell Joe: 'just ride winners. Just accept it if you get taken off horses and other people get put on. Don't get huffy about it – you won't achieve anything by that.'"

Though many Johnston horses break well from the stalls, and make the pace, there is no demand for this from high command. Johnston often emphasises that he never gives jockeys instructions. "Never, ever," he insists. "They may have been told the characteristics of the horse. What we know about it. But never instructions to sit somewhere in the field. That is stupidity. How can you ask someone to sit second when you don't know how fast the horse in first is going to go?"

He adds: "The Rules of Racing say you have to give jockeys what are deemed to be adequate instructions. They are supposed to include where the jockey should sit in the field, and when he should make his move. I'd love them to have me in and accuse me of giving inadequate instructions. I'd have to say 'I've given the same inadequate instructions in every one of those 4,000-plus wins.'

"There's a suggestion that we should declare 'tactics' [given to jockeys]. How ridiculous is that, in any sport. I don't have any tactics and I don't give any instructions. We were joking yesterday, about how Franny [Norton] said before mounting one of my horses at Newmarket, the day after Sir Ron Priestley's victory on 2,000 Guineas day: 'How was Sir Ron after yesterday?' I said, 'Fine'. They were the only words we exchanged in the paddock. "If the stewards had me in and asked me what instructions I'd given, I'd have told them that!"

The discussion brings us inevitably to women riders. As a long-time advocate of female riders, who I believed had merely required opportunities, I'd noticed that Hollie Doyle had won on a Johnston horse recently.

"I think my favourite jockey at the moment is Hollie Doyle," Johnston enthuses. "I think she's fantastic. If you had asked me the question five years ago 'what's your view on women jockeys', I'd have said, 'there'll never be a champion.'

"Ask me this year, and I think it'll be measured in months, not years, before there's a champion female jockey in Britain or Ireland. Could be Flat, could be jumps.

He adds: "Hollie's so dedicated; she can ride a horse from the front, back, anywhere. She could well be champion. And Rachael Blackmore is just phenomenal – one of the best things that's happened to racing, never mind jockeyship. Just wonderful."

He will concede that his attitude had changed. "I'd convinced myself that the man has this aggressive, competitive spirit which a woman doesn't have. It's not going to happen. But I now look back, and say they are so good, it must be that they didn't get the opportunity. Now we might see in my lifetime where female jockeys outnumber males. Female riders in the yards outnumber males."

We return to the subject of Ben Curtis. Purely in passing, I mention that he had incurred a two-day suspension for misuse of the whip after he had coaxed Zabeel Champion to victory by a nose in a handicap on 1,000 Guineas day at Newmarket.

It would instigate a conversation lasting several minutes, which started with the thought-provoking observation: "Misuse of the whip never did really happen."

USE OF WHIP PROVOKES FIERCE DEBATE

"Zabeel Champion?" Mark Johnston asks me to confirm the name of the horse Ben Curtis had been riding which was the subject of his ban. I confirm the name. "Not aware," says Johnston. Any thoughts? I ask. "No," he says. But with the Scot, one word never suffices. Pondering the question for a moment, he adds: "I think you just don't see misuse of the whip nowadays… because they ban them for things like that which are not misuse of the whip."

He laughs at what he's just said, but by way of elaboration, recalls an incident when jockey Ryan Moore won a juvenile event at York by 11 lengths on Richard Hannon's Mums Tipple in August 2019, after which the stewards handed him a two-day suspension for using his whip 'when clearly winning inside the final furlong'.

"The BHA put it out on Twitter. Yet, nobody had noticed, and Ryan Moore, if he has done that more than once I don't know, but it would be a very rare occasion for him to do it." The trainer emphasises the point: "If it was a regular occurrence, he would lose rides. That controls the whip. Not the BHA. All the BHA do is suggest there's been abuse of a horse when there hasn't. So, it's totally counterproductive and totally wrong – as was banning Ben Curtis. No horse has been abused. Rules have been broken, but the rule's an ass."

He adds: "We don't need the bloody BHA to control what people do to their horses. Owners and trainers are well capable of seeing if a jockey has abused a horse in some way – and the jockey won't be used any more. It's a complete nonsense."

I suggested to Johnston it would appear that, although his horses are often ridden vigorously, the whip is used sparingly by his jockeys. Was that at his insistence? "They are professional jockeys," Johnston retorts. "It's not for me to give them instructions. What I will say is that if jockeys go out and abuse horses, they won't stay riding for us for very long.

The whip, and use of it, however, remains contentious and rarely can two characters have been so ideologically and one could suggest, somewhat mischievously, as socially opposed as these two individuals in the aftermath of 2018 Royal Ascot.

In the blue corner: Charlie Brooks, the former amateur jockey and assistant to Fred Winter, who, when training in his own right, produced successes including Suny Bay, winner of the 1997 Hennessy Gold Cup, runner-up in the 1997 and 1998 Grand Nationals, and Couldn't Be Better, winner of the 1995 Hennessy Gold Cup. However, he was perhaps better known amongst the wider public as the husband of former *News of the World* editor Rebekah Brooks. Both were accused of perverting the course of justice in the wake of the phone-hacking scandal, but both were acquitted. "Mr Brooks, a horse trainer and an Old Etonian, was known for his luxurious lifestyle and his close connection to the

Prime Minister (David Cameron)," according to a profile in *The Telegraph*, for whom he writes a weekly column.

In the red corner: the never less than combative Mark Johnston, racehorse trainer for 34 years. Born in a Glasgow housing estate.

Apart from both being trainers (though Brooks last had a runner in the 2014–15 season), there could hardly be more contrast between them – other than that both can be provocateurs with the pen.

So, under the rather inflammatory *Telegraph* headline: "Ban whip or racing will be no more", Brooks referred to comments by Charlie Fellowes, 'a young, intelligent trainer from, importantly, a non-racing background', after he had stated that his horse Thanks Be, a winner of the Sandringham Handicap at Royal Ascot, should have been disqualified because the jockey Hayley Turner used her stick more than the authorised number of times. Turner received a nine-day suspension and was fined £1,600.

Brooks commented in his *Telegraph* column of 15 July 2019: "To be precise, she hit the horse 11 times, four more than the permitted level. So, a conscious infringement of the rules, rather than an accident. But as the rules stand, only the jockey, not the horse, gets penalised.

"The financial damage that the whip is causing is not apparent yet. But when the snowflake and millennial generations get control not only of their family purse but also the levers of power, horseracing as we know it today will be snuffed out."

Strong stuff, and he went for the jugular, stating: "But nobody in racing wants to hear this message. Some trainers such as Mark Johnston are committed to having their horses whipped because they think it makes them run faster. And Johnston seems to think it is his right to demand it."

It should be stressed that Brooks' comments are somewhat at

odds with what the BHA's view on what today constitutes the whip, and its use.

It states: "Whips are carried first and foremost as an essential aid to horsemanship and safety. The current ones, developed with input from the RSPCA, are 'foam-padded and energy absorbing, comprising a composite spine with a polymer surround, encased in thick foam padding.'

"The whip can be used a maximum of seven times in a Flat race or eight times in a Jump race. Any more than this will prompt the stewards to review the ride."

Use of the whip for encouragement is not about simply making a horse run faster. It is to focus and concentrate a horse so that it performs at its best during a race.

From 73,872 runners in 2020, no horse was found to have been marked, or 'wealed', by use of the whip.

Johnston says: "It's not about winning a race; it's about believing that whips are right. I think that whips are essential for riding horses. You cannot ride them properly without them. It's an essential tool for riding the horse, for making it go places you want it to go, for steering it, for making it behave itself, for preventing it from savaging another horse. I liken it to a second in a boxing corner. He's slapping the fighter in the face, shouting and swearing at him, telling him to wake up, keep his wits about him. He's saying, 'Keep your chin in and look after yourself. If you don't you'll get your head knocked off.' He's being aggressive to his man. He's getting the adrenalin flowing. It's the same with a jockey with the whip. We get an endorphin and adrenalin response which is conditioned into the horse both genetically and from the first time it runs; you get this response to the sting of the whip. It keeps it alert and on the ball on that run to the line so that it doesn't lose its action, doesn't let its head drop. You could well argue that a horse under the drive of a whip is far safer in terms of long-term injury to itself than a drive which is mostly hands and forward weight."

One can argue about who emerges the victor in that Brooks–Johnston bout. However, at the time of writing, an online consultation had begun which allows *anyone* (author's italics) with an interest in the subject to provide responses to a number of set questions related to whip rules and penalties. This had been recommended by the industry's independently-chaired Horse Welfare Board (HWB) as part of its five-year strategic plan for the welfare of horses bred for racing: "A Life Well Lived".

Johnston is well aware of the observations that will be forthcoming from certain quarters – as previously mentioned, one animal rights group Animal Aid campaigns for an end to racing altogether – and maintains:

"Those who argue against use of the whip aren't actually interested in the horse's welfare. They are only interested in the public's perception. They are more concerned about how it appears to be than how it actually is."

He adds, rhetorically: "Why is the whip such a big issue for the RSPCA? Why are racehorses such a big issue? Why, for that matter, are homes for ex-racehorses? Racehorses belong to rich people, and they stir emotions, and consequently they fill tin cans. Yet, laminitic ponies and neglected donkeys are a much bigger animal welfare issue in Britain than racehorses ever will be. We have far too much political correctness and nonsense on issues like that. We shouldn't be pandering to what the public at large want if they have no knowledge of the subject. We should be educating them."

CLASHING WITH
HIS CRITICS

I t's an occupational hazard for most trainers, but possibly more so for one whose entire operation has at its core the legend 'Always Trying'. There will always be the (often anonymous) malcontents who voice their displeasure, usually when an 'expected' stable runner is turned over.

One example was in August 2016, when a Johnston two-year-old named Sofia's Rock had been beaten at Hamilton, at 15-8 on. According to Johnston in his 'Bletherings': "An odds-on favourite gets beaten and the internet trolls crawl out from under their piles of losing betting slips. The latest one calls himself [he mentions a name] and comes, to me at least, from the highly unoriginal email address of 'alwayscheatings@gmail.com'.

This evening's offering read simply "Sofia's Rock – Always cheating at it's best Mark!" (Please note the grammatical error is his, not mine, Johnston is at pains to point out).

In the old days, a posted scribbled letter in green ink would have been the norm. Today, like many trainers and jockeys, he is the subject of social media barbs, or sometimes email or text.

Johnston wrote in the same piece: "I can cope with all the abusive mail I get, although I have to admit that it is an unpleasant side of the job."

However, he appreciates that many figures in the 'public eye' receive far worse – as he emphasised on *Desert Island Discs* in 2020. Commenting on his selection "Not Ready to Make Nice" by Dixie Chicks, he told Lauren Laverne: "I get hate mail on occasion, emails and text messages. Usually when favourites are beaten, some of them can be quite nasty. During the Iraq war, the lead singer of Dixie Chicks made a statement somewhere in Britain, I think at a concert, and she said 'not everybody from Texas supports the war, we're from Texas and we don't support the war,' and they had death threats. It brings everything into perspective for me, this track. It makes me realise there's people a lot worse off than me."

Returning to the issue of 'stopping a horse', Johnston, it should be added, boasts a clean record when it comes to the 'non-triers' rule. But then it would ill-behove a man whose branding is 'Always Trying' to be hauled before the stewards and found guilty, wouldn't it?

The only occasion he did fall foul of the local stewards was at Newcastle in July 2000. It involved a horse named Champfis, ridden by Darryll Holland, who finished fourth of eight in a one-mile maiden event. The *Racing Post* comment on its running was: "Steadied start, never near to challenge." Johnston was not at the meeting and, though he hadn't ridden the horse, jockey Bobby Elliott was called in as his representative. In his absence, Johnston was found to be in breach of the rule on 'non-triers' and was fined £750. "Basically, Bobby was stitched up," Johnston told me a few years later. "It's probably changed a bit now, but the way they ran these things was like a little kangaroo court. You had somebody [the Stewards' Secretary, the professional involved] who fancies himself as a Perry Mason, setting out to catch people who may be out of their depth, and trying to wring a confession out of them." Johnston won his case on appeal.

The trainer laid his position firmly on the line back in 1997 in his *Horse & Hound* column when the BHB (this was pre-BHA) declared that it was going to get tough on non-triers – and has not swerved from it since.

He wrote: "Frankly, I don't really feel that these rules are aimed at people like me and so I won't be losing any sleep over it. Most people know that, as far as I am concerned, every single one of my horses is trying to win on every occasion that it runs and if there is ever any suggestion that one of mine was 'stopped', then I'll be on the side of the prosecution."

However, he added: "A system which encourages and rewards cheats must be wrong, and if they are ever going to stamp out non-triers, they will have to change their own attitude to them and do away with the system that leads to them."

He refers, of course, to the whole ethos behind handicapping, which in the BHA's words: "enable horses of varied ability to race competitively against each other via the allocation of weight. The higher their handicap rating, the more weight a horse is required to carry." It doesn't require a particularly credulous nature to comprehend how this is open to abuse. Indeed, there has long been a euphemism applied to certain trainers; that they are 'laying out' a horse for a big race. They are not condemned, but admired.

The view, long-held by Johnston, is this: "I just think handicap racing is wrong," he says. "Which is not to say I don't think that the handicappers do a great job. If you're looking for something untoward in a race, that the result's not true, who would be better judges, a panel of stewards or a panel of handicappers? No doubt the latter. Probably if you had a panel of bookmakers they'd be ahead of the stewards as well."

In his 'Bletherings' in February 2021, he opined: "At all levels, the handicap system is failing British racing. I have asked the question before and never had an answer, so I'll ask it again: 'Who, apart from the betting industry, benefits from the handicap system?' The benefit to the betting industry is even debatable. Sure, their margins on handicaps are higher but, with nine of the top ten betting turnover races being non-handicaps, you will never convince me that punters prefer handicaps."

He added: "Is it really beyond the wit of man to devise a graded race system in which horses move up the grades according to what they have won and move down the grades when they fail to earn any prize-money for a period of time? It is how it works in most professional sport."

His preparedness to readily proffer opinions, frequently contentious ones, a prolificacy of winners, particularly given his backstory, tends to ensure that most media opinion of Johnston is positive. But that doesn't mean he is immune from the occasional gibe. In 2019, the *Racing Post*'s former editor Bruce Millington had referred to an earlier article by the paper's Stuart Riley, headlined: "Rich, poor or somewhere in between: how much does a trainer really earn?"

Riley had compared two trainers who both make their training fees public and wrote that the (then) daily fees of Tim Vaughan, predominantly a jumps trainer, based in the Vale of Glamorgan, at £37.50 (plus veterinary fees at cost), and Johnston's £78 (veterinary fees included) were at opposite ends of the scale.

Millington, in a comment piece, mused: "Why the difference, I wonder?

Surely horse food is horse food whether you are in Wales, Yorkshire or anywhere else? Admittedly Johnston bangs out a monthly magazine, the *Kingsley Klarion*, but that's just full of pictures of horses having operations and articles slagging off the Stewards, the *Racing Post* and anyone else who has happened to incur Braveheart's wrath. Still, he's trained more winners than many of us have had hot dinners and his yard is teeming with top-notch talent so good luck to him. Clearly, though, if you were thinking of entering the world of ownership and you didn't have a sheikh's budget it would pay to shop around fairly extensively for the best deal."

There was never any chance that Johnston would overlook such an observation. And, as the writer of the article correctly pointed out, the Scot does, indeed, have the mouthpiece to do so with the *Kingsley Klarion*.

In a lengthy article, Johnston turned those *Racing Post* observations on their head, claiming: "It is certainly a major concern that some, very competent, trainers are failing to make the job pay. The *Racing Post* should have been having a serious look at why that is happening and it should have been done by someone with a good understanding of training businesses and some grasp of the economics of small business in general. They would probably have quite quickly come to the conclusion that those trainers aren't charging a realistic fee and they should then ask why those trainers can't, or feel they can't, charge more."

The *Klarion* is a platform that has been increasingly important since Johnston's withdrawal from formal racing politics, the maelstrom in which he had frequently immersed himself right from his early days – until just after Royal Ascot 2006.

In his 'Times Diary' column in *The Times* on 29 June that year, the late Alan Lee reported that: "Mark Johnston, an articulate and forthright spokesman for his profession, has resigned from his prominent role on the National Trainers' Federation (NTF).

"I've been beating my head against a brick wall for 15 years and it's time to move on," he told 'Times Diary'. "Someone else can have a go now – I've had enough." The trainer explained to me soon afterwards: "I decided to go back to the back benches. It's nothing to do with the NTF, or what it may have done or failed to do, but there was a desperate frustration at my own failures."

Johnston added: "I had three years of influence on the NTF, as vice-president, president and past president, but I'll never retire entirely because I'll always have something to say." He shrugged and added: "It's a sad thing, isn't it? In industry, in politics, in every walk of life, people start off as radicals and end up as conservatives. I've always said I'm not arguing for me because I'm doing fine. I'm arguing for people that aren't doing fine, and arguing for British racing because I passionately believe it's not doing fine, or at least not getting what it should get. Frankly, I just got fed up. I thought, 'Never mind what everyone else does, let's just look after number one.' I may as well put all that energy into my own business. It's been said I should target complaints and issues I have through the NTF. Why? The sad reality is that I can achieve a lot more by writing about it in the *Kingsley Klarion*."

Predictably, that wasn't actually the end of Johnston's participation in the sport's politics. In 2011, he was appointed a director of the BHA. Better, it was possibly thought by racing's hierarchy, to have him inside the fortress, taking responsibility for running the sport, than firing cannons at it from the outside.

As Johnston explains this elevation: "I was active at the time on the NTF, and they said: 'we've got to get someone on the BHA board.' There was a crisis of some kind, and I said: 'I'll do it – that will upset them.' They had a rule that 'licenced personnel' could not be on the BHA. We thought that wrong and wanted to challenge it. The challenge to it was to put me forward..."

Ask him to recall what he brought to the role, and Johnston replies: "Little things. The marketing department would come around and suggest there should be multi-coloured silks, and I'd just say 'this is ridiculous'. The purpose of racing silks is to identify the horses. We shouldn't have zebra-striped ones and so on. And it got thrown out. A year later, it comes back again. It got thrown out. I left the board and it happened. It's not exactly important, but it sticks in my mind."

The trainer concedes: "I can't claim to have achieved anything dramatic at all, or anything important at all, either on the NTF or the BHA. That's probably why I've become disillusioned with it, and why I'm not active now."

'Not active' formally shouldn't infer not active at all. In April 2020, he became embroiled in a row over the timing of racing to return from lockdown. In April 2020, *The Telegraph* reported that: "A bitter row erupted over horse racing's delay in returning from lockdown last night after the head of the British regulator faced explosive calls to quit from a group of leading trainers."

Leaked emails from Johnston and fellow trainer Ralph Beckett, said to be furious at the BHA's reluctance to seek a government 'green light' to start racing again, called for chief executive Nick Rust – three months into a one-year notice period after resigning from his post in January – to quit immediately. This followed the issue of a statement, stating that it was "right to continue the suspension until the pressure on the NHS allows for a resumption, and we can assure the safety of those taking part."

In the event, the BHA supported Rust's stance. It would not be until 1 June that racing restarted – although it was the first major sport to do so.

It's in his nature. Johnston just can't help articulating his views, not least when he believes racing reacts to well-meaning, but often ill-informed public perception of certain issues rather than defending the correct course of action. In passing, he consults his smartphone and mentions to me a conference to be held in 2021, at which speakers were to address the topic: "Future-proofing the Racing Industry: Protecting People & the Planet".

The eyes roll at the title, and he says: "'Future-proofing the Racing Industry' is *this*," says Johnston. "It's about getting owners who are willing to invest money, income from betting and the media, jobs for people. Not all this bloody crap. This is like emperor's new clothes stuff. It's the same with this whip 'consultation.'" He pauses and spells out what he expects from the hierarchy of British racing: "Just. Get. On. With. Running. The. Industry."

CHAPTER 34

"HOW CAN YOU ENJOY OWNERSHIP WHEN YOU GET SO UPSET BY EVERY DEFEAT?"

The week before Royal Ascot 2021, the century of winners was on the scoreboard for the Johnston operation when the two-year-old Jadhlaan, in the familiar Sheikh Hamdan blue and white silks – but now under the name of Shadwell Estate – coasted home at York.

That change in name came about because, in March that year, His Highness Sheikh Hamdan bin Rashid al Maktoum, aged 75, was one of three highly prominent racehorse owners to have died.

Silks worn by that trio's jockeys have been instantly recognisable for many years. Apart from Sheikh Hamdan (owner of Dayjur, Nashwan and Battaash), Khalid Abdullah (Frankel, Dancing Brave and Enable) and David Thompson, joint-owner of Cheveley Park Stud (the flying sprinter Pivotal, Medicean and Russian Rhythm) had also passed away. Their colours were, and remain, synonymous with quality breeding; and as owners they have been serious players in British racing.

While their families grieved, their trainers have pondered the effect of the loss of such patrons, particularly members of the Maktoum family, and the effect on the industry,

Johnston told me in May 2021: "We've all been talking for years about what's going to happen to the Arabs – will there be a new generation of Dubai owners? Sheikh Hamdan, who we trained for was the biggest of the next generation in terms of ownership, but it's a really great concern as to whether things are going to carry on and be passed on.

"When Sheikh Maktoum died, none of his family took it on; it didn't get passed on to one of his family. Sheikh Mohammed absorbed the Sheikh Maktoum horses into Darley at the time. But this is a much bigger organisation than Sheikh Maktoum's was."

By late June, the position looked to have been clarified when the *Racing Post*'s Newmarket correspondent David Milnes wrote: "The future of Shadwell Estate is significantly clearer after it was confirmed Sheikha Hissa Hamdan Al Maktoum will succeed her late father Sheikh Hamdan as the head of one of Flat racing's most powerhouse owner-breeder operations."

Shadwell's racing manager Angus Gold told the *Racing Post* that Sheikha Hissa, in her late twenties, "had confirmed to me that she and her family are very keen to honour Sheikh Hamdan's legacy and keep the whole thing going, which is fantastic. It's wonderful for his memory that she has the passion and her brothers are going to support her taking it forward and we'll do our best to do the same."

Johnston told me: "I've not met her, but it's got to be great news for horseracing."

* * *

While the Maktoum empire remains the stable's most prominent owners, it is not alone, among patrons, in being well-resourced when it comes to bloodstock, notably Kirsten Rausing. Swedish-born, but based in Newmarket where, at her Lanwades stud, stand four stallions – Sir Percy, Study Of Man, Sea The Moon and Bobby's Kitten. The granddaughter of Ruben Rausing, who was the founder of the liquid food packaging company Tetra Pak, she was named as the 150th richest individual in the world in the Forbes 2020 list of The World's Billionaires.

Her seven horses trained by Johnston in 2021 include a two-year-old filly Madame Ambassador, by Churchill, out of Lady Jane Digby. Johnston trained Lady Jane Digby for Rausing to win an £81,000 ten-furlong Group 1 at Munich in 2010.

Other multi-horse owners include the previously-mentioned Dr Jim Walker, Mick Doyle, G.R. Baileys (of Mister Baileys fame), Markus Graff, and Paul and Clare Rooney. Paul Rooney, the man behind the Horsham-based Arun Estates, and his wife have long been more associated with high-profile successes over hurdles and fences, but in 2020 they transferred their interest to the Flat.

We discuss patronage in general at the Johnston yard. I assume owners will be, in no particular order: Expectant. Demanding. Easily disenchanted. You half-expect the trainer to play the diplomatic game. He doesn't.

"I remember when I started training, people saying to me that the worst thing about it was the owners," says Johnston. "That's ridiculous – saying that the worst thing about your business is your customers." Yet, he pauses before continuing, "It *is* the worst thing. It is such a relief, and is so pleasurable to have one running that you own yourself. If it gets beat, yes, you can be a wee bit disappointed. But I cannot understand the people who get so upset. I'm as competitive as anybody. And I want to win. But how can you enjoy it at all if you get so upset about every defeat and have to find someone to blame for every defeat, whether it's trainer or jockey? You shouldn't own horses [with that attitude] but people do."

He chuckles, and reflects on the 2021 2,000 Guineas victor Poetic Flare. What a superb set-up for a trainer. "It must be fantastic to be Jim Bolger. His wife owns it, he trains it and his son-in-law [Kevin Manning] rides it. And they won the Guineas. Must be absolutely wonderful." Narrowly defeated in the Irish equivalent, Poetic Flare would proceed to triumph in the St James's Palace Stakes at Royal Ascot.

He adds: "Why does no-one look at the stats which tell you that pound for pound at the sales, our Kingsley Park partnership horses out-perform everybody else. The reason is I control where I enter them, where I run them, who should ride it, or the ground it should run on – and nobody ever questions it. I can decide not to run them for a month or I can run them three times in a week. Nobody interferes. I run it where I believe it's got the best chance of winning."

The partnerships are run on the basis of 20 shares in three horses, purchased as yearlings, to run for up to two seasons. "And none of them get any say," continues Johnson. "And, so, they're a real pleasure to train for as well. I don't get any of the hassles or problems I get with other owners. Two runners today, they finish down the field. Nobody's going to moan or complain. I'm not going to get down in the dumps about it. Nobody's going to say it needs a rest or what I should do with it next. I may run it again quickly and it may win, but it can't win if the owner insists it needs a break. Nobody says: 'Take it to Chester because I love Chester and my gran lives nearby.'" It is also entirely his decision if a horse is sold out of the yard.

TRIUMPH AND TRIBULATIONS AFTER A CROWN DUEL AT ROYAL ASCOT

A still Covid-defined Royal Ascot 2021 was not quite like the 2020 edition when the enclosures were empty, but it was still deficient in spectating numbers, and its mounted participants were masked like bandits. And, for a second consecutive year, there was no Royal Procession, a tradition that dated back to 1825, when King George IV paraded in front of racegoers before taking his position.

In 1998, Mark Johnston had been invited to ride in the Royal Procession, preceded by lunch with the Queen. And did he accept? "Of course," he says, as though any other response was unthinkable, though he added: "Deirdre did – I didn't get any choice in the matter!"

He adds: "Whichever monarch it was, here, Dubai or wherever, I'd be delighted to do it. We had lunch at Windsor Castle, and I had what they call the 'hot seat', between the Queen and the Queen Mother. Of course, we talked mainly about horses. Deirdre was next to the Duke of Edinburgh. Then we rode in the Royal

Procession, down the course, and spent the afternoon in the Royal Box. It was very interesting. I'd do it again." That was the year Double Trigger was narrowly beaten by Kayf Tara in the Gold Cup.

Though this year, there were no Royal preliminaries, there was a battle for the crown – the stayers' crown. It was a tantalising prospect: the appearance of Stradivarius, the now seven-year-old Cup king, who would start at odds-on favourite to record a fourth consecutive Ascot Gold Cup – unless Subjectivist could become Mark Johnston's fourth Gold Cup victor, and subjugate him.

Even before the stalls opened the story would always be about Stradivarius, victor or vanquished. It was a vintage renewal, in terms of the talent on display. Three participants had already won more than £1m. They included Twilight Payment, winner of the 2020 Melbourne Cup.

The race itself was as uncomplicated for the Johnston horse as the Dubai Cup had been. Joe Fanning eased Subjectivist into the lead three furlongs out and the colt was never challenged as he strode clear and maintained his advantage to the line, securing first place by five lengths. He had won two races this year by an aggregate of just under 11 lengths, and won more than half a million pounds for his owner.

Subjectivist finished ahead of Princess Zoe, Spanish Mission and, in fourth place, Stradivarius.

"This horse has annihilated them," declared Sky Sports Racing's Alex Hammond. Fanning was accorded a standing ovation by his fellow riders as he and Subjectivist returned to the winner's enclosure. Hammond's colleague Freddy Tylicki, a former jockey, added: "We know Mark Johnston likes to have his horses up front or very handy. Joe Fanning is an absolute genius, riding from the front. It was a perfect ride – he put the race to bed very easily."

Inevitably, much of the post-race analysis would focus

on Stradivarius's 'traffic problems' turning for home, when Frankie Dettori's mount was denied a clear run, although it was inconceivable that he would have caught Subjectivist.

As Johnston, owner Jim Walker and Fanning received their trophies from the Princess Royal, Hammond enthused that the race had been won by: "This team, this family outfit, who have grown and grown over the years to become one of the most powerful stables in the world."

Describing his charge as "very much a young pretender against the old guard", Johnston told Sky Sport Racing's Hayley Moore: "There are more valuable races at Royal Ascot, there are races that can make a horse an awful lot more valuable at Royal Ascot, there are plenty of races I have still to win at Royal Ascot, but I say every year, there's no race I want to win more than this. It's the pinnacle of Royal Ascot."

Susan Hearn, Subjectivist's breeder reflected: "I felt sick, I always feel sick when my horses are running, it's a horrible feeling but I can't believe how easily he did that. It's a shame we sold him, but there you go!"

In the wake of the race, headline writers were clearly torn between putting the accent on Stradivarius suffering defeat and Subjectivist proving supreme.

Later, in his 'Bletherings', Johnston mused: "It was great to watch the race again and to read some of the newspaper reports... although it was a little frustrating, if not entirely surprising, to be damned with faint praise in some quarters where the emphasis was on Stradivarius having suffered interference in running rather than on the magnificent performances from Subjectivist and his jockey."

However, he added: "The reception that Subjectivist received and the overwhelmingly positive media coverage was all the more gratifying. Some of that was, most certainly, down to the popularity of his rider, Joe Fanning, but this was not Joe's first Group 1 win and not even his first on this horse. And, when he won the Middle Park on The Last Lion, he was lowering the colours of none other than Blue Point with an enterprising ride. The public reaction to that was muted by comparison.

"I think the difference this time was that most informed observers thought they had seen something quite special. They had witnessed a demolition job on a field jam-packed with staying talent by an extremely talented young horse, executed with precision by the most underrated jockey in the weighing room."

Ever the analyst, he added: "It should, perhaps, be noted that the Gold Cup was the only race on the day where the time dipped below standard, and by a full 1.22 seconds. ITV's analysis of the sectional times was also very interesting and it pointed out that Subjectivist covered the final furlong faster than any other horse so, if my very basic physics and maths isn't failing me, that tells me that, for anything to beat him, it would have had to be in front of him with 220 yards to go or it would have had to finish a lot faster than it did on the day.

"Stradivarius's owner, Bjorn Nielsen, was the first person to congratulate me when I managed to extricate myself from the winners' enclosure and he and the Gosdens were very magnanimous in defeat, as you would expect from such a professional team. They must have been very disappointed, but I am sure that they feel that their great horse owes them nothing.

"His earnings are quite staggering as, I believe, he collected two £1 million Weatherbys Hamilton Stayers bonuses to add to almost £3 million in prize money, and who is to say that he is finished yet. Subjectivist is highly unlikely to ever amass such earnings although, if this was a different sport, we would probably have

Subjectivist's breeder's husband, Barry Hearn, promoting a rematch with the bulk of the media rights earnings going to the 'players'. Wouldn't that be something?"

This was Alastair Down's droll take of the Subjectivist's triumph in the *Racing Post*: "Thursday was Mark Johnston's fourth Gold Cup triumph and as I recall the days when he trained on a gunnery range in Lincolnshire I have never begrudged him a scintilla of his success. He is an endearing mix of the charming and the mildly irritating.

"The winner now heads to the Goodwood Cup where Double Trigger gave me some of the indelible moments of my life on the Flat in 1995, '97 and '98.

"As for the winning trainer, I instinctively like the fellow, though there are times when you want to give him a gentle slap – as there are occasions when he will tell you he knows the name of the Unknown Soldier."

Meanwhile *The Times* couldn't resist placing a little political spin on the story: "An economist who stood unsuccessfully for Alex Salmond's Alba Party in the Scottish election in May has been celebrating a better result after winning Royal Ascot's Gold Cup. Dr Jim Walker's horse Subjectivist, ridden by Joe Fanning, claimed victory in Berkshire yesterday. Walker, chief economist with Aletheia Capital, told ITV Racing that the joy of winning the contest was 'the pinnacle' of his involvement in the sport."

* * *

Three weeks after Subjectivist's Gold Cup, the evening of 8 July, I meet up with the Johnstons at their property in Newmarket, situated conveniently almost within earshot of the Tattersalls auctioneer.

Sir Ron Priestley has just repelled all challengers to claim the

Princess of Wales's Stakes at the July course, his second Group 2 success of the year. However, the tone is subdued.

This sport always has the capacity for extreme emotions, and from that moment when his younger brother Subjectivist had been elevated to the pantheon of staying greats only three weeks earlier, there is now an air of despair.

Johnston has just told the media at Newmarket that his colt is out with a leg injury, at least for the season, possibly to never race again. "The best scenario is that he'll be back for the Gold Cup next year. Not before."

I take him back to his observation that his horse's Royal Ascot display had been a "demolition job". He nods. "That's why it's so devastating that he's injured. If you're now to say to me: 'Name the best three horses you've ever had', I would say: Shamardal, Attraction and Subjectivist. He's right up there with them. Not since I had them, have I had a horse that's likely to be superior to anything that's come up against him."

He adds: "I can't say I was doing that before Dubai. When he won in France last year, we knew he was top class. We were saying before Dubai 'we've got a fantastic team of stayers to take on Stradivarius next year.' But in Dubai, he just moved up a complete level to where he'd been before. He just won it so easily.

"Everybody was a little unsure – could he carry that form across to an even higher level? But that was an incredible Gold Cup field. Jam-packed full of Group 1 horses. Two Derby winners. I don't think there's been a better Gold Cup field in a long time and he didn't just win it, he won it by five lengths."

We talk pressure, something Johnston has said he only experiences when, like Attraction ahead of the 2003 Queen Mary Stakes, he would be devastated if his charge is defeated. That was not the case here. "We'd seen what we'd thought was a fantastic performance in Dubai. But we didn't know for *certain* he'd do that again. We never thought he was nailed on. And even if he did that again, was that as far ahead of Stradivarius and horses like him that we'd hoped." He pauses and adds: "It was, wasn't it?"

"You can debate whether Stradivarius could have finished second – but I don't think that anyone believes that Stradivarius could have won it, no matter how different he'd been ridden in the race. But Spanish Mission proved himself better than we thought he was. It was a rock-solid field.

"It meant a huge amount to Dr. Jim [Walker]. He had a good middle-distance horse in Austrian School before. But this is the first Cup horse he's had. His attitude was 'this is the race I wanted to win more than any other.'

"I phoned him this morning and told him: 'I think we have to accept that he's not going to race again this year.' He was very philosophical about it. He took probably the right attitude to say: 'We've got the Dubai Gold Cup and the Ascot Gold Cup. The horse owes us nothing.'

"It's heart-breaking, and heart-breaking for racing, too. The Goodwood Cup was looking like being a huge draw." It transpired, however, that Stradivarius was withdrawn on the day of the race because of the heavy going.

As for Subjectivist's future, Johnston explains: "He's relatively young in staying terms. It will be a purely economic decision. If someone offers enough for him to go to stud, he'll go to stud – because the odds are stacked against him coming back at the same level. But if they're not offering enough, then we may as well try and get him back. He can win £500,000 in one race.

"He will go to stud as a National Hunt stallion – not as a Flat sire. They're not worth an awful lot of money, not relative to what the Flat sires are."

So, no return bout with Stradivarius, probably ever – because the Gosden horse will be eight next year, and could be off to stud himself.

And as for Subjectivist's younger half-sister Alba Rose...she didn't make it to the German 1,000 Guineas either. In fact, for all the best-laid plans, Johnston reveals the filly is sidelined with a fractured pelvis and won't race again this Turf season.

Their big brother Sir Ron Priestley was soon back in action; he was supplemented, at a cost of £25,000, to contest the Goodwood Cup, and finished third behind Alan King's Trueshan. However, the five-year-old pulled up lame with a recurrence of a suspensory injury, which was described by Johnston as career- but not life-threatening. It meant all three members of the family had suffered injuries in the space of a few weeks.

It would be easy to trot out those oft-quoted Kipling lines:

"If you can meet with Triumph and Disaster.
And treat those two impostors just the same..."

As stoical as Johnston is, at times living by that principle must be damned hard.

"BEAUTIFULLY TURNED OUT, AS YOU'D EXPECT FROM THIS STABLE"

From the scene the Johnstons encountered in the late 1980s, when they rolled into town with their 13 horses of varied quality, it would have been almost unimaginable – *almost*, but perhaps not to one man – that they would create the establishment that confronts you today.

In 2021, there are around 230 equine athletes spread across the three yards: Kingsley Park, where the operation is now based, Kingsley House, and Warwick House.

With the groom-riders, office personnel and estate workers included, there is a total of 235 staff. Some to whom I speak should be recipients of long-service medals. Indeed, Jock Bennett *had* been winner of a lifetime in racing award in 2020 and in 2013 had been named Employee of the Year at the ninth annual Godolphin Stud and Stable Staff Awards.

Jock Bennett was here when Johnston passed the 1,000-winner mark and, in doing so, beating Henry Cecil's record for the fastest

1,000 Flat victories by a trainer in Britain by 90 days, when Double Honour won at Hamilton in September 2000.

They don't come any more insightful than this engaging character, who turned 65 in 2021. He arrived at Middleham in 1997 after 25 years with Bill Watts in Richmond.

As we talk, Bennett is overseeing horses in the water-walker. "Many horses benefit from it," he explains. "It's a great innovation – one of the best things I think we've put in. The swimming pool's very good as well, but I think the water-walker is a gem. They will get more popular. People will see the difference. Some of the older horses that move up here and start going in there, you see their form improve. It's a great exercise. If you ever try walking through water yourself, it's hard work. They're walking in two feet of water. Every muscle is covered."

This vast operation is a production line, of sorts, of winners. Yet, for raw material, we talk of fragile, occasionally fractious, beings of flesh and blood, all with their own idiosyncrasies and temperaments, and talent needing to be nurtured.

Some are biddable and comply quietly; others are nervous, cautious characters. Some have special needs. On the treadmill adjacent to the water-walker is one of the stable's lesser lights, although twice a winner. I'm told when she was taken to the gallops, she just stopped and the rest of the string couldn't get past her, so it was decided to train her on this equipment instead.

Bennett told me: "I'd left school at 15, with no qualifications. I was struggling, to be fair. I'd always fancied working outdoors, but hadn't ridden a horse in my life. I had a paper round and the guy that owned the shop was very keen on horseracing. He suggested, with my height and weight 'why don't you go away and be an apprentice jockey?'

"So, I wrote that day to four trainers. Bill Watts offered me a month's trial, which I did, and 25 years later, he still hadn't told me whether I'd got the job or not. It must have gone OK...

"I learned to ride pretty quick, but it was a lot different then. Fifty years ago, we were looking after two horses, wages were very poor, but you got a one-to-one training. You'd have an older lad looking after you, and the head lad would teach you to ride. It was different, it wouldn't work nowadays. But it did then."

He compares the operation now to the one he encountered when he arrived in the 1990s. "Staff, horses, everything has increased so much, and it's still not stopping. There's something different going on every year. We've just built a new indoor school. But that's Mark. From the start, it was always investment, investment, investment. Whatever was made was invested back into the business."

He adds: "I started as second head lad. We still called them that then. We then moved to the yard manager system. I moved from yard manager to assistant around 15 years ago at that stage when Mark was standing outside doing the boards until two in morning [doing 'the list']. One thing I appreciated about it all was that when he said he was going to have an assistant, he didn't advertise the job. Two of us went for it – but he kept it in-house.

"If he'd have advertised that job: 'Assistant trainer to Mark Johnston', he'd have had a load of applications that high". He gestures skywards. "Who knows who would have been turning up for it."

Bennett's previous employer had taken over from his father, the late Jack Watts. "Jack was private trainer to Lord Derby, and we trained for Lord Derby as well," says the Scot. "Having worked for Bill for 25 years, I was very much set in the ways of that. I'd been watching Mark's career from across the way [Hurgill Lodge] at Richmond and when I came here, I saw a completely different operation – which is just what I needed. He had learned so much in such a quick time."

He adds: "Most of his ideas were common sense. The first trainer I worked for, he would gallop a horse twice a week, no matter what – Tuesday and Friday was work day. He'd gallop these horses, and eventually he would run them. I can remember one of the horses had 14 gallops before he actually ran.

"Then I've seen Mark, how he trained – if they are two-year-olds, they'd have four gallops maybe. But they'd have done a lot of outside work, had a good education beforehand, but they're ready to run. And once he gets them running, he doesn't gallop them again. He doesn't need to. 'They gallop on the track for money', he used to say to me.

"That just hit a note with me. It was the most common-sense thing I've ever heard. Because I used to think it was stupid, towing a horse up the gallop twice a week when it should be doing it on the track. Feeding the horses through the night. The way he used to monitor the weights – we hadn't done that before. Maybe we were behind the times at Richmond. But Mark was ahead of the time. I learned that very quickly. He hasn't got much wrong."

Few Johnston horses cause problems at the stalls. That is not coincidence. "It starts with us as yearlings, they go through them [the stalls] every day in their life – even before they have a rider on their back. Any stall problem we come across is sorted straight away. Our percentage of horses with stalls problems is very low. Once they do this, and they're fast out, they're ready to run," says Bennett.

Going racing with the horses has never lost its appeal. "I enjoy being with the owners. I love seeing them first time they have a winner, or a lad with his first winner, a jockey with his first winner, a trainer. You don't see that in any other walk of life. It's a unique experience, that first winner. To see the joy and expressions on people's faces – it's quite something."

We discuss the boss, and his, shall we say, more irascible side. "Yes, he can start an argument in an empty house," says Bennett. "I find two sides to him. He doesn't suffer fools. I don't either. He talks so much common sense, and has a good sense of humour – people don't often see. His demeanour on the track doesn't always tell you about the person he is. There's a side that you guys [journalists] don't see. He has a very kind side. If I was in trouble, he'd be one of the first people I'd ask, and I'm sure he would help."

As for Charlie's eventual take over, albeit with a joint licence initially, Bennett says: "It's a huge responsibility. On the horse side of it, I've no doubt he'll do a very good job. He's more than capable. He's very good with owners as well. This young man never ceases to amaze me. As he matures, as he gets older, I would say there's nothing that would faze him. He will get round whatever it is."

Bennett confirms Johnston's constant striving to accentuate the need for teamwork, whatever your status. "Our ethic for the staff, if you read the handbook, right from the introduction, is to say: 'You Are Part Of A Team'. I think we're more of a team than a lot of other yards. We still have our fringe problems with staff, but generally it's pretty good. Take that lad there, Paddy. He's Mark Johnston through and through."

'Paddy' is **Patrick Trainor**, a groom-rider at the yard. He has been here for more than 20 years, and if anyone was selected to be the poster boy for Johnston Racing, it would probably be him. In the reception of the Kingsley Park office, there's an enormous poster-size photograph of Frankie Dettori undertaking one of his flying dismounts from the stable's grey filly Nahoodh after a 10-1 triumph in the Group 1 Falmouth Stakes at Newmarket in 2008. But you can't help being struck by the character in the foreground, ecstatically punching the air.

"That's me in the picture," says Trainor, his features wreathed in a grin. "First Group 1 winner I'd ever led up. I was also lucky enough to lead up Dee Ex Bee, when he was second in the 2018 Derby. For me, it was like winning the Lottery, even though he wasn't the winner. That horse came to us as a yearling, and I was lucky enough to lead Dee Ex Bee to his first-ever race when he won at Goodwood, and then at The Derby."

That old cliché 'infectious enthusiasm' could have been created for this character. Indeed, I hadn't asked to speak to him – he simply ambled up and introduced himself.

It should never be underestimated what unadulterated elation a victory, be it a charge like Nahoodh in Group 1, or a humble selling race, brings to a member of staff at the racecourse. Even a best-turned-out award is greatly prized.

At the racecourse, the horses are so impeccably-groomed you can almost see your reflection in their gleaming coats, and you can only admire the immaculately-crafted quarter marks. Many of the public do not fully appreciate the meticulous attention that goes into capturing a 'best-turned-out' prize.

"Beautifully turned out, as you'd expect from this stable." Sky Sports Racing's Hayley Moore would say of a Johnston horse, Silver Kitten, in July 2021, at Yarmouth, before a hard-fought victory. It is just the end of a long process of different roles which culminates at the racecourse with the jockey being legged up into the saddle.

Trainor, fiercely proud of his Scottish lineage – he was born in London, the son of a Scottish mother – says: "We grooms are best-turned out, too. When we got the tartan waistcoats, our ties, we got a lot of stick from other stables. Not now. I'm proud to wear it, even though it's not my Tartan. You could go into the paddock, and there'd be three runners from our stable, and the cameras would be straight on to us."

These individuals will not be the one interviewed by press and TV; they will never earn big bucks. But it's what sustains them through perishingly bitter winters, and not always sociable hours.

They are committed to their charges from the moment they arrive as unbroken yearlings to the moment the elite amongst them go to stud or to the paddocks as broodmares, just move on to another stable, or are retired. And, regrettably, very occasionally don't return from the racecourse.

"I always loved horses and, at 17, went on a course at The British Racing School at Newmarket," says Trainor. "I've been here 23 years. I love it. My wife Sam now works for National Racing College at Doncaster. She's an assessor, and comes into our stable and assesses new staff from that college, the NVQs 1, 2 and 3, whether it's bandaging, plaiting up, recognising lameness. She's been there around 10 years. She worked here for a few years before that."

He adds: "When I got married, the boss [Johnston] came to my wedding. I remember on the day, knocking on his door and asking for a kilt belt. He was so proud. I'm here for life now – even if I was offered a lot more money at another stable, that would mean nothing. I still wouldn't go because this is my home. I help break in the yearlings in winter as soon as those horses come in on day one. I usually take them first time to the racecourse, and lead them up. I'm involved in the whole process. I have my four two-year-olds I look after year after year. I like chatting about my job when I go racing, I chat to anyone." Indeed, he does.

Andrew Bottomley, another of the yard's assistant trainers, arrived here in 2002, just before the Attraction–Shamardal era. "The second year I was here, we had something like 18, 19 Group winners," he recalls, adding: "Dad [John] was a trainer in Malton, and I worked for him straight from school, but when he packed up, I left racing for two years and worked in a factory – the worst two years of my life."

Johnston says of him: "We think of Andrew as the 'ideas man', always coming up with something new. A lot of man-management stuff he got from working in the factory." Bottomley, who is much involved with staff training, has produced a skills video for staff with Angus Johnston.

I ask him about Charlie's involvement, and eventual takeover. Does he have any problems working for a younger man? "I thought when I heard he was going to become Mark's assistant it might – there is a big age difference – but it hasn't. When I first started here, he was, what, seven years old. Now he's my boss. But he's a down-to-earth lad. He doesn't go around throwing his authority about. Everybody gets on with him and he's really approachable. The fact is that everything's done on such a professional scale that if Mark was to disappear for a year it would continue to run. The attention to detail is unbelievable."

Hayley Kelly joined the staff at Middleham as a teenager. Within four years, she was travelling with horses to Australia, and later her adventures would take her to Canada, the U.S. and Hong Kong, as well as throughout Europe.

"I had work experience here for three weeks and was on a British Racing School ten-week course and started off as groom-rider," she says. "But in my first year, I became travelling manager, and did that for 17 years. I was 17, going on 18, when I first started travelling, going racing every day, all over Britain, but there were also a lot of trips abroad as well. Obviously, it's a big responsibility, taking the horses away, because you're in charge of the horses and the staff.

Today, Kelly is an assistant trainer, having been a yard manager for eight years. Staff training is one of her responsibilities. She says: "Some of the young ones, I ask how old they are. If they're early twenties, I tell them: 'Do you know what I was doing when I was 21? I was on the other side of the world with a horse. And I tell them about that Australia trip, to the Melbourne Cup with Yavana's Pace in 1999. Nobody was with me. Mark and everybody else were here. It was me and the horse for seven weeks. To be allowed to do that was a massive, massive responsibility – although, at the time, I took it for granted."

Jukebox Jury was another of her charges who would establish himself as a seasoned European and North American tourist and become almost as experienced a world traveller as Michael Palin.

The Irish St Leger victor – he dead-heated with John Gosden's Duncan for first place at The Curragh – had been bought by Johnston for €270,000 and proceeded to secure the four Group 2 events here, the Royal Lodge Stakes and Jockey Club Cup, and two at Deauville and included the Group 1 Preis von Europa at Cologne 2009 amongst his haul of nine victories. He was retired in 2011 after finishing lame in the Melbourne Cup.

Hayley Kelly would partner the horse in his work and accompany him on his travels. "He really wasn't very straightforward," she recalls. "He had a fear of trees. See that one there [pointing at one particular tree], he hated it when it was windy and the branches were moving. And he hated birds suddenly flying out. I loved him, but he was really soft when he wanted to be. When I took him to Canada [for the 2009 Canadian International, in which he was runner-up, beaten half a length] I was cantering him one morning, and he was suddenly confronted by about 30 geese. I can tell you I held on a bit tighter than usual! We managed to get through it. I took him all over the world. He now stands as a stallion, and because he was a 1m 4f–1m 6f horse, the jumping boys absolutely love him."

She adds: "It's funny to see horses like him, lots of horses we've trained, that are now standing at stud. And you get the fillies and because I've been here so long, they're mares and you're finding yourself riding the offspring of something you used to have in your own barn. You don't realise that time goes so quickly."

Johnston had only just bought Warwick House when Kelly arrived. "To see this place grow, in horses, staff and facilities, it's an amazing place to work, and to train," she says. "In winter time, I love breaking in the yearlings, when they're babies. It's great to break them and see them come on to be good racehorses. There's always a difficult one, and you think 'Oh, my God!' and it turns out a good horse. To know that that horse took me so long to break it, but I got there in the end. It's a bit of an achievement to do that."

Kelly adds: "I don't usually travel to races here any more, but I went on the Dubai trip with Subjectivist because Mark knows I still enjoy that side of it. The horse ran so well – I was chuffed to bits with him. In 2018, I was lucky enough to go to America twice [to Keeneland and Arlington], with the filly Nyaleti [a Group winner, here and abroad], who I used to ride at home. She was quite a stubborn filly. I used to take her racing in Britain because she wouldn't go into the stalls. I had to go down to the start and help put her in. Another one was Bijou D'Inde, I used to ride him a lot at home when I was younger. I took him over to Ireland when he ran in the Irish 2,000 Guineas."

We discuss Charlie's impending partnership with his father, and how he will ultimately become trainer here in his own right. "It's funny because when I started, Charlie was this size [she lowers her hand to just above floor level]. Charlie has always been a big part, even since he was tiny. When he was four, five, six, he was always out in the yard. He'd go and see the horses at night time. Was always very knowledgeable about the horses and owners. He used to ride out when he was younger, was always riding out with the lads. So, he knows what it's like to work in the yard."

Though an assistant trainer, Kelly still rides out, and does so on some of the yard's best horses. "I'm riding Nayef Road and Thunderous at the moment. Thunderous won the Dante last year, but got injured and has some screws in a back leg. He's such a lovely horse, and such a gentleman, but doesn't do a tap at home. So, you never know how fit he is." The colt has been placed in Group races in 2021. As for Kelly's own future, she says simply: "If I was to leave, I wouldn't work for any other trainer bar Mark...so looks like I'm here for life!"

* * *

One suspects, if Mark Johnston could clone Hayley Kelly, he would. Staff like her are worth their light weight in gold. He has told me that if a dozen lightweight riders arrived at the yard, he would employ them – even if he had no vacancies.

It explains why, although he admits to being in general "anti-charity", he does have a concept for one.

I interrupt and ask why 'anti-charity'? Again, it goes back to his upbringing, a belief, he says that: "Charity is conscience money for people who should be paying more income tax."

He admits that this will not be the consensus view. "I was out cycling with a friend, and we discussed this. He didn't agree. He said 'the fairest tax is income tax – *if* you could trust the government to spend it wisely. But most of us don't trust the government to spend it wisely. Charity gives you an opportunity to give money where you think it should be spent.'"

Johnston returns to his idea for a charity. "I think it's wrong that there are only two racing schools. I would like to see a situation where if you went into any riding school in Britain, there'd be a poster on the wall which said 'Become a jockey' or 'Work in racing – learn here'. We need to get to more people. As I've said, I'm not particularly into charities…but I have this vision. I would like to see free riding lessons for anybody. Not means-tested, so anyone could go along, rich or poor, and have free riding lessons. Group riding lessons, ten, or whatever. The rich would want individual tuition – they can pay for that."

He adds: "If someone wants to sit on a horse, we should make it possible, regardless of whether they're 12 or 50, in the country or inner city. Long-term that would have an impact on the perception of horseracing, and the number of people who wanted to be involved.

"That should be a charity, and the racing industry should put money into it. Instead of wondering about the public perception of horseracing and the whip, and so on. The problem is that many of those people out there have never even *seen* a horse.

"Even when I was a kid, the rag man used to come around with a horse and cart in East Kilbride. When my Dad was a kid, there were horses and carts everywhere. The Army had horses right up until World War II, and beyond. People were much more aware of horses – as the Irish still are."

As we talk, in the office at Kingsley Park, one work-rider returns. She removes her riding-out hat. It is the colours of the Saltire. "Different styles of it, but I've had that for 33 years," says Deirdre. "It's familiarity. I love things I've had a long time. My whip I've had for about 18 years."

The job, if you can describe it as such, is one she's had for over 30 years. For this individual, it is something she has done for love, not necessity, at least not since those early days on the beach in Lincolnshire.

THE POWER BEHIND
THE THRONE

From a young girl with a pony in 'Mark's field' at Aberfoyle, near Stirling, Deirdre Johnston's life has become dominated by horses of one kind or another; of one colour or other.

"I ride racehorses in the morning, and if I don't go to the races afterwards, I ride my own horses in the afternoon," she tells me, embracing her large labradoodle, and saying: "Horsey-daft, aren't we Doogs [full name Doogle]." She adds: "I have five horses in work, plus a mare and yearling in the field. And I've actually cut down a bit!

"All my hobbies involve my own horses, and going to places with them. I own event horses with Nicola Wilson, the Olympic rider. I met her family hunting, and took a share in a horse with Nicola, who lives nearby, about 15 years ago."

Deirdre also has a half share in an event horse, named JL Dublin, purchased by Wilson in Germany. The other share is owned by Jo and James Lambert, owners at Johnston Racing. In the weekend before Royal Ascot 2021, Deirdre and her fellow owners spent the weekend at Bicton in Devon where JL Dublin, with Wilson in the saddle, won a highly competitive event, "one I would equate with a Group 1 in racing terms," she says. It was JL Dublin's 10th top-10 finish at international events, but his first win.

Deirdre adds: "I do some eventing on Kingsleypark Patch – all my home-breds are called Kingsleypark something – he's 13 now, I do some riding club activities, a bit of everything. I've got a lovely coloured[10] that I've bred that I want to do showing classes with. If I go away for a weekend, it's to do with horses. That's what I love."

Deirdre did consider race-riding. "I did the amateur course at the British Racing School, but then I decided I'd let it go too long. I wish I'd done it when no one knew who I was. I didn't fancy being out there on the public stage. That's why I go with a horsebox with no writing on it. I like to go incognito."

She confesses to one other passion. "I don't like fancy handbags or shoes or designer clothes, anything like that, but if I'm going to have a little treat it'll be a piece of jewellery. I used to buy a piece from Harriet Glen at Glorious Goodwood if we'd had a winner, like Double Trigger. Nearly all have an association with a horse."

Deirdre's husband has no interest in any other equine-related sports, and admitted to me when his sons were young that, though he would occasionally attend to watch Charlie in action, "mostly it's Pony Club competitions and one-day events he goes to. But when I do go, I think that these are the most boring sports under the sun."

He is essentially a man who needs racing to fulfil him and, if it's not horses, then greyhounds are an excellent alternative. Indeed, a few years ago, he did turn his hand to training greyhounds. It was the consequence of a challenge he couldn't resist.

---

[10] Coloured horses are skewbald (marked with spots and patches of white and some colour other than black) or piebald (colours are properly white and black).

The story began in a pub in Naas in Ireland, over a few pints of Guinness. An owner, Peter Kelly, had introduced him to a friend Mick O'Dwyer. Johnston told Mick he could train greyhounds better than greyhound trainers – a belief dating back to when he trained whippets as a teenager. Mick offered to give the Scot a half-share in three pups in return for him training them.

Johnston approached his new role with deadly seriousness. He bought the owner's friend's share of the dogs – named Crush (pet name: Sooty), Idolize (Sweep) and Affection (Soo) and during the winter, he installed an electric lure, put them on the horse walker, ran them up the gallops and fed them prime steak.

"I was officially the trainer, but Lyn, my sister, did most of the work. Two won five races apiece at quite a high level, and the other won ten, but at a much lower level. The dogs would often run at Pelaw Grange in County Durham, but our last winner was at Newcastle, and was televised. When Lyn died [in 2014], we carried on for maybe six months, but the dogs were getting on towards the end of their careers, so we didn't continue."

As related previously, throughout her life Lyn wrote poems. Her brother recites one that's very relevant:

> "*Mark, Oh Mark, you do make us smile.*
> *We pups, we come from the Emerald Isle.*
> *We don't like porridge. Oh no, we do not.*
> *We don't like it cold and don't like it hot.*
> *Porridge is Scottish and really won't do.*
> *Give us, please give us a good Irish Stew.*
> *Calcannon and Skirlie and Boxty are fine.*
> *Just stop feeding us horrible slime!*
> *Mourne mutton and Clapshot are really quite good.*
> *Porridge is nasty and horrible food.*

We feel we are in prison in this cage on the hill.
Add insult to injury, feed us on swill!
Porridge we've seen it, that programme on telly.
But the food it is awful, and lies in the belly.
So, bring on the eggs, the beef and the lamb,
Or even some fish with warm milk and ham.
Just please not the porridge, we've had quite enough.
It's yukky and foul and tasteless old stuff."

Johnston says: I took the hint. I changed their feed and I'd like to think that, by the end of my short flirtation with greyhound training, I wasn't getting it too far wrong."

On another sombre note, Deirdre's mother Kathleen died in June 2020. It was the passing of one half of the couple who made crucial contributions to Johnston's early career.

The early scenes in Lincolnshire which feature on the home video were all shot by Deirdre's father Duncan. "What memories to have now, fantastic," says Deirdre – though she knows better than any that it was her father who produced the deposit for the purchase of the Lincolnshire yard and, without his intervention, there may have been no future at Middleham when that VAT bill had to be paid in the early nineties.

"My mum absolutely loved the racing," she says. "She watched every runner. It really kept her going – she loved it. I'd phone her to see how she was, and she'd say, 'that jockey didn't give it a very good ride.' But she loved Joe Fanning."

Deirdre adds: "She was housebound, in a wheelchair, with MS, which progressively got worse, although she died of cancer in the end, aged 80, just seven weeks after discovering it – and all during Covid, which made it awful."

The Fergusons clearly recognised the latent talent in their son-in-law, and no doubt took the view that their daughter would provide wise counsel when required, a power behind the throne. "I always wanted to work with horses, but my Dad insisted 'you've got to get your education'. I did all that, but my heart was always with horses," says Deirdre. "It was right up my street, what Mark was planning to do – even though I knew nothing about racing. I learned that on the job basically."

The point, made early in this book, remains. Many would have been wary indeed of following the dreams of such an intractable character all those years ago. Did she really have no qualms? "No. No, none at all," Deirdre says firmly. "I never thought about it like that. That's what we were going to do. Remember, he did try to get a job in racing to begin with, but nobody would employ him. They just said, 'we don't need a vet,' so we just took the plunge and bought that first yard."

Deirdre adds: "Looking back, I think: 'Oh, God – all the things we did.' Even coming here, the money we spent on the yard, with Brian Palmer. I used to do a daily cash-flow. Literally, I couldn't pay out until one of the owners had paid us. It was that tight for quite some time. The interest on the money we had borrowed to do up the yard, build the swimming pool, had rocketed to 17 per cent. It was scary stuff at the time."

I asked if she felt she had been a restraining influence? The question provokes a knowing smile. "I've always had to hold him back," she says. "I remember this ice machine for horses he bought [the injured horse stands in ice water to above its knees and water is circulated against the legs]. 'Oh, this is the new thing. We'll have two,' he said. I said: 'No. we'll have one, and see how we get on with it. If we really think it's amazing, maybe we'll get a second one.'"

Deirdre adds: "That's why I hold the purse strings. I look after the money." When I enquire if she still does that, her response is:

"Yes, I check the wages, and the invoices, the bills. I get the monthly bank statement."

Today, with a reported turnover of around £8m a year, and a wage bill of £4m, that will make much more agreeable reading than it once did.

Did she ever, in those early days, envisage what they would achieve? "No," she says. "When we moved to Kingsley House with about 40 boxes, I didn't think we'd ever fill it. You have to remember, we'd left a place with 20 boxes, where we'd started with three and a half paying owners and got to about 11 paying. We moved here with 13 horses, and I was looking at all these boxes, and thought, 'God, we'll never fill these.' So, no, I could never have imagined that we'd get to where we are now."

And from that, you've created an empire? She nods. "And where do you stop it? It's just great for us that Charlie's here. So, we don't have to worry about that. It continues. That's the great thing. The only thing that we wished, and we tried really hard, was that he had gone to work for someone else – at least for a while. We'd say: 'you don't have to go as a vet. You could be a pupil–assistant, whatever you want. Just go – when you finish uni.' But we couldn't get him to go away. I just think it would have done him good, from his overall perspective, looking at different ways, different approaches to things. Just like me, this is the only thing he knows, apart from school and uni. He's never been in another job. I was in another job but never a racing one."

Both Mark and Deirdre had struck it lucky in finding partners whose talents and temperaments complemented each other. How important is it for Charlie to do the same? "At the moment, he just looks at the owners, the horses, and racing, and not everything else we've got to cope with – the properties, the estate side. And he's on his own. He needs a 'me' to come and support him, as it were," says Deirdre. "When you start with nothing, there's no other agenda. He's got to find the right person, for the right reasons. He's obsessed with racing. So, you need someone like-minded. Lots of racing marriages don't work because they can't stand the seven days a week and racing all the time."

Deirdre updates me on the latest news of her versatile younger son, Angus. "He was a trainee accountant, but hated it," she says. "So, he gave it up to be a singer. He was in a band, was a singing waiter at weddings – and really enjoyed it. Just before Covid hit, we were off, seeing him at La Folie Douce in Val d'Isère."

She adds: "We've always sung as a family, at Christmases, all the time, just at home, and then we didn't do any for quite a while. He was in France at La Folie, but came home for the whole of that first lockdown. That was why we started singing together [with the aforementioned 'Kingsley House Acoustic Sessions'], just to cheer people up."

Angus also has a business sideline, as Deirdre explains: "He does lots of singing, but he's always had three or four flats he's looked after, and built it up to about seven and then at the beginning of last year, when he was home and couldn't sing, he got more and more and has established a flat-renting business for students in Glasgow. He has 30 flats on his books now. It's amazing. He finds the students – it's mostly students – using Facebook. He'll tell me: 'Oh, I've got five viewings this afternoon.' It's great. He plans to go back to singing, and hopes then, if necessary, he might employ somebody to do all the day-to-day maintenance on the flats."

As will become apparent, it's just possible that Angus may also have a role to play at Middleham.

CHAPTER 38

THE RECORD-BREAKER PREPARES FOR 'YEAR ZERO'

As I complete this book on one man and his wife's odyssey, in early August 2021, it has crossed my mind that, if this was a movie, the final scene would be the completion of the full circle: for Mark Johnston and Deirdre to tearfully depart Middleham and return to Scotland, to enjoy the fruits of their labours, their work here having being done and leaving their son in charge. Who knows? Maybe they could even move back to Aberfoyle…

But real life's not like that.

Apparently, their elder son had that impression, too – that his parents would be Scotland-bound, to live. I'd asked Johnston where he saw himself in a decade's time. To answer that, he told me two or three years ago how he'd asked the same question of Charlie.

Johnston recalls: "We were trying to press Charlie on making future plans, and at one of our board meetings, we asked him: 'Where did he see himself in ten years' time?' He said, 'here'. We went into how many horses he'd have, and where would he live? And he said: 'Here – in this house.' He meant *our* house, Kingsley House.

"We asked, 'where do you think *we'll* be?' And he said: 'Scotland. You've always said you want to live in Scotland.' It's true we're always looking for a house in Scotland, Deirdre and me. But purely as a holiday home.

"So, I think I'll still be here in ten years' time though I'll be doing an awful lot less of it, if anything at all. I'm not going anywhere until they carry me out in a box."

A mention of Johnston's beloved Scotland leads us to depart tangentially on to his ideologies; specifically to Scottish nationalism – and the campaign for independence – and religion.

A few years ago, following that column in *The Times* in which Johnston had written of his "rapacious desire to plunder south of the border" he had attempted to articulate his feelings on the whole issue of Scottish nationalism. Looking ahead to his eventual retirement, I had suggested to him, only half in jest, that perhaps he would be knighted when the time came. "I won't get a knighthood," he had retorted. "I'm a Jacobite."

Not quite the response I had anticipated, and though presumably not a strict adherent of the political movement dedicated to the restoration of the Stuart kings to the thrones of England and Scotland, what he meant was that, despite his years in the South, he remained a staunch advocate of Scottish nationalism.

"Quite," Johnston had responded. "Well, very, I suppose. But I can't always equate that to my other beliefs. Second to religion, there's terrible things done in the name of nationalism. I'm not a believer in it in that sense. But I suppose, like so many Scots, there's still a bitterness bred into us, taught into us at school even, through Scottish history. We're taught that for 800 years we've been persecuted by the English, and we rebel against it – as do the Irish."

I asked if this explained why Scots frequently appear more

driven, more ambitious than their English counterparts? "You can say that's just a chip on Scottish shoulders. On the other hand, there's an immense pride, confidence and arrogance about Scots. We all think we're better than the English. I was brought up with that as well. That the best brains in Britain come from Scotland; that our biggest export is people; that we invented anything that has been worth inventing; that we fought all the battles. We were brought up *not* to feel inferior, but to feel downtrodden, and therefore rebellious."

Johnston added: "I remember from quite a young age, my father used to tell me: 'One of your great advantages is your Scottish accent. Never lose it. You will be able to move in all circles.' Because in Scotland, a Scottish accent is perceived as being working class. The upper classes, the landed classes, were Anglo–Scots educated in England or in Scottish public schools in the Highlands or in Edinburgh, and they emerged with an English accent. In England, a Scottish accent is classless to most Englishmen. It's not like having a Liverpool or Geordie accent."

I put it to him that despite today's cosmopolitan society, history and ancestry still shapes many of our attitudes. "Of course," he said. "I take the mickey out of Deirdre because she's got a great-grandfather who was an English soldier. I never let her forget that. I will maintain that my father is pure Scottish. I don't actually know, not beyond two generations – my parents and their parents. I joke about that."

Recently, in light of that comment, I asked him whether he had considered taking one of those DNA ethnicity tests? "No," he asserted. "I'd be scared to – in case I find I'm an Englishman!" I also asked him what he had entered in the national census under the question of how he would describe his national identity? "I didn't complete it – maybe Deirdre did it. But Scottish…" Johnston says he would have answered, as though it was quite obvious. Not British.

Like his parents, Johnston is an SNP member, and insists: "We've never been closer to independence, and it could well happen." A good thing? I ask. "A fantastic thing."

And yet, he adds: "One of the policies that I just do not understand [about SNP politics] is how you can want to be out of Westminster and into Brussels. Independence is about being independent, and how small is beautiful, about running your own shop. You can be friendly with all these people, you don't have to be at war with them, but you don't have to be ruled by them, either. So, I am a Scottish Nationalist Brexiteer…which I suppose is contradictory!"

You expect nothing else.

As for religion, Johnston once told me he was brought up as a Scottish Protestant – and a Rangers supporter – but "hates the bigotry" on both sides of the divide. He added: "Funnily enough, at times I think of joining the Secular Society, or the Humanists. I'm a bit anti-religion. The only time I've been to church was at school, when I was dragged along, and I've attended some funerals. I got married in a church, of course – Deirdre insisted – though I always thought it was wrong. But the kids weren't christened. I wouldn't have it."

Returning to less spiritual matters, one thing is certain: the Scot does not intend to be obsessing forever on such dilemmas as who rides for the stable in the 3.10 at Newmarket. He has an enormous bucket list of travel destinations.

"At the end of 2019, we went to India, and I'd say that was the best holiday of my life. Partly because India is a fascinating country, but also because it was structured and organised, and we had a guide. We want to do more of that kind of thing," he says, reading a list which includes: the Calgary stampede, Channel

Islands, Barra, Sicily, Athens, Shetland, Russia, a cruise around the Scottish islands, Jamaica, Sandy Lane, Ireland North and South.

His other indulgence is cars. He has a 1965 E-type, a 1980 MG Midget, and (for regular driving) a Range Rover and Jaguar F-type.

However, the fact remains he will be a significant, not to say immovable, presence at Kingsley House and Kingsley Park for many years yet. "Maybe I'll become superfluous, and..." Put out to grass? – I suggest is the most appropriate phrase. He nods in agreement.

We consider other major trainers who have entrusted their operations to their sons. Ian Balding was 64 when he handed over his yard in 2002; Richard Hannon was 68 when he handed over to Richard Jnr in 2013; John Gosden was 70 when he switched to a partnership with son Thady this year. In comparison, Johnston, 62 in 2021, is still a young man.

When I suggest that he could have half his life again remaining, he looks incredulous. "I wish I thought so. No! My father died at 65, my grandfather died at 35, my sister [Lyn] died at 61. So, I'm not counting on it..."

More important than age, of either father and son, is what Johnston wouldn't want to do was hand the business over if it was in a state of decline. That remains a primal instinct.

"I'd seen how some of the great trainers of the past can just slide away. It can happen to anybody. So, I'm still driven by that. I'm still acutely aware of how fast this can haemorrhage money," he says.

Never mind the maxim: 'Always Trying'. His mission is rather more encapsulated by the declaration: Always innovating. Always prepared for adversity. He is a man who is proactive rather than reactive.

Intriguingly, it's conceivable that Charlie's younger brother could play a pivotal role, too, in the future of the yard. Johnston had mentioned that Angus had unofficially attended board meetings. "Angus came home and wrote what we jokingly called 'The Angus Book of Office Procedures'. He taught himself, and wrote a manual for the office staff to refer to. Angus is good at doing things like that, and we'll set him on projects to deal with various issues. He helped put together the staff training video [with Andrew Bottomley]."

Johnston adds: "Deirdre and I would have more confidence in Angus looking after our property interests and things like that than we would Charlie who has a one-track mind. We can imagine an ideal situation where Charlie ran the training and Angus ran the business. But who knows – it'll be up to them."

There have been periods in his career when the Scot, who continues to question conventional wisdom while challenging all limits placed on his ambition, has enjoyed a magic carpet ride; others when he has fallen to earth from it.

Some years ago, I asked him to address his flaws, his shortcomings. He told me then: "I'm a bad loser. For someone who wants to win so much, it's very hard to accept losing. I don't think there's any virtue about being a good loser, is there, although everybody likes to say there is? I don't think you become very competitive if you're a good loser. I want to be a good winner."

However, he paused and conceded: "I sometimes realise, in managing the business and in general life, that I've looked for someone to blame for something that was my own fault. I'm then pretty disappointed with myself. It's one of my flaws. I'm sure I do it far too often. But maybe everybody has that?"

When I return to that question today, Johnston insists he has mellowed. His staff would generally concur with that. However, he does confess: "Looking back I'm embarrassed about how angry I got with people. I would hate to think that I ever bullied people who couldn't answer back. I'd hate to think that I was a bear with a sore head and that I put people under unfair pressure."

He smiles ruefully and adds: "I still can't help it, but I *do* put people under pressure because I *want* them to feel the pressure. I *want* them to be as self-critical as I am. I want them to feel *we* failed, if we have. So, sometimes I do it, but I'm not as bad as I was. So, yes, that's changed. I've learned. I don't want to be like that."

It is apparent that what he doesn't like is to be defined, categorised – as writers like myself are apt to do. As previously mentioned, he dislikes intensely being labelled a 'businessman' rather than a man who understands horses, and when I broach the fact that he remains the principal trainer in the north to train for the Maktoum family and friends, he interrupts sharply. "I'm not a Northern trainer – I don't see myself as that. Everything we've done has been about smashing that North–South divide."

On that subject, it must be said that stables in and around Middleham, and North Yorkshire generally, are flourishing. Richard Fahey (Malton), Karl Burke (Middleham), Kevin Ryan (Hambleton), David O'Meara (Upper Helmsley) and Tim Easterby (Great Habton) were all in the 2021 season Flat trainers' top 20 table in terms of prize money won, at the time of writing.

Johnston was fourth in that table, but way ahead of all his rivals in terms of winners as he headed for another double century, for the final time under his own name. That is what has sustained him, year in, year out.

I recall an interview he did with my former *Independent* colleague Brian Viner in 2013, when the trainer said: "When I moved to Middleham at the end of '88, I did a television interview with *Look North* in which I said that I dreamt of training Classic winners. Some people thought that was hilarious. Well, I've wiped the smiles off their faces."

That, essentially, is what has empowered him: an almost religious zeal to convert all those disbelievers who didn't give him a prayer.

Now, from 2022, Johnston is faced with a different challenge. The business will operate under the dual names of Mark and Charlie Johnston, and there will be a complete re-set in the statistics, a kind of year zero. Nil winners. It will be a fascinating transformation to witness.

Soon, they will be at the sales installing *their* team for next year – his 35th as a trainer, Charlie's first – while awaiting their latest consignments of yearlings from Arab and other patrons and attending the autumn sales.

That will be followed by yet another winter of speculation: could there be a Mister Baileys, an Attraction, a Double Trigger, a Royal Rebel, a Shamardal, a Subjectivist amongst them? More Group 1 prospects?

All you can be certain of is that Johnston's well-honed competitive edge will be at the fore once more as an atmosphere of rich expectancy permeates the moorland around Middleham, those rich acres of North Yorkshire which will be forever part of Scotland...

INDEX